AMERICAN SOCIAL FICTION

JAMES TO COZZENS

AMERICAN SOCIAL FICTION

JAMES TO COZZENS

MICHAEL MILLGATE

BARNES & NOBLE, INC. · NEW YORK

PUBLISHERS · BOOKSELLERS · SINCE 1873

First published, 1964
by Oliver & Boyd, Ltd

Copyright 1964 by Michael Millgate

Reprinted in this series, 1967 by Barnes & Noble, Inc.
through special arrangement with Oliver & Boyd, Ltd

L. C. Catalog Card Number: 64-5659

Printed in the United States of America

TO
MALCOLM COWLEY

Preface

The novelists discussed in this study are alike in that they set out deliberately to create an image of the society in which their characters move; with the exception of James, and possibly of Fitzgerald, they are also writers whose work we read and value primarily for reasons arising directly from the social presentation they attempt. In other ways they differ widely, and I have purposely avoided speaking of "the American social novel" or suggesting a formal categorisation of any kind. Indeed, I have been led to the approach followed in this book by a sense that recent attempts to define *the* American novel have resulted, all too often, in a narrowed and impoverished conception of American fiction. Critics have realised, and quite rightly, that any claim they wished to make for the American novel as an autonomous form must be supported by unimpeachable literary evidence; most recent attempts to establish canons, traditions, and genealogies of the American novel have therefore involved a heavy dependence on the great novels of the American classic period, and the characteristics of these works have been adduced again and again as the standard or pattern by which the central tradition of American fiction is to be identified.

Such a method inevitably excludes many novels which, if not of the very first rank, are nevertheless of such quality and importance that they cannot be ignored in any satisfactory account of American fiction as a whole, and it has led in particular to a serious undervaluation of those American novelists who have been specifically concerned with the presentation of American society. Even Lionel Trilling, a critic who is thoroughly convinced of the importance of social fiction, can say, in "Manners, Morals and the Novel," that Americans seem to have "a kind of resistance to

looking closely at society," and that the novelists who have
attempted to treat of American society have been incapable of
reporting the "social fact" with accuracy or of using it with
imagination.[1] Such criticism, though applicable to all too many
American novelists, seems unduly severe as an overall judgment,
and I have taken as my starting-point the contrary hypothesis that
it might be possible to obtain a different and richer impression of
American social fiction, and hence of American fiction as a whole,
by exploring the work of novelists other than those normally
regarded as constituting the major tradition, and by considering
this work in its relation, not to the literary achievements of the
mid-nineteenth century, but to its own historical and social context,
which might be radically different from that of the American
classic period.

The period embraced by this study is roughly eighty years,
from 1877, when Henry James's *The American* first appeared, to
1957, the year of publication of James Gould Cozzens's latest novel,
By Love Possessed. The writers I have considered are novelists all
of whom, apart from James, fall outside the acknowledged first rank
and all of whom it seemed useful to approach as social novelists,
as authors of novels which are especially concerned with the
presentation of society. The term "social fiction" is clearly too
limiting to apply to James's achievement as a whole, but a few of
his novels are touched upon in an attempt to discover some of the
possibilities of social fiction and define some of the technical problems involved. I have not attempted to re-examine the "proletarian" novels of the nineteen-thirties so admirably discussed
by Walter B. Rideout.[2] In approaching the question of social
presentation in the work of a number of novelists who differ from
each other in so many ways I have found it helpful to follow, at
least in the first instance, a common line of inquiry—specifically,
the way in which they treat of that figure of the businessman who
has played such an important role in American social history and
been such an obsessive image of American literature. Thus,

[1] Lionel Trilling, *The Liberal Imagination*, London 1951, p. 213.
[2] Walter B. Rideout, *The Radical Novel in the United States, 1900–1954*, Cambridge,
Mass. 1956.

although it has in no way been my central concern, I have found myself following the development of the image of the businessman through both its "epic" and its "obscure" phases and watching its gradual supersession by the image of the individual in his relation to the ever-increasing institutionalisation of modern American society.

I am indebted for advice and criticism to many friends and colleagues, and especially to M. Bryn Davies, Douglas Grant, Walter Isle, A. Norman Jeffares, D. W. Jefferson, Bert James Loewenberg, and Arthur Mizener. The greatest of my debts, however, are to Malcolm Cowley, who first suggested to me the subject of this book and for whose friendship and wisdom I shall always be deeply grateful, and to my wife, whose encouragement, practical assistance, and immensely perceptive criticism have done more than anything else to sustain me in my endeavours. My thanks are also due to Mr Thomas L. McHaney, for research services, and to Miss Audrey Stead, for her patient and highly competent secretarial assistance. The editors of the *Critical Quarterly*, *English Studies*, *Modern Language Review*, *Neophilologus*, and *Studi Americani* have generously given me permission to include material which first appeared in those periodicals, and I am grateful to the Modern Humanities Research Association for permission to include an article previously published in the *Modern Language Review*.

Acknowledgments

ACKNOWLEDGMENTS are due to the following for permission to quote from the works indicated: Edward Arnold Ltd (E. M. Forster, *Howards End*); The Bodley Head Ltd (F. Scott Fitzgerald, *The Great Gatsby*, *The Last Tycoon*, *Tender is the Night*, *This Side of Paradise*, *The Beautiful and Damned*); Brandt & Brandt (J. P. Marquand, *So Little Time*, *Sincerely, Willis Wayde*); Jonathan Cape Ltd (Sinclair Lewis, *Dodsworth*, *Arrowsmith*, *Elmer Gantry*, *Main Street*, *The Man Who Knew Coolidge*, *Babbitt*, *The Job*); The Cresset Press (Arthur Miller, *A View From the Bridge*); Curtis Brown Ltd and the Booth Tarkington Estate (Booth Tarkington, *The Midlander*, *The Plutocrat*); Doubleday & Company, Inc. (Richard Chase, *The American Novel and its Tradition*; Vladimir Nabokov, *Pnin*; Booth Tarkington, *The Midlander*, *The Plutocrat*); E. P. Dutton & Co. Inc. (Van Wyck Brooks, "America's Coming of Age," in *Three Essays on America*); John Farquarson Ltd and the Henry James Estate (Henry James, *The Reverberator*, *Lady Barbarina* etc, *The American*, *The Golden Bowl*, *The Ivory Tower*, *The American Scene*, *The Bostonians*, *The Ambassador*, *The Portrait of a Lady*, *The American Essays of*

Henry James); *Esquire* (George Jean Nathan, "Memories of Fitzgerald, Lewis and Dreiser") Faber and Faber Ltd (Randall Jarrell, *Pictures from an Institution*); Harcourt, Brace & World, Inc. (James Gould Cozzens, *Men and Brethren, Guard of Honor*; Alfred Kazin, *On Native Ground*; Sinclair Lewis, *Dodsworth, Arrowsmith, Elmer Gantry, Main Street, The Man Who Knew Coolidge, Babbitt, The Job*; Mary McCarthy, *The Groves of Academe*); Harvard University Press (William Miller, *Men in Business*); William Heinemann Ltd (Mary McCarthy, *The Groves of Academe*; John Steinbeck, *The Grapes of Wrath*); Houghton Mifflin Company and Mr John Dos Passos (John Dos Passos, *District of Columbia*; W. D. Howells, *The Lady of Aroostook*); Mr W. W. Howells (W. D. Howells, *A Hazard of New Fortunes, A Traveller from Altruria, The Quality of Mercy, Through the Eye of the Needle, The World of Chance, The Rise of Silas Lapham*); Margot Johnson Agency (Howard Nemerov, *The Homecoming Game*); Alfred A. Knopf Inc. (E. M. Forster, *Howards End*; Richard Hofstadter, *The Age of Reform*; Randall Jarrell, *Pictures From an Institution*; Carl Van Vechten, *Spider Boy*); Little, Brown & Company (Sherwood Anderson, *The Letters of Sherwood Anderson*; J. P. Marquand, *So Little Time, Sincerely, Willis Wayde*); Longmans, Green & Co. Limited (James Gould Cozzens, *Men and Brethren, Guard of Honour*); Macmillan & Co. Ltd (C. P. Snow, *The Masters, The New Men*; Edith Wharton, *The House of Mirth, The Custom of the Country*); The Macmillan Company (Miriam Beard, *A History of the Businessman*; Granville Hicks, *The Living Novel*); Mr Norman Mailer (Norman Mailer, *The Naked and the Dead*); Harold Matson Company, Inc. (Herman Wouk, *The Caine Mutiny*); Methuen & Co. Ltd (F. O. Matthiessen, *Theodore Dreiser*); New Directions (F. Scott Fitzgerald, *The Crack-Up*; Nathanael West, *The Day of the Locust*); New York University Press (W. D. Howells, *Criticism and Fiction and Other Essays*); N. V. Martinus Nijhoff and Mr James E. Miller (James E. Miller, *The Fictional Technique of Scott Fitzgerald*); Harold Ober Associates (Sherwood Anderson, *The Portable Sherwood Anderson, A Story Teller's Story, Windy McPherson's Son, Poor White, The Letters of Sherwood Anderson*); Oxford University Press, Inc. (F. O. Matthiessen, *The Notebooks of Henry James*); G. P. Putnam's Sons (Norman Mailer, *The Deer Park*); Random House, Inc. (H. E. Maule and M. H. Crane, *The Man From Main Street*; Budd Schulberg, *The Disenchanted, What Makes Sammy Run?*); Alvin Redman Limited (Harvey Breit, *The Writer Observed*); Richards Press Ltd (Frank Norris, *The Pit, The Responsibilities of the Novelist, The Octopus, A Deal in Wheat*); Charles Scribner's Sons (F. Scott Fitzgerald, *This Side of Paradise, The Beautiful and Damned, Tender is the Night, The Great Gatsby, The Last Tycoon, Afternoon of an Author*; James Jones, *From Here to Eternity*; C. P. Snow, *The Masters, The New Men*; Edith Wharton, *The House of Mirth, The Custom of the Country*); Simon and Schuster, Inc. (Stringfellow Barr, *Purely Academic*; Howard Nemerov, *The Homecoming Game*); University of Texas Press (W. P. Webb, *The Great Frontier*); The Viking Press Inc. (Sherwood Anderson, *Winesburg, Ohio*; Arthur Miller, *A View from the Bridge*; Theodore Morrison, *The Stones of the House*; John Steinbeck, *The Grapes of Wrath*); Arnold Watkins, Inc. (Edith Wharton, *A Backward Glance*); A. P. Watt & Son (*The Complete Short Stories of Mark Twain*, ed. Charles Neider); The World Publishing Company (Harvey Breit, *The Writer Observed*; Theodore Dreiser, *Sister Carrie, The Titan, The Financier, The "Genius," A Hoosier Holiday*).

Contents

I

Henry James and the Business Hero

I

In the opening pages of Henry James's novel *The American* (1877), Christopher Newman is discovered sitting in the Louvre: "An observer with anything of an eye for local types would have had no difficulty in referring this candid connoisseur to the scene of his origin, and indeed such an observer might have made an ironic point of the almost ideal completeness with which he filled out the mould of race. The gentleman on the divan was the superlative American . . ."[1] Newman is a wealthy businessman, and there was certainly ample justification in the late nineteenth century for casting such a figure in the role of *the* American. The industrialisation of America, because it was fostered by war, came swiftly; because it came late, it came already highly developed; because it came into what amounted to an economic power-vacuum, it was able for many years to grow and spread almost unhindered. The businessman himself was subject to few social or legal restraints, and he rapidly became a dominating figure in the life of the nation, and in the national imagination. From the time of the Civil War until quite recent years business seems to have been widely regarded as the most important, most interesting, and most characteristic of all American activities, and when President Coolidge declared that the business of America was business he echoed a point made long before by Henry James.

As early as 1877 James had seen the appropriateness of making Christopher Newman a businessman, and in 1898 he wrote one of the earliest critical discussions of the peculiar relevance of business

[1] Henry James, *The American*, London 1921, p. 2. All quotations from James's novels are taken from the London edition of 1921-23. The original version of *The American* shows extensive textual variation, but not of a kind to affect the argument of this chapter.

and the businessman as a subject for the American novelist. For
this is what interests us here: not merely the incidence of novels
portraying, with varying directness and thinness of disguise, the
greed, glamour, villainy, and magnificence of the American captains
of industry and finance—the Goulds, Hills, Rockefellers, and Morgans—but the whole question of how far, in what ways, and for
what purposes the business theme proved usable to James, his
contemporaries, and their successors. It was in an article for the
English magazine *Literature*, in March 1898, that James wrote:

I cannot but think that the American novel has in a special, far-
reaching direction to sail much closer to the wind. "Business"
plays a part in the United States that other interests dispute much
less showily than they sometimes dispute it in the life of European
countries; in consequence of which the typical American figure
is above all that "business man" whom the novelist and the
dramatist have scarce yet seriously touched, whose song has still
to be sung and his picture still to be painted. He is often an obscure,
but not less often an epic, hero, seamed all over with the wounds
of the market and the dangers of the field, launched into action and
passion by the immensity and complexity of the general struggle, a
boundless ferocity of battle—driven above all by the extraordinary,
the unique relation in which he for the most part stands to the life
of his lawful, his immitigable womankind, the wives and daughters
who float, who splash on the surface and ride the waves, his terrific
link with civilization, his social substitutes and representatives,
while, like a diver for shipwrecked treasure, he gasps in the depths
and breathes through an air-tube.

This relation, even taken alone, contains elements that strike
me as only yearning for their interpreter—elements, moreover, that
would present the further merit of melting into the huge neigh-
boring province of the special situation of woman in an order of
things where to be a woman at all—certainly to be a young one—
constitutes in itself a social position. The difficulty, doubtless, is
that the world of affairs, as affairs are understood in the panting
cities, though around us all the while, before us, behind us, beside
us, and under our feet, is as special and occult a one to the outsider
as the world, say, of Arctic exploration—as impenetrable save as a
result of special training. Those who know it are not the men to
paint it; those who might attempt it are not the men who know

it. The most energetic attempt at portrayal that we have anywhere had—*L'Argent*, of Émile Zola—is precisely a warning of the difference between false and true initiation. The subject there, though so richly imagined, is all too mechanically, if prodigiously, "got up." Meanwhile, accordingly, the American "business man" remains, thanks to the length and strength of the wires that move him, *the* magnificent theme *en disponibilité*. The romance of fact, indeed, has touched him in a way that quite puts to shame the romance of fiction. It gives his measure for purposes of art that it was he, essentially, who embarked in the great war of 1861-4, and who, carrying it on in the North to a triumphant conclusion, went back, since business was his standpoint, to his very "own" with an undimmed capacity to mind it. When, in imagination, you give the type, as it exists today, the benefit of its great double luster —that of these recorded antecedents and that of its preoccupied, systematic, and magnanimous abasement before the other sex—you will easily feel your sense of what may be done with its overflow.[2]

The first point James makes—that the American novelist should "sail closer to the wind," be more adventurous, take more risks— must be taken in the context of the essay as a whole. His title is "The Question of the Opportunities," and he has been discussing the implications for the American writer of the huge new reading public he saw coming into existence: "they hang before us a wide picture of opportunities—opportunities that would be opportunities still even if, reduced to the *minimum*, they should be only those offered by the vastness of the implied habitat and the complexity of the implied history. It is impossible not to entertain with patience and curiosity the presumption that life so colossal must break into expression at points of proportionate frequency. These places, these moments will be the chances."[3] James sees the world of business as the heart of this "colossal" life and as offering the outstanding "opportunity" for the novelist, and when he goes on to draw attention to the general acceptance of the businessman as the "typical American figure" he simply reaffirms the conception he had had many years earlier when writing *The American*.

[2] Henry James, "The Question of the Opportunities," in *The American Essays of Henry James*, ed. Leon Edel, New York 1958, pp. 202-03.
[3] *Op. cit.*, p. 200.

When James turns to the problem of writing on the business theme, he points out that the businessman may be either an "obscure" hero or an "epic" one. Although it is not wholly clear what James intended by this distinction, it presumably relates to the contrast between the businessman as a representative middle-class figure—a man of no particular eminence, importance or ability, working furiously, even desperately, to keep his head above water and his family supplied with all their multifarious wants—and the businessman as great industrial captain or merchant-prince. When speaking of "the immensity and complexity of the general struggle, a boundless ferocity of battle," James must have had in mind the great contemporary contests for commercial and industrial power, and at such a period the images of battle no doubt sprang readily to mind. They nonetheless carry with them strong suggestions of medieval romance, and the great captain of finance, if sometimes an evil figure, was certainly a romantic one: "The romance of fact, indeed," writes James, "has touched him in a way that quite puts to shame the romance of fiction." In his subsequent remarks upon the relationship of the businessman to his "immitigable womankind" James touches, most perceptively, on fundamental questions likely to be encountered by any novelist attempting to present a businessman as a central figure. How far is the business life compatible with the cultivation of personal relationships, or of the arts? What, in particular, of the relationship between the businessman and his wife: can it be other than a yoked incompatibility?

Having suggested what the ideal business novel should do and what it should be about, James proceeds to demonstrate the very good reason why it was unlikely ever to be written. The world of business, he declares, is "impenetrable save as a result of special training. Those who know it are not the men to paint it; those who might attempt it are not the men who know it." Although James recognises this difficulty, he nevertheless continues to be fascinated by the businessman as "*the* magnificent theme *en disponibilité*." We can appreciate the significance of the *disponible* for James from the Preface to *The Portrait of a Lady*, where he recalls Turgenev's remark that his own novels began "almost always with the vision of some person or persons who hovered before him, soliciting him."[4] James observes:

> So this beautiful genius, and I recall with comfort the gratitude I drew from his reference to the intensity of suggestion that may reside in the stray figure, the unattached character, the image *en disponibilité*. It gave me higher warrant than I seemed then to have met for just that blest habit of one's own imagination, the trick of investing some conceived or encountered individual, some brace or group of individuals, with the germinal property and authority. I was myself so much more antecedently conscious of my figures than of their setting—too preliminary, a preferential interest in which struck me as in general such a putting of the cart before the horse.[5]

Thus for James, too, it was the figure and not the setting that first seized the imagination, and this is the progression which reveals itself in the passage from "The Question of the Opportunities." In the middle of the passage James acknowledges the near impossibility of dealing convincingly with the "world of affairs," the businessman's setting, but at the beginning of the passage, and again at the end, it is the businessman himself—both as an extraordinary phenomenon in his own right and as "the typical American figure" —whom James finds so irresistible.

2

The excitement which sweeps through the passage quoted from "The Question of the Opportunities" has all the marks of a "shock of recognition," of a prospector come suddenly upon a vein rich beyond expectation. Yet the idea of the businessman as hero was not new to James, nor were most of the ideas in the essay. In the *Notebooks*, for example, under the date 26 November 1892, we find a reference to

> the whole subject, or question, about which Godkin, as I remember, one day last summer talked to me very emphatically and

---

[4] Henry James, Preface to *The Portrait of a Lady*, London 1921, p. viii.
[5] *Op. cit.*, p. ix.

interestingly—the growing divorce between the American woman (with her comparative leisure, culture, grace, social instincts, artistic ambitions) and the male American immersed in the ferocity of business, with no time for any but the most sordid interests, purely commercial, professional, democratic and political. This divorce is rapidly becoming a gulf—an abyss of inequality, the like of which has never before been seen under the sun.[6]

The passage appears between a discussion of the international marriage (24 November) and an outline of the situation which was later to evolve into *The Golden Bowl* (28 November). *The Golden Bowl* (1904) portrays two international marriages and is centrally concerned with the relationships between a businessman, Adam Verver, his daughter and his wife, but it scarcely touches upon the kind of problem which James was discussing in the *Notebooks* and in "The Question of the Opportunities." Indeed, the treatment of Verver recalls that of Mr Dosson in *The Reverberator* (1888), which James discusses in the later "Preface" to that tale:

Before the American business-man, as I have been prompt to declare, I was absolutely and irredeemably helpless, with no fibre of my intelligence responding to his mystery. No approach I could make to him on his "business side" really got near it. That is where I was fatally incompetent, and this in turn—the case goes into a nutshell—is so obviously why, for any decent documentation, I was simply shut up to what was left me. It takes but a glance to see how the matter was in such a fashion simplified.[7]

James, that is to say, acknowledges his own insuperable ignorance of business, but pleads that by ignoring altogether the "business" side of the businessman and confining himself to what was left he had contrived at least to simplify the problem. The businessmen of the early tales—Mr Dosson, Mr Westgate in "An International Episode" (1879), Mr Ruck in "The Pension Beaurepas" (1881)— are not seen in action, apart from the charming moment when Mr Westgate takes it as a great joke that the two aristocratic Englishmen should come to America to do business: " 'Leave that to the

[6] *The Notebooks of Henry James*, edd. F. O. Matthiessen and Kenneth B. Murdock, New York 1961, p. 129.
[7] Henry James, Preface to *The Reverberator*, etc., London 1922, p. xix.

natives,' said Mr. Westgate."[8] But if James does not let us see his American businessmen in action, he often shows them in relation to their "immitigable" womankind, and the peculiar aptness of the surprising adjective is nowhere better demonstrated than in the portrayal of that "obscure" businessman, Mr Ruck, and his family in "The Pension Beaurepas." The American narrator is here explaining their situation for the benefit of a fellow-expatriate:

"Mr. Ruck's a broken-down man of business. He's broken-down in health and I think he must be broken-down in fortune. He has spent his whole life in buying and selling and watching prices, so that he knows how to do nothing else. His wife and daughter have spent their lives, not in selling, but in buying—with a considerable indifference to prices—and they on their side know how to do nothing else. To get something in a 'store' that they can put on their backs—that's their one idea; they haven't another in their heads. Of course they spend no end of money, and they do it with an implacable persistence, with a mixture of audacity and of cunning. They do it in his teeth and they do it behind his back; the mother protects the daughter, while the daughter eggs on the mother. Between them they're bleeding him to death." . . .

"But haven't they common sense? Don't they know they're marching to ruin?"

"They don't believe it. The duty of an American husband and father is to keep them going. If he asks them how, that's his own affair. So by way of not being mean, of being a good American husband and father, poor Ruck stands staring at bankruptcy."[9]

James more than once suggests that there is a conflict, or even a "divorce," between the sexes—between the civilised female and the uncivilised male—and in *The Portrait of a Lady* Isabel's difficulties stem partly from her desire to supply the intellectual distinction in her marriage. It seems clear from "The Pension Beaurepas" that, long before his discussion with Godkin, James's own observations had convinced him that between the over-worked businessman and

[8] Henry James, "An International Episode," in *Lady Barbarina*, etc., London 1922, p. 256.

[9] Henry James, "The Pension Beaurepas," in *Lady Barbarina*, etc., pp. 408-09.

his leisured womankind such differences were of a particularly radical nature. In *The American* Christopher Newman had specified of his ideal wife: " 'She may be cleverer and wiser than I can understand, and I shall only be the better pleased.' "[10] Much later, in *The Golden Bowl*, Adam Verver spends money lavishly on his wife and on his daughter, and when he marries Charlotte Stant his ostensible reasons are largely social; indeed, it is because he so constantly uses her as his "social representative" that Charlotte and the Prince are able to be alone together.

Christopher Newman and Adam Verver are, of course, the most important of James's business characters; Newman is a very early creation while Verver appears in James's last completed novel. Superficially, at least, the two have a good deal in common. They are both comparatively young—Newman is forty-two, Verver forty-seven—but they have already made great fortunes from small beginnings. Newman is certainly a self-made man, Verver apparently so. Both have made their money in the American West, and both finally return there. In both novels the action arises from the same point of departure: a businessman making an acquisitive expedition to Europe becomes deeply involved with members of the European aristocracy. Newman comes to Europe frankly in search of a wife: " 'I want, in a word, the best article in the market.' "[11] Verver comes to Europe primarily to purchase rare *objets d'art* but he also obtains a real Italian prince as husband for his daughter: Prince Amerigo is " 'a part of his collection',", as Maggie tells her husband, " 'You're a rarity, an object of beauty, an object of price.' "[12] This kind of acquisitiveness is perhaps less unattractive in Newman than it is in Verver. In Newman it springs from warmth, eagerness, and naïve aspiration; in Verver it issues from a deliberate, cultivated connoisseurship. When Newman speaks of wanting " 'the best article in the market,' " he does so jocularly; it is characteristic of his appealing straight-forwardness that he should use such down-to-earth and, to him, customary imagery. There is little conscious humour, however, in Verver's habitual "application of the same measure of value to such different

[10] Henry James, *The American*, p. 44.   [11] *Ibid*.
[12] Henry James, *The Golden Bowl*, London 1923, I. 11.

pieces of property as Old Persian carpets, say, and new human acquisitions"[13]—acquisitions, that is, such as Prince Amerigo and Charlotte Stant.

Newman and Verver both experience some revulsion from their financial success, but their reactions differ considerably in kind and in quality. Early in *The American* Newman tells Tristram how he was on the point of concluding a spectacular business transaction when he suddenly experienced " 'the most extraordinary change of heart—a mortal disgust for the whole proposition.' "[14] Later, reflecting upon the opposition of the Bellegarde family to his "commercial" background, he recognises that he would have given up his business for the sake of Madame de Cintré—and indeed that he no longer has the same appetite for business as before. At the same time, he retains some pride in his achievement: "his financial imagination was dead [but] he felt no contempt for the surviving actualities begotten by it. He was glad he had been prosperous and had been a great operator rather than a small; he was extremely glad he was rich. He felt no impulse to sell all he had and give to the poor, or to retire into meditative economy and asceticism."[15] Verver, on the other hand, seems to look back over the whole of his business career with a kind of shame, regarding it as "the years of darkness [which] had been needed to render possible the years of light."[16] Perhaps not actually with guilt, but with the hope of justifying himself, he is devoting these latter years to building and furnishing a magnificent museum, "a palace of art . . . a receptacle of treasures sifted to positive sanctity," which he will present to "the people of his adoptive city and native State, the urgency of whose release from the bondage of ugliness he was in a position to measure," as a "house from whose open doors and windows, open to grateful, to thirsty millions, the higher, the highest knowledge would shine out to bless the land."[17]

The irony here[18] is sufficient both to define James's attitude

[13] *Op. cit.*, I. 175.   [14] *The American*, p. 28.
[15] *Op. cit.*, p. 462.   [16] *The Golden Bowl*, I. 128.   [17] *Op. cit.*, I. 129.
[18] It seems possible to speak of irony in *The Golden Bowl* without necessarily accepting the more extreme views expressed in Joseph J. Firebaugh's essay, "The Ververs," *Essays in Criticism*, IV (1954), 400-10. On this point see D. W. Jefferson, *Henry James*, Edinburgh and London 1960, p. 111.

towards Verver and to mark the contrast with the presentation of Newman. The "innocence" of both Newman and Verver has often been commented upon and has usually been regarded as practically identical: they are in fact innocent in quite different ways. Newman's innocence is naïvety, a genuine ignorance of all affairs which are not business affairs. Verver, on the other hand, in his devotion to the aesthetic principle, in his enslavement to "the exemplary passion, the passion for perfection at any price,"[19] has wilfully cut himself off from "life." Where Newman—though undoubtedly the cruder, the brasher of the two—remains conspicuously uncorrupted to the end, James seems to suggest that Verver has, in some measure, been corrupted by his success and by the power he consequently has over things and people. Verver has, it is true, developed a conscience, but its quality is called into question by the sheer coldness of the impersonality into which he has withdrawn and which colours his entire role in the action of the novel. We can perhaps detect here the first hints of the overt moral criticism of *The Ivory Tower* (1917).

In neither *The American* nor *The Golden Bowl*, of course, does James come near to fulfilling his own prescription for the business novel. Neither Newman nor Verver is seen in action as a businessman. No clue is given to the sources of Verver's fortune, though he has obviously augmented it on the stock market, and we learn little of Newman's career except that he has " 'been in everything' "[20] including railways, wash-tubs, leather, oil, and copper. The whole question is, in *The American*, rather lightly dismissed: Newman's account of his career to Tristram "was, with intensity, a tale of the Western world. . . . It dealt with elements, incidents, enterprises, which it will be needless to introduce to the reader in detail; the deeps and the shallows, the ebb and the flow, of great financial tides."[21] This is as near as James ever comes, in his own novels, to the "boundless ferocity of battle," to what is referred to in *The American* as "transcendent operations in ferocious markets"[22]

[19] *The Golden Bowl*, I. 129.   [20] *The American*, p. 108.
[21] *Op. cit.*, p. 23. For a more detailed comment on this point see John Robert Moore, "An Imperfection in the Art of Henry James," *Nineteenth Century Fiction*, XIII (1959), 351-6.
[22] *The American*, p. 302.

and in *The Golden Bowl* as "transcendent calculation and imaginative gambling."[23]   The recurrent reliance on "transcendent" conveys clearly James's sense that it was not for him to attempt the portrayal of the business world as such.

Even in *The Ivory Tower* the two rival businessmen, Abel Gaw ("incapable of thought save in sublimities of arithmetic")[24] and Frank Betterman, are seen only when retired from business and at the point of death.   As the rather Bunyanesque naming of Betterman suggests, there is a specific moral intention in the book, stronger perhaps than anywhere else in James's work.   Once again, however, the emphasis is not on business enterprise itself but on its results, in this case on the moral issues arising from the inheritance of wealth commercially acquired.   In the notes appended to the unfinished book James comments:

> Enormous difficulty of pretending to show various things here as with a business vision, in my total absence of business initiation; so that of course my idea has been from the first *not* to show them with a business vision, but in some other way altogether; this will take much threshing out, but it is the very basis of the matter, the core of the subject, and I shall worry it through with patience.[25]

James had to make Gaw and Betterman businessmen or the whole point of the novel might have been compromised, and he proposed to follow the familiar method, dating back to *The American* and *The Reverberator*, of avoiding the necessity to present the businessman in a business setting.   In this instance, however, the problem was complicated by James's changed attitude towards his material, and we may wonder whether, even if the book had been finished, he could have successfully performed the necessary sleight of hand.

Largely as a result of his 1903-04 visit to America, James had suffered a powerful moral and aesthetic revulsion from "the dreadful American money-world."[26]   This becomes evident not only in *The Ivory Tower*, but in the short story, "The Jolly Corner," in which Spencer Bryden confronts at last the terrible image of that

---

[23] *The Golden Bowl*, I. 128.
[24] Henry James, *The Ivory Tower*, London 1917, p. 6.
[25] *Op. cit.*, p. 285.   [26] *Op. cit.*, p. 278.

monster of business he might have become if he had stayed in America, and in that other disturbing story, "A Round of Visits," in which the hero, returned to New York to find that his funds have been embezzled by his best friend, makes the round of other acquaintances only to find all of them caught up in one form or another of moral and financial corruption. This is not to say, however, that James felt himself to be any nearer than he had ever been to a real understanding of the business situation. In *The American Scene* (1907), the direct product of the 1903-04 visit, some of the comments on the business section of New York indicate that James had come to think of the American "world of affairs" as too vast and complex for any fictional treatment—except, possibly, in the hands of a Zola. He recalls

> how from the first, on all such ground, my thought went straight to poor great wonder-working Émile Zola and *his* love of the human aggregation, the artificial microcosm, which had to spend itself on great shops, great businesses, great "apartment-houses," of inferior, of mere Parisian scale. His image, it seemed to me, really asked for compassion—in the presence of this material that his energy of evocation, his alone, would have been of a stature to meddle with. What if *Le Ventre de Paris*, what if *Au Bonheur des Dames*, what if *Pot-Bouille* and *L'Argent*, could but have come into being under the New York inspiration?
>
> The answer to that, however, for the hour, was that, in all probability, New York was not going (as it turns such remarks) to produce both the maximum of "business" spectacle and the maximum of ironic reflection of it. Zola's huge reflector got itself formed, after all, in a far other air; it had hung there, in essence, awaiting the scene that was to play over it, long before the scene really approached it in scale. The reflecting surfaces, of the ironic, of the epic order, suspended in the New York atmosphere, have yet to show symptoms of shining out, and the monstrous pheno-mena themselves, meanwhile, strike me as having, with their immense momentum, got the start, got ahead of, in proper parlance, any possibility of poetic, of dramatic capture.[27]

It is hardly surprising that James should shrink from any attempt to capture such a scene. The solution he proposed in *The Ivory*

[27] Henry James, *The American Scene*, London 1907, pp. 82-3.

Tower represented no perceptible advance on his previous practice with regard to the business milieu: the novel may mark a new development in James's social and moral attitudes at a late moment in his life, but nothing in the book makes it necessary to qualify Edith Wharton's remark, in *A Backward Glance* (1934), about James's

> total inability to use the "material", financial and industrial, of modern American life. Wall Street, and everything connected with the big business world, remained an impenetrable mystery to him, and knowing this he felt he could never have dealt fully in fiction with the "American scene", and always frankly acknowledged it. The attempt to portray the retired financier in Mr. Verver, and to relate either him or his native "American City" to any sort of concrete reality, is perhaps proof enough of the difficulties James would have found in trying to depict the American money-maker in action.[28]

3

We must be clear, of course, that we have been approaching James on what he himself recognised as his weakest side. James's ignorance of economic issues, with the limitations this imposed upon him as a novelist of American manners and of American society, has been frequently commented upon,[29] and it is worth reminding ourselves at this point that in most of his novels James's treatment of society is both skilful and shrewd. *The Bostonians* (1886), for example, is masterly in the richness and precision of its notation, and the physical setting of the novel is vividly presented: the house in which Basil Ransom lived

> had a red, rusty face, and faded green shutters, of which the slats were limp and at variance with each other. In one of the lower windows was suspended a fly-blown card, with the words "Table Board" affixed in letters cut (not very neatly) out of coloured paper, of graduated tints, and surrounded with a small band of stamped gilt.[30]

[28] Edith Wharton, *A Backward Glance*, New York and London 1934, p. 176.
[29] See, for example, F. O. Matthiessen, *Henry James: the Major Phase*, New York 1944, pp. 89–90, and Bradford A. Booth, "Henry James and the Economic Motif," *Nineteenth Century Fiction*, VIII (1953), 141–50.
[30] Henry James, *The Bostonians*, London 1921, I. 223.

The surroundings of the house are described in equally concrete terms:

> a strong odour of smoked fish, combined with a fragrance of molasses, hung about the spot; the pavement, toward the gutters, was fringed with dirty panniers, heaped with potatoes, carrots, and onions; and a smart, bright wagon, with the horse detached from the shafts, drawn up on the edge of the abominable road (it contained holes and ruts a foot deep, and immemorial accumulations of stagnant mud), imparted an idle, rural, pastoral air to a scene otherwise perhaps expressive of a rank civilization.[31]

James's notation of manners is even richer, and throughout the novel he is concerned to show the private lives of his characters interacting with the larger social world in which they move. F.R. Leavis has rightly argued that James's settings are never as solidly created as George Eliot's,[32] but in *The Bostonians*, as in *Washington Square* (1880) and *The Europeans* (1878), James shows himself to be supremely capable of exploiting certain limited areas of American society in ways similar to those found in English novels of the time.

When in his later novels James moved from the American scene to the European, he did not lose that awareness of social reality which he had demonstrated in his early work. Even in *The Golden Bowl* the much-criticised insubstantiality of the social setting may in part represent a deliberate comment on the unreality, the impossibly sheltered and rarefied lives of the characters, while in *The Ambassadors* (1903) the fact that the whole of the action is set in Europe does not prevent Woollett, Massachusetts, from attaining an extremely important position in the life of the novel and of its characters.

In *The Ambassadors* the treatment of the Paris setting is unobtrusive but extremely effective. At the beginning of Book Sixth, for example, there is a description of Madame de Vionnet's apartment:

> She occupied, his hostess, in the Rue de Bellechasse, the first floor of an old house to which our visitors had had access from an old clean court. The court was large and open, full of revelations,

[31] *Op. cit.*, I. 223-4.
[32] F. R. Leavis, *The Great Tradition*, London 1948, p. 91.

for our friend, of the habit of privacy, the peace of intervals, the dignity of distances and approaches; the house, to his restless sense, was in the high homely style of an elder day, and the ancient Paris that he was always looking for—sometimes intensely felt, sometimes more acutely missed—was in the immemorial polish of the wide waxed staircase and in the fine *boiseries*, the medallions, mouldings, mirrors, great clear spaces, of the greyish-white salon into which he had been shown. He seemed at the very outset to see her, in the midst of possessions not vulgarly numerous, but hereditary cherished charming. While his eyes turned after a little from those of his hostess and Chad freely talked—not in the least about *him*, but about other people, people he didn't know, and quite as if he did know them—he found himself making out, as a background of the occupant, some glory, some prosperity of the First Empire, some Napoleonic glamour, some dim lustre of the great legend; elements clinging still to all the consular chairs and mythological brasses and sphinxes' heads and faded surfaces of satin striped with alternate silk.[33]

This is not mere scene-setting; it charts, as the phrase "full of revelations" promises, a dawning awareness on Strether's part of the quality and style of the apartment and of its owner; it marks a crucial stage in his growing appreciation of Madame de Vionnet, and of Europe, and in his revaluation of Chad, and of Woollett. James does not describe Woollett itself because he does not need to do so. He treats Woollett as something so familiar to his readers that it need only be evoked, not described, and he is undoubtedly right in doing so. The distinctive note of Woollett is heard in the orders and communications of Mrs Newsome; Woollett is sufficiently present in the persons of the Pococks, its travelling representatives; above all Woollett is progressively defined in terms of Strether's gradual realisation of all the ways in which Europe differs from it. A more direct or more detailed treatment of society, especially of the society of Woollett, might have upset the artistic balance of the novel as a whole and would not appreciably have increased our understanding of the central situation.

Jim Pocock, that man of Woollett, is perhaps what remained

[33] Henry James, *The Ambassadors*, London 1923, I. 213-14.

to James of the businessman whom he briefly considered as a possible hero for *The Ambassadors*. In the *Notebooks* we find James musing: "A mere man of business—he's possible; but not of the intellectual grain that I mean."[34] Jim Pocock is certainly not of the "intellectual grain" of Strether, and he is far from being the hero of the book, but he is a Jamesian businessman quite as much as Newman and Verver—even if he is, in the line of Mr Ruck, a representative of the obscure rather than of the epic variety—and he is present in the book as a realised character more convincingly than Verver ever is in *The Golden Bowl*:

> Small and fat and constantly facetious, straw-coloured and destitute of marks, he would have been practically indistinguishable hadn't his constant preference for light-grey clothes, for white hats, for very big cigars and very little stories, done what it could for his identity. There were signs in him, though none of them plaintive, of always paying for others; and the principal one perhaps was just this failure of type. It was this that he paid, rather than with fatigue or waste; and also doubtless a little with the effort of humor—never irrelevant to the conditions, to the relations, with which he was acquainted.[35]

Our pleasure in this passage derives largely from the delight of recognition. Jim Pocock is not presented in any depth, but we accept him as a character for much the same reasons as we accept the indirect presentation of Woollett—because we feel sufficiently familiar with the underlying social fact, because there is between author and reader a considerable area of shared understanding, and because James exploits this area with great skill.

James's achievements as a social novelist are not, of course, confined to his portrayal of the businessman, and the term "social novelist" itself would be ridiculously limiting as a final categorisation. He is discussed here primarily because of his exemplary importance, because we see in his criticism and in his fiction a clear demonstration—deliberate in "The Question of the Opportunities," involuntary in *The American* and *The Golden Bowl*—of some of the difficulties which face the American novelist who attempts to

---

[34] *The Notebooks of Henry James*, p. 227.   [35] *The Ambassadors*, II. 72.

mirror at all accurately the most representative areas and types of his society. James felt himself impelled, largely for purposes of cultural definition, to write about businessmen of epic stature. However, the world in which such men moved *as* businessmen was unknown to James as to his readers; they might share a common knowledge of the Woollett-scale activities of a Jim Pocock, but they could share only a common ignorance of the "transcendental" operations of an Adam Verver. James sought to solve this problem by ignoring the businessman's business life and presenting only his private life: he was fairly successful in treating in this way characters like Mr Dosson, Mr Ruck, and Jim Pocock—small businessmen not at the centre of the novels or tales in which they appeared— who did not need to be developed in any depth; he might have been more successful with his major business characters if he had presented them more nearly as men whom we could possibly imagine as operating also in a business environment. Newman, for all his innocence, is perhaps just made credible by his brashness; Verver, who has not only innocence but a typically Jamesian "fine intelligence" as well, is ultimately unacceptable: James seems to have forgotten that he had ruled out a businessman as the hero of *The Ambassadors* because he would be "not of the intellectual grain that I mean." James never solved the contradiction between his need to write about the businessman and his inability to do so, and we shall find other American novelists unable to resist the beckoning figure *en disponibilité*, while remaining, at the same time, ill-equipped to present that figure in any comprehensive or deeply revealing way.

2

William Dean Howells

W hen, in "The Question of the Opportunities," Henry James spoke of business as a theme which "the novelist and the dramatist have scarcely yet seriously touched," he was perhaps a little unfair to some of his literary predecessors and contemporaries. As early as 1857, in *The Confidence-Man*, Melville had sketched, if confusingly and only very tangentially, the figure of that promoter and speculator who was such a familiar part of the American nineteenth century scene, and who reached his fullest development in the portrait of Colonel Sellers in *The Gilded Age* (1873) of Mark Twain and Charles Dudley Warner. It is not certain that James ever read *The Confidence-Man*, but even if he did it seems likely that he would have considered neither of these presentations to be entirely "serious." In *The Confidence-Man*, as in *Pierre* (1852), Melville leaves no doubt of his attitude towards the increasing commercialisation of American society, but his main concerns are metaphysical and the social insights merge into the overall pattern of fantasy-parable. In *The Gilded Age*, on the other hand, there is direct satire of the political corruption which all too often accompanied financial speculation, but the satire is blurred by the authors' reliance on ill-defined middle-class values: as W. F. Taylor observes of the economic criticism in the book, "notwithstanding the late date of its appearance, [it] is curiously pre-machine."[1]

Nowhere, in fact, does Twain develop any criticism of contemporary society that can be described as either direct or coherent. *A Connecticut Yankee in King Arthur's Court* (1889), which aims at satire through the medium of fantasy, is an uncomfortably

[1] W. F. Taylor, *The Economic Novel in America*, Chapel Hill, N.C. 1942, p. 124.

ambivalent book testifying to a motivation more emotional than intellectual and to a disabling division in Twain himself between, on the one hand, admiration for the machine, with its implications of democratic progress, and, on the other, a deep attachment to the lost pre-industrial past. Even Edward Bellamy, in his famous Utopian novel *Looking Backwards, 2000-1887* (1888), was not so much criticising contemporary society as projecting an egalitarian industrial paradise of the future. There can be no question, in fact, that William Dean Howells was the first important novelist to embark upon a "realistic" and critical presentation of the American urban-industrial society of the post-war period.

It has to be said that Howells, though an extraordinarily acute social observer, had an inadequate grasp of economics. He adhered at different times to a wide variety of social and economic theories, so that the followers of Henry George, Edward Bellamy, William Morris, Tolstoy, and various other prophets have all with some justification claimed him as one of their number, and it is easy to see why the proletarian writers of the nineteen-thirties were so impatient of this uncommitted crusader, this *soi-disant* Progressive with socialist leanings and one foot firmly in the Brahmin world. At the same time, Howells is of special interest to us now precisely because his lack of a narrowly-defined political commitment left him unusually receptive to new ideas, so that his novels of the eighteen-eighties and eighteen-nineties record sensitively the changing mood of the times. In particular, to compare *The Rise of Silas Lapham* (1885) and *A Hazard of New Fortunes* (1890) is to chart with surprising accuracy that decisive change in the American intellectual climate which took place around 1890 and gave rise to the Progressive movement.

Silas Lapham has made his fortune by exploiting a high-quality mineral paint discovered on the family farm, but in the main Howells is less concerned with Lapham's business career than with the comic situations which develop when the Lapham family attempts to enter aristocratic Boston society. Although Howells exploits the social ineptitude of the Laphams, he never does so unsympathetically. Simple principles and pieties give them strength, and the novel, in one of its aspects, is another variation on Howells's customary theme of the New England conscience. In such a view, not only do the business details serve as the framework for the social drama, but they also furnish the conditions in which Lapham can work out his personal moral drama—they become exercises, so to speak, for the testing of Lapham's conscience, and the book might have been accurately entitled "The Trying-out of Silas Lapham." Lapham appears as an honest man in a predominantly dishonest business world; he is duped by Rogers, his former partner; the two Englishmen who try to do a deal with him are tricksters; he feels that men of the world like Bellingham will think him a fool for his moral delicacy; he refuses to sell property for more than he thinks it is worth, though to do so would prevent his going bankrupt. With such scruples he is perhaps bound to fail. In the final paragraph of the book he recognises that his honesty does not necessarily pay, for he is now poor when he might have been still rich, but he knows that his sense of what is right will not allow him to behave otherwise.

Lapham is nevertheless presented as having been corrupted by his business success: he has been dishonest in his early dealings with Rogers, he gambles unwisely on the stock market, he grows conceited, he indulges in foolish ostentation in his attempts to enter Boston society. Then the unfinished house that is the outward expression and symbol of his vanity is burned down, he goes bankrupt, and the family return to the farm where the paint was originally found, to the rural source not only of their good fortune but of their solider virtues:

> All those who were concerned in his affairs said he behaved well, and even more than well, when it came to the worst. The prudence, the good sense, which he had shown in the first years of his success, and of which his great prosperity seemed to have bereft him, came back . . . He saw himself that it was useless to try to go on in the old way, and he preferred to go back and begin the world anew where he had first begun it, in the hills at Lapham.[2]

They take with them from their Boston house only the "simpler moveables" and the statues of Prayer and Faith.[3] At the farm they

[2] William Dean Howells, *The Rise of Silas Lapham*, New York [1885], pp. 496-7.
[3] *Op. cit.*, p. 513.

are contented: "In the shadow of his disaster they returned to something like their old, united life."[4]   Although Lapham is a somewhat pathetic figure after his business failure—his "spring" has gone and he appears suddenly elderly—he is unquestionably a *better* person. "Adversity had so far been his friend that it had taken from him all hope of the social success for which people crawl and truckle, and restored him, through failure and doubt and heartache, the manhood which his prosperity had so nearly stolen from him."[5]   Since prosperity steals manhood, Lapham's rise as a man is not merely accompanied by but actually dependent upon his fall in terms of conventional financial success.

The Rise of Silas Lapham seems to be innocent of political overtones; *A Hazard of New Fortunes* is full of them. In this novel, set in New York instead of Boston, the social and economic conflicts in contemporary society are extensively and explicitly explored. Old Dryfoos is a capitalist; his son Conrad is an idealistic reformer; Colonel Woodburn, a Southerner, is an agrarian-conservative critic of modern commercial society who regrets the passing of slavery; Lindau is a socialist; Fulkerson, publisher of the magazine *Every Other Week* round which the story revolves, is a cheerfully amoral minor entrepreneur; March, through whose eyes the action is most often viewed, is an uncommitted moderate with a social conscience.

These seem obviously the *dramatis personae* of a fierce ideological drama, but that is not quite the way things work out. Dryfoos is crude and avaricious, a hater of unions and an enemy of reform, yet by the end of the novel he has become less a villain than a representative of suffering humanity. Lindau the socialist is presented sympathetically as a man of generous impulses and high ideals, but he gets drunk and behaves obnoxiously and his final action, which brings about his own and Conrad's death, is to condone if not actually to encourage the use of violence in a street-car strike. The presentation of Colonel Woodburn is particularly ambiguous, and he emerges as a sympathetic but rather comic figure. As a novel *A Hazard of New Fortunes* is undoubtedly enriched by Howells's

[4] *Op. cit.*, p. 495.　　　　　　　[5] *Op. cit.*, p. 506.

interest in his characters as particular individuals with destinies of their own, but as a social statement it suffers a certain blurring of the issues. It becomes difficult to distinguish Howells's own point of view, and we can only say that *apparently* Howells identifies himself most closely with the final, cautiously pro-socialist position of March, into whose mouth is put a passionate complaint against

> this economic chance-world in which we live, and which we men seem to have created. It ought to be law as inflexible in human affairs as the order of day and night in the physical world, that if a man will work he shall both rest and eat, and shall not be harassed with any question as to how his repose and his provision shall come. Nothing less ideal than this satisfies the reason. But in our state of things no one is secure of this. No one is sure of finding work; no one is sure of not losing it. I may have my work taken away from me at any moment by the caprice, the mood, the indidigestion of a man who has not the qualification for knowing whether I do it well or ill. At my time of life—at every time of life—a man ought to feel that if he will keep on doing his duty he shall not suffer in himself or in those who are dear to him, except through natural causes. But no man can feel this as things are now; and so we go on, pushing and pulling, climbing and crawling, thrusting aside and trampling underfoot; lying, cheating, stealing; and when we get to the end, covered with blood and dirt and sin and shame, and look back over the way we've come to a palace of our own, or the poor-house, which is about the only possession we can claim in common with our brother-men, I don't think the retrospect can be pleasing.[6]

Old Dryfoos, as the only capitalist in the book, bears the brunt of the author's protests against the existing system, and it must be said at once that he makes a poor target for such an attack. Like James's Christopher Newman, but unlike Silas Lapham, Dryfoos is never seen actually conducting his business: he makes his money off-stage. When he does appear it is always out of his chosen sphere of action and in the company of men who are better educated than he is and have more social graces. Dryfoos remains, therefore, a

[6] William Dean Howells, *A Hazard of New Fortunes*, New York 1889, II. 252-253.

grotesque or, at best, a pathetic character—a poor punch-bag for Howells's indignation to work out on.

This is perhaps surprising, for, on the face of it, Dryfoos has a good deal in common with Lapham. Like Lapham he begins as a farmer. Like Lapham he originally prospers from the discovery of rich natural resources on his land, in this case natural gas. Having sold out his farm he turns to speculation in real estate, makes still more money, and eventually, by an almost inevitable progression, arrives in Wall Street. This is his moral undoing. As a farmer "other things besides his money seemed admirable to him,"[7] and he was known for his public service among his country neighbours. But once he had sold his land all this quickly changed:

> His moral decay began with his perception of the opportunity of making money quickly and abundantly, which offered itself to him after he sold his farm . . . He devolved upon a meaner ideal than that of conservative good citizenship, which had been his chief moral experience: the money he had already made without effort and withour merit bred its unholy self-love in him; he began to honour money, especially money that had been won suddenly and in large sums; for money that had been earned, painfully, slowly, and in little amounts, he had only pity and contempt. The poison of that ambition to go somewhere and be somebody which the local speculators had instilled into him began to work in the vanity which had succeeded his somewhat scornful self-respect; he rejected Europe as the proper field for his expansion; he rejected Washington; he preferred New York, whither the men who have made money and do not yet know that money has made them, all instinctively turn. He came where he could watch his money breed more money, and bring greater increase of its kind in an hour of luck than the toil of hundreds of men could earn in a year. He called it speculation, stocks, the street; and his pride, his faith in himself, mounted with his luck.[8]

Dryfoos has now left Lapham far behind. Lapham's stock market gambles had always been guilty, clandestine adventures: he had never become one of "the men who have made money and do not yet know that money has made them." At the end of the

[7] Op. cit., II. 14-5.   [8] Op. cit., II. 16-7.

novel Dryfoos is a little softened by his son's death, but there is no question of his sharing Lapham's experience of moral regeneration. Howells's presentation of Dryfoos's family is equally unrelenting in its comment on the social evils which may accompany financial success, for whereas the attempt of the Lapham women to enter society is presented with humour and sympathy, the social climbing of the Dryfoos women is seen as a crude barbarian assault.

Howells has moved away from the "uncommitted" attitude towards business displayed in *The Rise of Silas Lapham* and now, in *A Hazard of New Fortunes*, emerges as an indignant social reformer. The author's Preface to the 1909 edition recalls the social and political context in which the book had been written:

> We had passed through a period of strong emotioning in the direction of the humaner economics, if I may phrase it so; the rich seemed not so much to despise the poor, the poor did not so hopelessly repine. The solution of the riddle of the painful earth through the dreams of Henry George, through the dreams of Edward Bellamy, through the dreams of all the generous visionaries of the coast, seemed not impossibly far off. That shedding of blood which is for the remission of sins had been symbolised by the bombs and scaffolds of Chicago, and the hearts of those who felt the wrongs bound up with our rights, the slavery implicated in our liberty, were thrilling with griefs and hopes hitherto strange to the average American breast. Opportunely for me there was a great street-car strike in New York, and the story began to find its way to issues nobler and larger than those of the love-affairs common to fiction. It was in my fifty-second year when I took it up, and in the prime, such as it was, of my powers. The scene which I had chosen appealed prodigiously to me, and the action passed as nearly without my conscious agency as I ever allow myself to think such things happen.[9]

The final sentence is illuminating. *A Hazard of New Fortunes* is fully as powerful as any of Howells's books, but it lacks the formal qualities which distinguish *The Rise of Silas Lapham* as well as some of the lesser novels; Howells's intimation that the novel evolved with little conscious direction on his part may help to explain this.

[9] *A Hazard of New Fortunes*, New York 1952, p. xxii.

It may also help to explain the similarities already noted between *A Hazard of New Fortunes* and *The Rise of Silas Lapham*, in particular between Dryfoos and Lapham himself: Howells was conscious of dealing with issues "nobler and larger" than those of the earlier book; but he seems not to have realised how extensively he was in effect rewriting the story of Silas Lapham from a different point of view.

2

The comparison between *The Rise of Silas Lapham* and *A Hazard of New Fortunes* can be taken further. When, in his Utopian novels *A Traveller from Altruria* (1894) and its sequel *Through the Eye of the Needle* (1907), Howells is free to write purely as a propagandist, he proposes a Utopia in which business and money have been abolished and men set free from the anxieties of that "economic chance-world" against which March had protested in *A Hazard of New Fortunes*. Business has been done away with, says Mr Homos, the representative Altrurian, because it was "nothing structural" but only "the sterile activity of the function interposed between the demand and the supply."[10] Since everyone in Altruria must devote three hours a day to manual labour, no one need work longer hours and no one need suffer unemployment. The result is a society of cleanliness, friendliness, and light, a rural paradise where men live close to the soil. Mr Homos speaks of

> the cultivation of the earth. We believe that this, when not followed slavishly, or for gain, brings man into the closest relations to the Deity, through a grateful sense of the divine bounty, and that it not only awakens a natural piety in him, but that it endears to the worker that piece of soil which he tills, and so strengthens his love of home. The home is the very heart of the Altrurian system . . . our country is our mother, and we love her as it is impossible to love the step-mother that a competitive or monopolistic nation must be to its citizens.[11]

This very positive presentation of a rural ideal puts us in mind of books such as *New Leaf Mills* (1913) or the explicitly

[10] William Dean Howells, *A Traveller from Altruria*, New York 1908, p. 209.
[11] *Op. cit.*, pp. 195-6.

autobiographical *A Boy's Town* (1890), in which Howells recalls with great tenderness the scenes of his Ohio boyhood, and it contrasts violently with the sordid urban life of *The World of Chance* (1893), where one of the characters speaks of " 'the hideousness of a competitive metropolis. All these abominations of sight and sound, these horrible discords, that offend every sense, physically express the spiritual principle underlying the whole social framework. . . . No one can imagine the horror, the squalor, the cruel and senseless turpitude which these things typify, except in their presence.' "[12]

It seems clear that Howells shares to a considerable extent that essentially conservative "agrarian myth" of the Populists which Richard Hofstadter so skilfully analysed in *The Age of Reform*:

> The utopia of the Populists was in the past, not the future. According to the agrarian myth, the health of the state was proportionate to the degree to which it was dominated by the agricultural class, and this assumption pointed to the superiority of an earlier age. The Populists looked backward with longing to the lost agrarian Eden, to the republican America of the early years of the nineteenth century in which there were few millionaires and, as they saw it, no beggars, when the laborer had excellent prospects and the farmer had abundance, when statesmen still responded to the mood of the people and there was no such thing as the money power. What they meant—though they did not express themselves in such terms—was that they would like to restore the conditions prevailing before the development of industrialism and the commercialization of agriculture.[13]

The land is good, and so are those who belong to it, who live on and by it. Cities and money-men are evil. So Farmer Lapham, who returns at last to his land, is saved, while Farmer Dryfoos, who sells his land to the natural gas interests and his soul to "the street," is damned. This is perhaps to over-simplify the moral pattern, but the important point, that the pattern is fundamentally the same in both books, remains. By the time he comes to write *A Hazard of New Fortunes* Howells has changed his political viewpoint, but he has not changed his moral and emotional assumptions—his

---

[12] William Dean Howells, *The World of Chance*, New York 1893, pp. 296–7.
[13] Richard Hofstadter, *The Age of Reform*, New York 1955, p. 62.

sense of justice and his profound feeling for simple rural values. Indeed, these assumptions have made the political change inevitable: the heart has dictated to the head. Following the brutal Haymarket riots of 1886 and their tragic aftermath, his basic emotional commitment remained unchanged, but it found overt expression in a different political and intellectual commitment.

The comparison between the two novels makes it clear that the new commitment, bringing Howells into the Progressive movement, is more strictly a shift of emphasis than a decisive break with the past, and that Howells, the Progressive, remains in many ways a Populist at heart. Precisely because it is the heart that is in control, however, and not the head, the political and intellectual commitment will remain unsure of itself, will waver and perhaps change once more. The economic and social issues in a novel like *A Hazard of New Fortunes* will almost necessarily be blurred, for while Howells feels deeply, and is distressed by, the sufferings of individuals, he seems never to grasp the essential economic and social facts of the situation nor even the logical consequences of his own position.

The reasons why Dryfoos fails as a character now become more apparent. Lapham is a successful character because, even at the height of his prosperity, he never becomes a real money-man and never abandons the simple beliefs and standards of behaviour in which he was brought up: that is to say, he remains within the range of Howells's own experience and sympathies. But Dryfoos is a man of a new and quite different order: Howells knew little about men of that type, and his prejudices prevented him from making any imaginative leap of understanding. Accepting, unconsciously or otherwise, a substantial part of the "agrarian myth," Howells was bound to feel an instinctive revulsion when faced by a man like Dryfoos. And so Dryfoos becomes, for most of the book, a kind of half-baked and quite unconvincing ogre; the portrait is not a penetrating indictment of the ruthless, amoral Wall Street speculator, but a gesture of moral indignation at something thoroughly disliked but insufficiently understood.

The essential conservatism of Howells's attitude to business appears again in *The Quality of Mercy* (1892), in which a more sympathetic portrayal of a businessman reveals a similar failure of characterisation. The story concerns an American embezzler, Northwick, who escapes over the border into Canada, and the practical and moral effects of his behaviour on himself, his family and his business associates. The French priest whom Northwick encounters in Canada is deeply puzzled by him:

It took the young priest somewhat longer than it would have taken a man of Northwick's own language and nation to perceive that his gentlemanly decorum and grave repose of manner masked a complete ignorance of the things that interest cultivated people, and that he was merely and purely a business man, a figment of commercial civilization, with only the crudest tastes and ambitions outside of the narrow circle of money-making. He found that he had a pleasure in horses and cattle, and from hints which Northwick let fall, regarding his life at home, that he was fond of having a farm and a conservatory with rare plants. But the flowers were possessions, not passions; he did not speak of them as if they afforded him any artistic or scientific delight. The young priest learned that he had put a good deal of money in pictures; but then the pictures seemed to have become investments, and of the nature of stocks and bonds. He found that this curious American did not care to read the English books which Bird offered to lend him out of the little store of gifts and accidents accumulated in the course of years from bountiful or forgetful tourists; the books in French Père Étienne proposed to him, Northwick said he did not know how to read. He showed no liking for music, except a little for the singing of Bird's niece, Virginia, but when the priest thought he might care to understand that she sang the ballads which the first voyagers had brought from France into the wilderness, or which had sprung out of the joy and sorrow of its hard life, he saw that the fact said nothing to Northwick, and that it rather embarrassed him. The American could not take part in any of those discussions of abstract questions which the priest and the old woodsman delighted in, and which they sometimes tried to make him share. He apparently did not know what they meant. It was only when Père Étienne gave him up as the creature of a civilization too ugly and arid to be borne, that he began to love him as a brother; when he could make nothing of Northwick's mind, he conceived the hope of saving his soul.[14]

[14] William Dean Howells, *The Quality of Mercy*, New York 1892, pp. 262-3.

This elegant paragraph, which sums up admirably the reasons for the cultivated man's disdain of the "typical" businessman, suggests once more that instinct and emotion played as large a part as rational analysis in determining many of Howells's own economic and social attitudes. Unfortunately the novel as a whole falls short of this level of writing and of interest, and its fatal flaw is Howells's own inadequate conception of Northwick. He is seen sometimes from within, sometimes externally, and at critical moments it is the external view that we are almost invariably given, with that apparent shirking of the difficult which is so common in Howells's work. The novel is too long and, like so many other novels by Howells, it is too much diluted by mild and peripheral romantic interludes and by the unravelling of complicated inter-relationships. Howells's stock formulae of suspense, delay, complication and compromise were invaluable to him as a prolific writer of novels for serial publication, but they seriously impeded the working out of his central themes.

3

After *The Quality of Mercy* Howells attempted no more full-length portraits of businessmen, but from the late eighteen-eighties onwards he wrote a number of other novels on specifically economic subjects—notably *The Minister's Charge* (1887), *Annie Kilburn* (1889), *The World of Chance*, and the two Utopian novels, *A Traveller from Altruria* and *Through the Eye of the Needle*. None of these is a good novel; even *The World of Chance*, probably the best of them, is a meandering, heavily conversational book, indecisive and inconclusive despite the violent events which occur. *The World of Chance*, however, is interesting for the stage it marks in the development of Howells's political ideas, and memorable for the figure of Denton, the mad inventor, who hates and eventually destroys, because it would put men out of work, the engraving machine he has devised. There is in the book a revealing passage of dialogue when one of the characters tries to explain the success of *Uncle Tom's Cabin*:

"But that had an immense motive power behind it—a vital question that affected the whole nation."

"I seem to have come too late for the vital questions," said Ray.

"Oh, no! oh, no! There are always plenty of them left. There is the industrial slavery, which exists on a much more universal scale than the chattel slavery; that is still waiting its novelist."

"Or its Trust of novelists," Ray scornfully suggested.

"Very good; very excellent good; nothing less than a syndicate perhaps could grapple with a theme of such vast dimensions."[15]

There is perhaps an element of self-justification, or of self-mockery, in this. Howells was certainly aware of the vastness of the economic theme; there is little doubt that he was also conscious of his own inability to deal with it in any very direct way. His adventure into Utopian fiction was in part an attempt to find a solution to this problem and to resolve the conflict, particularly observable in *A Hazard of New Fortunes*, between the novelist's sense of verisimilitude and the reformer's commitment to economic and social theory.

In *A Traveller from Altruria* Howells almost abandons his role as a novelist to become little more than the unseen moderator of a middle-class discussion group. He even goes so far as to dispense with the "romantic interest" which had been an essential ingredient of all his earlier books and which even Edward Bellamy, in *Looking Backward, 2000–1887*, had felt obliged to supply. In *Through the Eye of the Needle* the romantic complications seem to exist for purely technical reasons: Howells marries an American woman to an Altrurian so that she can describe Altrurian life in letters to a friend back in the United States. The first half of the book is devoted to a satirical portrayal of American society: Mr Homos, the Altrurian, finds that Mrs Makely is

infinitely superior to her husband in cultivation, as is commonly the case with them [American women]. As he knows nothing but business, he thinks it is the only thing worth knowing, and he looks down on the tastes and interests of her more intellectual life with amiable contempt, as something almost comic. She respects business, too, and so she does not despise his ignorance as you would

---

[15] *The World of Chance*, pp. 336–7.

suppose; it is at least the ignorance of a business-man, who must have something in him beyond her ken, or else he would not be able to make money as he does.[16]

The same point has already been rather ponderously made in the Introduction: with the great increase in the production of books and periodicals "even our business-men cannot wholly escape culture, and they have become more and more cultured, so that now you frequently hear them asking what this or that book is all about."[17] The satire is at much this level of superficiality and coyness throughout: it is lightweight material heavily handled.

Considered simply as novels, then, the books have severe limitations, and only their bland style and occasional touch of whimsical humour makes them readable today. As propaganda they suffer from their failure to come to grips with the practical problems of contemporary life or to suggest a coherent political programme which might bring nearer the realisation of the social ideals they embody—although Utopian novels clearly need not expound political programmes, and Howells could hardly be blamed for omissions of this kind were it not for his own reformist pretensions. It is by no means easy to judge Howells fairly as an author of propagandist fiction. Although his Utopia seems an impossible and even forbidding dream-world of Morrisian craftmanship, innocent rusticity and clinical cleanliness, Howells himself, both as writer and as man, had greater distinction and greater courage than he is normally given credit for. It was no light thing for a man in his position to take up so strongly the cause of reform, and the attacks made upon him at this time caused personal suffering which should not be underestimated. The fact that in later years men, movements and ideas moved on past Howells—so that *Through the Eye of the Needle*, appearing in 1907, must have seemed strangely anachronistic to reformers who had read Upton Sinclair's *The Jungle* (1906) and were soon to greet Jack London's *The Iron Heel* (1908)—does not invalidate the novels of the eighteen-nineties.

Yet even in these books it is difficult to take Howells entirely

[16] William Dean Howells, *Through the Eye of the Needle*, New York and London 1907, pp. 12-13.
[17] *Op. cit.*, p. xi.

seriously as a reformer or, except in a superficial sense, as an important social novelist. His inadequacies in dealing with the business world are a case in point. He gives us some insight into the businessman at home, but he has a very limited understanding of how people behave in factories and offices, and the only kind of business activity he discusses convincingly is publishing, which he knew from personal experience. Thus we hear about the production of newspapers in *A Modern Instance*, of books in *A World of Chance*, and of magazines in *A Hazard of New Fortunes*—it is the publication of a magazine, after all, and not an industrial enterprise, which brings together the characters of this most ambitious of Howells's social novels. There is a reference in *A Traveller from Altruria* to the "killed, wounded and missing" in "the battle of life,"[18] but nowhere in Howells do we sense the excitement, exhilarating yet terrifying, of the "boundless ferocity of battle." Howells's sense of propriety, his awareness of a predominantly feminine audience, leads to the almost total exclusion from his pages of even metaphorical blood and sweat. The battles in his novels are mostly of the parlour-game variety, with social advancement the prize.

4

This, however, cannot be the final word on Howells. It may be true that his work is limited in range and that he too often shirks the difficult, but it may be fairer to say that he had an acute sense of his own limitations as an artist and that, even so, he did not shrink from exploring some areas, at least, of that prodigious American scene which James felt that only a Zola could confidently have confronted. Throughout his life Howells was always alert to new ideas and new areas of material, and in his criticism he discussed the possibilities of social fiction with a shrewdness of judgment that other American novelists, to the frustration of their own best talents, have too often lacked.

In 1912 Howells published an essay on "The Future of the American Novel" in reply to Arnold Bennett's essay of the same title which had been written in 1903 but not published until January

[18] *A Traveller from Altruria*, p. 139.

1912. Bennett had argued, much as James had done in 1899, that the great opportunity for American fiction lay in "the strenuousness, the variety, and the essential romance of American life," and in such things as the "intensity of competition, this interplay of warring activities, this havoc of operation in Wall Street, these monstrous concatenations of dollars."[19] In opposing this view, Howells points first of all to the developments that had taken place in American fiction since 1903 and says that he believes Bennett "would write in 1912 a better paper on the future of our novel than he wrote in 1903":[20]

> We do not believe, for instance, that he would now look at the phenomena of our enormous enterprise in all kinds, as the best material for fiction, as the material with which art would prosper most. That material is the stuff for the newspaper, but not for the novel, except as such wonders of the outer world can be related to the miracles of the inner world. Fiction can deal with the facts of finance and industry and invention only as the expressions of character; otherwise these things are wholly dead. Nobody really lives in them, though for the most part we live among them, in the toils of the day and the dreams of the night. . . .

> We must not, therefore, suppose that if he were writing now he would imply that our objective bigness was the stuff of our art. He must have learned from his own achievements that it could not be so, and that if we were ever to discover our greatness to others we must withdraw from our bigness to the recesses of that consciousness from which characters as well as camels are evolved. The American, no more than any other man, shall know himself from his environment, but he shall know his environment from himself. In the measure of his self-knowledge only shall he truthfully portray his neighbor, and he shall instinctively keep to his neighborhood, to his experience of it for his chance of knowledge beyond it. This has been instinctively so with the localists whom Mr. Bennett finds to have written novels of the States, but not of the United States. We for our part do not believe that the novel of the

---

[19] Quoted in William Dean Howells, *Criticism and Fiction and Other Essays*, edd. Clara Marbug Kirk and Rudolf Kirk, New York 1959, p. 335.

[20] *Op. cit.*, p. 346.

United States ever will be, or ever can be, written, or that it would be worth reading if it were written. In fiction, first the provincial, then the national, then the universal; but the parochial is better and more to be desired than either of the others. Next to the Italians and the Spaniards the Americans are the most decentralized people in the world, and just as there can never be a national Italian fiction, or national Spanish fiction, there can be no national American fiction, but only provincial, only parochial fictions evermore. The English cannot imagine this because of their allegiance to a capital, such as we feel to no supreme city of ours; and yet the English have no national novel, no United Kingdom novel. Mr. Bennett, who has written novels on a scale nobly vast, is strictly provincial in his scope; as provincial as Ibsen himself. When he goes to Paris with his scene he takes the Five Towns folk with him, and he realizes Paris to us through them, whom alone he perfectly knows. We could not wish it otherwise, and if we did we could not have it; or he, either.

Can any one, when he comes to it, really conceive of a United States novel? No more than of a novelist who should make our giant operations, our tremendous industries, our convulsive finance, our seismic politics, our shameless graft, stuff of an imaginative work.[21]

These are wise observations, and we shall see that not even such a remarkable book as John Dos Passos's *U.S.A.* (1938) can prove that Howells was fundamentally mistaken. The passage provides, among many other things, an excellent justification of Howells's own practice as a novelist, and it also suggests why he did not again attempt the ambitious scale of *A Hazard of New Fortunes*. His novels may be parochial, but in the best of them he achieves a presentation of American manners and of limited areas of contemporary American society that is both sensitive and incisive. Thus some of the scenes in *The Rise of Silas Lapham* are splendidly done, especially the encounters of the female Laphams and the female Coreys, and the dinner party at the Coreys' when Lapham gets drunk:

He was in this successful mood when word came to him that Mrs. Lapham was going; Tom Corey seemed to have brought it,

[21] *Op. cit.*, pp. 346–7.

but he was not sure. Anyway, he was not going to hurry. He made cordial invitations to each of the gentlemen to drop in and see him at his office, and would not be satisfied till he had exacted a promise from each. He told Charles Bellingham that he liked him, and assured James Bellingham that it had always been his ambition to know him, and that if any one had said when he first came to Boston that in less than ten years he should be hobnobbing with Jim Bellingham, he should have told that person he lied. He would have told anybody he lied that had told him ten years ago that a son of Bromfield Corey would have come and asked him to take him into the business. Ten years ago he, Silas Lapham, had come to Boston a little worse off than nothing at all, for he was in debt for half the money that he had bought out his partner with, and here he was now worth a million, and meeting you gentlemen like one of you. And every cent of that was honest money—no speculation—every copper of it for value received. And here, only the other day, his old partner, who had been going to the dogs ever since he went out of the business, came and borrowed twenty thousand dollars of him! Lapham lent it because his wife wanted him to: she had always felt bad about the fellow's having to go out of the business.[22]

The fidelity of presentation in this passage shows Howells at his finest; James could never be so downright, so close to the natural speech rhythms, and Howells himself was rarely to come so close again.

Howells's sensitivity shows itself in the delicately handled situations of that slight but engaging novel *The Lady of the Aroostook* (1879). Although the action takes place on board ship and in Venice, the essential concern of the book is the interplay of American manners. A beautiful young American girl—too innocent, too unsophisticated and too middle-class to realise that her position might be lacking in social propriety—finds herself the only woman aboard an American ship bound for Venice and the focus of attention not only for the three young male passengers but for the captain of the ship and all the crew:

As the first week wore away, the wonted incidents of a sea voyage lent their variety to the life on board. One day the ship

[22] *The Rise of Silas Lapham*, pp. 290-1.

ran into a school of whales, . . . At another time some flying-fish came on board. The sailors caught a dolphin, and they promised a shark, by and by. All these things were turned to account for the young girl's amusement, as if they had happened for her. The dolphin died that she might wonder and pity his beautiful death; the cook fried her some of the flying-fish; someone was on the lookout to detect even porpoises for her. A sail in the offing won the discoverer envy when he pointed it out to her; a steamer, celebrity. The captain ran a point out of his course to speak to a vessel, that she might be able to tell what speaking a ship at sea was like.[23]

The young men bring out their private stores so that the girl may feed upon delicacies, and one of them finds her a chair to sit on:

After that, as she reclined in this chair, wrapped in her red shawl, and provided with a book or some sort of becoming handiwork, she was even more picturesquely than before the centre about which the ship's pride and chivalrous sentiment revolved. They were Americans, and they knew how to worship a woman.[24]

Although much of Howells's work is insipid and tedious, the reader is always sustained by the clarity and easy flow of the style and by the hope of a sharply observed scene of social comedy. This comic sense, so evident throughout even such a minor work as *The Lady of the Aroostook*, is perhaps Howells's greatest strength; certainly it constitutes the pervasive mood of his best work. His impulse to deal directly with social "problems" and "questions" arose from the same essential generosity of spirit, but it was an impulse which ran counter to his true talents as a novelist. From the beginning of his career the imperious demands of social serious-ness tended again and again to lead Howells artistically astray; although *Dr. Breen's Practice* (1881), as a study of that modern phenomenon the woman doctor, is doubtless a more "worthy" book than *The Lady of the Aroostook*, it is much less successful, and much less enjoyable. In *A Modern Instance* and *The Rise of Silas Lapham*, which certainly rank among Howells's very best work, certain elements of social seriousness are successfully carried off, but

[23] William Dean Howells, *The Lady of the Aroostook*, Boston 1880, p. 94.
[24] *Op. cit.*, p. 95.

this is largely because of Howells's vigorous portrayal of the central character in each book. Bartley Hubbard and Silas Lapham are Howells's most vital creations, and one of the high points in his work is the scene in the opening chapter of *The Rise of Silas Lapham* when one of these aggressively self-made men is interviewed by the other. Indeed, Howells's principal contribution as an American social novelist is perhaps to be found not in the earnest economic novels but in these more ebullient books of his earlier period, in which, for the first time, he gives vivid fictional realisation to the self-made man in his American setting.

James was not absolutely unfair to Howells when he spoke of business as a theme which novelists had "scarcely yet seriously touched"—he may, indeed, have had Howells in mind when he introduced that qualifying "scarcely"—but if *The Rise of Silas Lapham* and *A Hazard of New Fortunes*, together with *A Modern Instance* and the best of the other novels, are not finally "serious" when judged by the highest critical standards, there can at least be little doubt of their lasting literary value or of their historical importance as novels of American society. Howells is perhaps of greater significance as a social novelist in terms of what he attempted rather than of what he achieved. Although he is not in the first rank of American novelists, he is the first important novelist to treat of American life in its normal rather than its abnormal aspects and to treat it comprehensively—not in the form of "the great American novel," a conception which both as a novelist and as a critic he emphatically rejected, but rather by numerous explorations of a more episodic nature, limited in scope but always acutely observed.

3
Frank Norris

rank Norris's *The Pit* (1903) is perhaps the first American novel of literary importance to derive its central interest from detailed descriptions of business activities; it certainly contains the first large-scale fictional presentation of an American captain of finance. The story of *The Pit* concerns Curtis Jadwin's attempt to corner the world wheat market through speculation on the Chicago wheat exchange, the "Pit" of the title, and the way these business activities affect his relationship with Laura, his "artistic" wife. It is a carefully, even self-consciously, structured novel: the whispers about the wheat which spoil Laura's evening at the Opera foreshadow the intrusion of the wheat into her own life and reflect the indifference of the world of business to what Chicago took to be the world of art and gracious living; the subject of those whispered discussions, the failure of an attempt to corner the market, is ironically related to Jadwin's own failure later in the book; and at the very end of the novel, as Jadwin and Laura are leaving to start a new life in the West, the early description of the brokers' offices working overtime is repeated, almost word for word. But the structuring only intensifies the sense of artificiality, of contrivance, that the novel gives. It becomes only too clear only too soon what the end will be—it is simply a matter of time.

What does engage the reader's attention is Norris's ability to squeeze excitement from the sheer audacity of Jadwin's attempt and from the details of the business operations in the "Pit" itself: he describes the changing mood of the "Pit" at critical moments, the violent fluctuations of triumph and disaster, and successfully conveys the all-absorbing nature of the speculative fever. The choice of the Chicago Wheat Exchange as a subject had one very great advantage: speculation in wheat is sufficiently straightforward for the ordinary reader to understand the essentials without needing to be bombarded with detailed explanations, as tends to happen in Dreiser's business novels. This makes for a nice management of that problem of comprehension mentioned by James. Moreover, Norris concentrates on the operations, visible and audible, of the "Pit" itself, tending to ignore or minimise the importance of political and other pressures. Unlike Dreiser, he does not feel impelled to give the whole picture, to present all the ascertainable facts, and this helps to give the narrative a certain clarity and strength. It is not clear that Norris had these factors particularly in mind when he chose his setting for the novel; in large measure, his choice must have been determined by his overall design for a three-volume "Epic of the Wheat," but it also seems likely that the Chicago Wheat Exchange attracted him as a possible setting for an American novel along the lines of Zola's *L'Argent* (1891).

Certainly, as Lars Åhnebrink has pointed out,[1] there is a remarkably close relationship between *L'Argent* and *The Pit*. *L'Argent* deals with speculation on the Paris Bourse and in particular with the history of one company, the Universal Bank, whose shares are pushed up to fantastic prices before collapsing in general ruin. M. Saccard, the promoter, perhaps resembles Dreiser's Frank Cowperwood more than Curtis Jadwin; he is intensely self-centred, unscrupulous, with a fierce appetite for women. Yet Saccard and Jadwin have much in common. Both engage in speculation for the love of battle rather than for the hope of gain. Both are known, more or less justly, for their kindness to the unfortunate. Both are frequently described as "Napoleonic."[2] Both commit themselves unreservedly to the enterprises in which they are engaged, Jadwin expending his personal fortune to support the price of wheat, Saccard using his to sustain the price of the Bank's shares. Both are driven on beyond what is wise and prudent in their ambition to achieve an unreasonable goal; when defeat eventually comes, each loses more heavily than his associates. Saccard is

[1] Lars Åhnebrink, *The Beginnings of Naturalism in American Fiction*, Uppsala and Cambridge, Mass. 1950, pp. 301-04.
[2] Emile Zola, *Money (L'Argent)*, tr. Ernest A. Vizetelly, London 1894, pp. 349, 411, 415; Frank Norris, *The Pit*, London 1903, pp. 197, 262, 332.

driven on by a desire to revenge himself upon the Jewish bankers; Jadwin does not have quite this personal revenge motive but he does desire to crush one particular speculator (Scannell) as punishment for his dishonest treatment of a former partner (Hargus). Both are loved by good women much gentler and more civilised than themselves, and loved above all because they are men of courage, activity, and intense vitality. An example of the more detailed resemblances between the two books is the false rumour that almost panics the market: in *L'Argent* the rumour is of an English ultimatum to France to stop work at Suez;[3] in *The Pit* it is of an English ultimatum to Turkey.[4] It seems clear, in fact, that *The Pit* represents a fairly sustained attempt to transpose *L'Argent* into an American context.

Unfortunately, *The Pit* remains a much less ambitious book than *L'Argent*, and a lesser achievement. Norris avoids the sordid lower depths of the financial world and only hints at the suffering caused by unscrupulous manipulators; he has, as it were, creamed off the top of finance, emphasising the excitement and romance, omitting the dirt and crime. Thus *The Pit* expresses, with few qualifications, a romantic conception of business. As Laura sits in the Opera she hears in the occasional silences fragments of the whispered conversation about the failure of the wheat "corner":

> And abruptly, midway between two phases of that music-drama, of passion and romance, there came to Laura the swift and vivid impression of that other drama that simultaneously—even at that very moment—was working itself out close at hand, equally picturesque, equally romantic, equally passionate; but more than that, real, actual, modern, a thing in the very heart of the very life in which she moved.[5]

A little later in the book Laura, though attracted by the artist Corthell, comes to realise that her feeling for Jadwin, the man of business, is far more powerful:

> Then suddenly Laura surprised herself. After all, she was a daughter of the frontier, and the blood of those who had wrestled with a new world flowed in her body. Yes, Corthell's was a

---

[3] *Money*, p. 9.   [4] *The Pit*, pp. 90-1.   [5] *Op. cit.*, p. 34.

beautiful life; . . . But the men to whom the woman in her turned were not those of the studio. Terrible as the Battle of the Street was, it was yet battle. Only the strong and the brave might dare it, and the figure that held her imagination and her sympathy was not the artist . . . but the fighter, unknown and unknowable to women as he was; hard, rigorous, panoplied in the harness of the warrior, who strove among the trumpets, and who, in the brunt of conflict, conspicuous, formidable, set the battle in a rage around him, and exulted like a champion in the shoutings of the captains.[6]

Norris's adaptation of Biblical imagery is not particularly successful, but it does suggest how earnestly he is attempting to invest business with an aura of antique splendour and romance.

The romantic possibilities of business had been recognised by Zola, whom indeed Norris claims as "the very head of the Romanticists,"[7] and Norris seized on these possibilities with immense enthusiasm. In *The Responsibilities of the Novelist* (1903), he writes:

The desire for conquest—say what you will—was as big in the breast of the most fervid of the Crusaders as it is this very day in the most peacefully disposed of American manufacturers. Had the Lion-Hearted Richard lived to-day he would have become a "leading representative of the Amalgamated Steel Companies," and doubt not for one moment that he would have underbid his Manchester rivals in the matter of bridge-girders. Had Mr. Andrew Carnegie been alive at the time of the preachings of Peter the Hermit he would have raised a company of *gens d'armes* sooner than all of his brothers-in-arms, would have equipped his men better and more effectively, would have been first on the ground before Jerusalem, would have built the most ingenious siege-engine and have hurled the first cask of Greek-fire over the walls.

Competition and conquest are words easily interchangeable, and the whole spirit of our present commercial crusade to the Eastward betrays itself in the fact that we cannot speak of it but in terms borrowed from the glossary of the warrior. It is a commercial "invasion," a trade "war," a "threatened attack" on the part of America, business is "captured," opportunities are "seized,"

[6] *Op. cit.*, p. 65.
[7] Frank Norris, *The Responsibilities of the Novelist*, London 1903, p. 215.

certain industries are "killed," certain former monopolies are "wrested away." Seven hundred years ago a certain Count Baldwin, a great leader in the attack of the Anglo-Saxon Crusaders upon the Old World, built himself a siege-engine which would help him enter the beleaguered city of Jerusalem. Jerusalem is beleaguered again to-day, and the hosts of the Anglo-Saxon commercial crusaders are knocking at the gates. And now a company named for another Baldwin—and, for all we know, a descendant of the Count—leaders of the invaders of the Old World, advance upon the city, and, to help in the assault, build an engine—only now the engine is no longer called a *mangonel* but a locomotive.

The difference is hardly of kind and scarcely of degree. It is a mere matter of names, and the ghost of Saladin watching the present engagement might easily fancy the old days back again.[8]

The point about military imagery is well taken. In *The Pit*, as in *L'Argent*, images of battle appear again and again in descriptions of commercial operations. Business as battle, and both as romance: James had a similar vision. Elsewhere in *The Responsibilities of the Novelist* Norris writes: "Romance does very well in the castles of the Middle Ages and the Renaissance chateaux, . . . but, if you choose to look for her, you will find her equally at home in the brownstone house on the corner and in the office-building downtown."[9] Norris also suggests that commerce is perhaps only the latest form to be taken by that great, uniquely American romance of the frontier which had seemed on the point of extinction ("we must look for the lost battle-line not toward the sunest, but toward the East.")[10], and we may recall how Laura's recognition that she was "a daughter of the Frontier" spurred her admiration for Jadwin, the "warrior" of business, rather than for Corthell, the artist.

The weakness of Norris's opposition between the artist and the practical man of affairs lies in his failure to make Corthell a convincing character: in dealing with the "artistic" Norris is hardly more at ease than Dreiser. Indeed, the characterisation throughout the novel is inadequately developed, even in comparison with what Norris had shown himself capable of in *McTeague* and in characters like Annixter and Magnus Derrick in *The Octopus*. Laura remains

[8] *Op. cit.*, pp. 74-5.   [9] *Op. cit.*, p. 218.   [10] *Op. cit.*, p. 76.

a misty, somewhat Pre-Raphaelite figure, but Norris presents effectively, if too melodramatically, the picture of a woman who sees not another woman but her husband's business as her deadly rival: "'It's wheat—wheat—wheat, wheat—wheat—wheat, all the time. Oh, if you knew how I hated and feared it!'"[11] Jadwin is intermittently convincing, especially in his moments of more relaxed speech, and Norris does manage to convey something of his "Napoleonic" quality. But the character never hangs together. Kind and even lovable at home, unscrupulous and brutal in the "Pit," Jadwin is too much of the Jekyll-and-Hyde to seem human. Norris repeatedly emphasises the gulf between Jadwin's sentimentality on the one hand and his ruthlessness on the other, but fails to suggest what unites them in a single personality. Everything is subordinated to Norris's dominating idea that Jadwin is defeated not by his fellow-men but by the Wheat, acting in accordance with inexorable natural laws: "He had laid his puny human grasp upon Creation and the very earth herself, the great mother . . . had stirred at last in her sleep and sent her omnipotence moving through the grooves of the world, to find and crush the disturber of her appointed courses."[12] Jadwin, in the grip of the speculative fever, becomes a *different* person, a man possessed: "'Corner wheat! It's the wheat that has cornered me'."[13] His behaviour seems to be dictated by the demands of Norris's over-riding economic and philosophical theories: it does not grow naturally out of his character as previously revealed.

2

The Pit was left unrevised at Norris's death in 1902, but when all allowances have been made it remains only partially successful, and there can be no doubt that it appears crude and limited, a distinctly minor work, by comparison with a James or a good Edith Wharton novel. At the same time, we must recognise how nearly *The Pit* fulfils James's conception of what the American business novel might be. The epic heroism, the "wounds of the market," the "ferocity of battle," the imagery of war and the aura of romance, the central importance of the relationship between the businessman and his

[11] *The Pit*, p. 231.   [12] *Op. cit.*, p. 374.   [13] *Op. cit.*, p. 352.

"immitigable womankind"—Norris gives fictional substance to just those elements which James propounded in theory. But these elements in *The Pit* are precisely the ones which Norris seems to have taken from *L'Argent*, and we may here recall the reference which James himself makes to *L'Argent* in "The Question of the Opportunities" as "The most energetic attempt at portrayal [of 'the world of affairs'] that we have anywhere had." James criticises *L'Argent* on the grounds that its subject "is all too mechanically, if prodigiously, 'got up,'" yet he does acknowledge the energy and the "richly imagined" quality of the book.[14] Though there is no evidence of James having in fact read *The Pit*, it seems likely that he would have judged it in similar terms, if with greater reservations.

Looking back at "The Question of the Opportunities" with both *L'Argent* and *The Pit* in mind it is hard to resist the conclusion that, far more than he may have realised, James's reading of *L'Argent* had profoundly influenced his prospectus of the potential novel of American business. It is perhaps worth noting that after his 1903-04 visit to America, when James became aware for the first time of the full effect of contemporary American business activity, he seems to have respected Zola's gifts more than ever: in the passage already quoted from *The American Scene*, for example, he speaks of Zola, with almost envious admiration, as the only writer who might have measured up to the New York business spectacle.[15] It seems unlikely, though not impossible, that Norris was influenced by James's essay, but it is interesting to think of James as a possible theoretician for such a practitioner. What emerges so impressively from the juxtaposition is not the narrowness of James's art but the catholicity, the comprehensiveness of his sympathies and insights; he was quite as aware as younger writers of the "opportunities" offered by an expanding society, and no one responded more eagerly to the appearance of such new novelistic material, however far it might seem to lie outside the conceivable boundaries of his own interests as a creative artist.

[14] All quotations in this paragraph: *The American Essays of Henry James*, pp. 202-03. Howells also admired *L'Argent*: see *My Literary Passions*, New York 1895, pp. 246-7.
[15] See also Henry James, "Emile Zola," *Notes on Novelists* (1914). Reprinted in *The Future of the Novel*, ed. Leon Edel, London 1901, p. 608.

3

The Pit deserves consideration as a more important and more impressive novel than critical opinion generally allows, but there can be no doubt that Norris's power as a novelist finds fuller expression in *The Octopus* (1901), an earlier and much larger work. The "Octopus," a predatory and monopolistic railroad, exerts pressures upon a group of wheat farmers in the San Joaquin valley of California, gradually but inexorably squeezing them to death. But this is far from being the usual type of "muckraking" novel; at least, Norris does not draw the usual "muckraker's" moral. Certainly he presents the railroad as evil, its agents as cruel, unprincipled and avaricious, its magnates as excessively wealthy at the expense of the farmers: "Because Magnus had been beggared, Gerard had become Railroad King; because the farmers of the valley were poor, these men were rich."[16]   Near the end of the book Norris juxtaposes scenes of the Gerard family dining in luxury with scenes of Mrs Hooven, widow of a farmer killed in a fight with railroad employees, dragging homeless, penniless, and dying through the streets outside.   Presley, the poet turned from aestheticism to solidarity with "the People," is an unwilling guest at the Gerard mansion, and at the very moment when, unknown to him, Mrs Hooven falls and dies, he is thinking:

> Yes, the People *would* turn some day, and turning, rend those who now preyed upon them.   It would be "dog eat dog" again, with positions reversed, and he saw for one instant of time that splendid house sacked to its foundations, the tables overturned, the pictures torn, the hangings blazing, and Liberty, the red-handed Man in the Street, grimed with powder smoke, foul with the gutter, rush yelling, torch in hand, through every door.
>
> ———
>
> At ten o'clock Mrs. Hooven fell.[17]

The juxtaposition is so deliberate that Norris must mean us to sympathise with Presley's bitterness and indignation.   Yet Presley has already penetrated to the office of Shelgrim, the president

[16] Frank Norris, *The Octopus*, London 1901, p. 608.
[17] *Op. cit.*, pp. 608-09.

of the railroad, whom he had imagined to be the cold, calculating villain of the piece, and found him a man of cultivated tastes, wide sympathies and vast energies. Shelgrim explains that though he "runs" the railroad he cannot "control" it:

> "You are dealing with forces, young man, when you speak of Wheat and the Railroads, not with men. There is the Wheat, the supply. It must be carried to feed the People. There is the demand. The Wheat is one force, the Railroad, another, and there is the law that governs them—supply and demand. Men have only little to do in the whole business."[18]

Conflicts that had seemed real are revealed as merely illusory. The situation is potentially ironic, but Norris, writing with impetuous earnestness, sweeps this possibility impatiently aside. At the end of the book he tries, by sheer accumulation of disasters, to induce a sense of tragedy and despair, but on the very last page he turns the tables upon himself and the reader, asserting faith in progress and the emergence of good from evil:

> Falseness dies; injustice and oppression in the end of everything fade and vanish away. Greed, cruelty, selfishness, and inhumanity are short-lived; the individual suffers, but the race goes on . . . The larger view always and through all shams, all wickednesses, discovers the Truth that will, in the end, prevail, and all things, surely, inevitably, resistlessly work together for good.[19]

Nothing in the book has adequately anticipated this conclusion: there is no "objective correlative" for it, unless the mystical renewal of life, the "Allegory of the Wheat," which the shepherd Vanamee experiences can be regarded as a symbolic enactment of the theme.[20]

It is possible that the ending may have been determined, at least in part, by Norris's plan for a "Trilogy of the Epic of the Wheat," of which *The Octopus* was to form the first volume, *The Pit* the second. The germ of this idea appears in Norris's story "A Deal in Wheat." Sam Lewiston, a wheat farmer, is ruined by a disastrous fall in wheat prices brought about by the activities of

---

[18] *Op. cit.*, p. 576.　　　　[19] *Op. cit.*, pp. 651-2.
[20] See, however, the very interesting analysis in Donald Pizer, "Another Look at *The Octopus*," *Nineteenth-Century Fiction*, x (1955), 217-24.

a "bear" group on the Chicago exchange. He comes into the city to find work and, while still unemployed, is standing one night in a breadline when the handouts are stopped because a "bull" market has driven the price of wheat to prohibitive heights. The story ends:

> He had seen the two ends of a great wheat operation—a battle between Bear and Bull. The stories (subsequently published in the city's press) of Truslow's countermove in selling Hornung his own wheat, supplied the unseen section. The farmer—he who raised the wheat—was ruined upon one hand; the working-man —he who consumed it—was ruined upon the other. But between the two, the great operators, who never saw the wheat they traded in, bought and sold the world's food, gambled in the nourishment of entire nations, practised their tricks, their chicanery and oblique "shifty" deals, were reconciled in their differences, and went on through their appointed way, jovial, contented, enthroned, and unassailable![21]

In developing this idea Norris not only changed its emphasis, apparently deciding that it was an over-simplification to lay all blame on the Chicago speculators, but he enormously expanded its scope. The final plan was that *The Octopus*, sub-titled "a Story of California," would portray the production of the wheat, *The Pit*, "a Story of Chicago," its distribution, and the projected but never written third volume, *The Wolf*, "a Story of Europe," its consumption. In a prefatory note to *The Pit*, Norris says that *The Wolf* " will probably have for its pivotal episode the relieving of a famine in an Old World community."[22] The three novels were to be quite separate, related only by the theme of the wheat and by the laws of economics, as Norris saw them, and although *The Pit* was written after *The Octopus* the whole book has only one passing reference to the San Joaquin valley. But, had Norris lived, it is conceivable that he might have been able, in *The Wolf*, to round off the trilogy into a satisfactory whole, making the apparent inconsistencies within individual works fully comprehensible as parts of an overall pattern.

[21] Frank Norris, *A Deal in Wheat: and Other Stories of the New and Old West*, London 1903, pp. 25-6.
[22] *The Pit*, p. [vii].

4

It seems quite likely that the completed trilogy would have been recognisable as an agrarian or Populist parable on a huge scale, reflecting somewhat the pattern of "A Deal in Wheat." As Richard Chase points out, it is clear from Norris's novels that he accepted a good deal of the Populist mythology described by Richard Hofstadter, in *The Age of Reform*.[23] Chase takes an example from *The Octopus*, where Norris opposes the fruitful land to the evil city, corrupter of Hyman Derrick, son of the soil. He might also have pointed to the presentation of the railway engine, representative of the encroaching "Octopus," as an iron monster,[24] or to the remarkable description of the harvesting machine near the end of the book:

> The harvester, shooting a column of thick smoke straight upward, vibrating to the top of the stack, hissed, clanked, and lurched forward. Instantly, motion sprang to life in all its component parts; the header knives, cutting a thirty-six foot swath, gnashed like teeth; beltings slid and moved like smooth flowing streams; the separator whirred, the agitator jarred and crashed; cylinders, augers, fans, seeders and elevators, drapers and chaff-carriers clattered, rumbled, buzzed, and clanged. The steam hissed and rasped; the ground reverberated a hollow note, and the thousands upon thousands of wheat stalks sliced and slashed in the clashing shears of the header, rattled like dry rushes in a hurricane, as they fell inward, and were caught up by an endless belt, to disappear into the bowels of the vast brute that devoured them.
>
> It was that and no less. It was the feeding of some prodigious monster, insatiable, with iron teeth, gnashing and threshing into the fields of standing wheat; devouring always, never glutted, never satiated, swallowing an entire harvest, snarling and slobbering in a swelter of warm vapour, acrid smoke, and blinding, pungent clouds of chaff. It moved belly-deep in the standing grain, a hippopotamus, half-mired in river ooze, gorging rushes, snorting, sweating; a dinosaur wallowing through thick, hot grasses, floundering there, crouching, grovelling there as its vast jaws crushed

[23] Chase, *The American Novel and its Tradition*, London 1958, p. 201. For Hofstadter see Chapter Two above, p. 26.
[24] *The Octopus*, p. 51.

and tore, and its enormous gullet swallowed, incessant, ravenous, and inordinate.[25]

Significantly, the machine is the special delight of S. Behrman, the villainous agent of the railroad.

The passage looks forward to the very similar anti-machine imagery in Steinbeck's *The Grapes of Wrath* (1939),[26] but it also recalls the underlying agrarian pattern which, in Chapter Two, we have already discerned in some of the novels of William Dean Howells. There are many obvious differences between Norris and Howells, but the similarities are no less important. Certain elements in *The Pit*, for example, recall *The Rise of Silas Lapham*: the new house as a symbol of success, Jadwin's delight in the open-air life of fishing and boating, and the way in which Jadwin is "saved" by his failure and leaves the city at the end of the novel to begin a new life in the West. There are also several specific references in *The Pit* to Howells and *The Rise of Silas Lapham*. Howells, we learn, is Jadwin's "abiding affinity":

> "Nothing much happens," he said. "But I *know* all those people." He never could rid himself of a surreptitious admiration for Bartley Hubbard. He, too, was "smart" and "alive." He had the "get there" to him. "Why," he would say, "I know fifty boys just like him down there in La Salle Street." Lapham he loved as a brother.[27]

In *The Octopus*, too, we are sometimes reminded of Howells by the realism which is one of the most important elements in the book and one of the main sources of its strength:

> Next the appointments of the sitting-room occupied her—since Annixter, himself, bewildered by this astonishing display, unable to offer a single suggestion himself, merely approved of all she bought. In the sitting-room was to be a beautiful blue and

[25] *Op. cit.*, p. 616.

[26] John Steinbeck, *The Grapes of Wrath*, New York 1939. See, for example, p. 48: "The man sitting in the iron seat did not look like a man; gloved, goggled, rubber dustmask over nose and mouth, he was a part of the monster, a robot in the seat . . . . He could not see the land as it was, he could not smell the land as it smelled; his feet did not stamp the clods or feel the warmth and power of the earth. He sat in an iron seat and stepped on iron pedals."

[27] *The Pit*, p. 216.

white paper, cool straw matting, set off with white wool rugs, a
stand of flowers in the window, a globe of goldfish, rocking chairs,
a sewing machine, and a great, round centre table of yellow oak
whereon should stand a lamp covered with a deep shade of crinkly
red tissue paper. On the walls were to hang several pictures—
lovely affairs, photographs from life, all properly tinted—of choir
boys in robes, with beautiful eyes; pensive young girls in pink
gowns, with flowing yellow hair, drooping over golden harps;
a coloured reproduction of "Rouget de Lisle, Singing the Mar-
seillaise," and two "pieces" of wood carving, representing a quail and
a wild duck, hung by one leg in the midst of game bags and powder
horns,—quite masterpieces, both.[28]

Despite the mild irony running through the passage, we recognise
here a delight, quite as strong as that of any local colourist or
Howellsian realist, in the quality and variety of objects and in their
sheer multiplicity. Even the big set pieces, such as the dance at
Annixters and the rabbit-drive, are built up by ample if not especially delicate notation. Howells responded to this quality in Norris
even while acknowledging the scope of Norris's ambition:

> We do not forget what Frank Norris did and wished to do. His
> epic of the wheat was to have run from California to Chicago,
> and from Chicago to Paris; but he, too, was a localist, and *The
> Octopus* was better than *The Pit*, because he had lived more in
> California than in Chicago, and was more vitally intimate with
> his scene and action there. Closer, firmer, truer than even *The
> Octopus* is Norris's other great book, *McTeague*, which scarcely
> ever leaves the shabby San Francisco street where the irregular den-
> tist hangs out his sign of a golden tooth.[29]

There can be no doubt of Norris's central concern with the
presentation of social reality. In the chapter on "An American
School of Fiction" in *The Responsibilities of the Novelist* he assumes
that American writers have a duty to American literature and goes
on to criticise Henry James for his abandonment of the American

[28] *The Octopus*, p. 282. This particular passage is reminiscent not only of Howells
but, more specifically, of Twain's description of the Grangerford household in
Huckleberry Finn.
[29] Howells, "The Future of the American Novel," in *Criticism and Fiction and
Other Essays*, pp. 348-9.

scene. In the chapter on "Novelists of the Future" he declares firmly that fiction is not for aesthetes: "Dependent solely upon fidelity to life for existence, it must be practised in the very heart's heart of life, on the street corner, in the market-place, not in the studios."[30] This last point he develops further in the chapter called "Salt and Society":

> If the modern novelist does not understand the Plain People, if he does not address himself directly to them intelligibly and simply, he will fail. But he will never understand them by shutting himself away from them. He must be . . . a Man of the World. None more so. Books have no place in his equipment, have no right to be there; will only cumber and confuse him. His predecessors never read the newspapers, but for him the newspaper is more valuable than all the tomes of Ruskin, all the volumes of Carlyle. And more valuable than all are the actual, vital affairs of Men. The function of the novelist of the present day is to comment upon life as he sees it. He cannot get away from this; this is his excuse for existence, the only claim he has upon attention. How necessary then for him—of all men—to be in the midst of life. He cannot plunge too deeply into it.[31]

The feeling of determined effort about this passage perhaps reflects Norris's own difficulties as a novelist—difficulties which are dramatised in The Octopus in the figure of Presley, an aesthete coming to terms with the West and the "People." Moved by the grandeur of his native California and by the story of the Southern Pacific's activities in the San Joaquin valley, Norris seems able to approach his material only with certain inhibitions, certain doubts about his role as an artist. Thus in The Octopus a fundamental preoccupation with social reality is combined with a "romanticism" of treatment which reveals itself in a melodramatic manipulation of plot and incident, as in the counterpointing of Mrs Hooven's collapse against the luxury of the Gerards' dinner party, in a deliberate writing-up of the Vanamee sub-plot, with its crudely allegorical overtones, and in the injection of verbal excitement into evocations of the wrath of the "People," the villainy of the railroad, or the omnipotence of "forces."

---

[30] The Responsibilities of the Novelist, p. 208.   [31] Op. cit., p. 282.

Chase does not rate Norris very highly as a novelist, but he makes a good deal of the chapter entitled "A Plea for Romantic Fiction" in *The Responsibilities of the Novelist* and claims Norris as an important figure in the maintenance and transmission of the tradition stemming from Hawthorne and Melville and "the older romancers"[32] generally. He argues in particular that in Norris's novels we find new versions of "two of the leading imaginative ideas of Melville," the ideas of the golden age and of the "power of blackness," and that Norris derived these ideas mainly from his "instinctive imaginative sympathy" with Populism and its folk-lore.[33] As we have seen, strong romantic elements appear in both *The Pit* and *The Octopus*, while others equally strong are present in those violent novels, *McTeague* (1899) and *Vandover and the Brute* (written 1894-5, published posthumously 1914), but in view of what we have already seen of Norris's interest in realism and of the similarities between his work and Howells's—especially their common indebtedness to Populist "folklore"—we can hardly accept Chases's suggestions in their entirety. It certainly seems too much to claim for Norris that his imagery and his "imaginative profundity"[34] make him into a romance-writer in the line of Hawthorne and Melville.

Obviously we cannot talk of Norris without using the term "romance," if only because Norris himself makes such play with it, but clearly the term does not carry the same connotations for him as for Hawthorne, say, in the Preface to *The House of the Seven Gables*. *The Octopus* is melodrama on the grand scale—just as another response to the West of that period, Owen Wister's *The Virginian* (1902), with a similar progression of set scenes and contrived tensions, is melodrama on the small scale—and it is romance only in so far as Norris responds in a crudely "romantic" way, as business-men speak of "the romance of commerce," to the facts on which the book is based and the scenes in which it is set. It was just this habit of giving melodramatic elaboration to fundamentally "realis-tic" material which Norris recognised in Zola when claiming him as "the very head of the romanticists," and it is this quality in

[32] Chase, *The American Novel and Its Tradition*, p. 199.
[33] *Op. cit.*, p. 201   [34] *Op. cit.*, p. 203.

Norris which may make it seem more appropriate to link his novels not with those of Hawthorne and Melville but rather with those of Upton Sinclair and Jack London, even of Booth Tarkington and Sinclair Lewis.

Norris's importance as a social novelist derives primarily from the sense of liberation that we experience in coming to his work from that of Howells. For all their acuteness of observation, Howells's novels sometimes tend to present social activity less than life-size; it seems more limited in scope, smaller in scale, than it would be in actuality. In Norris's novels, on the other hand, we find a coarse vitality, an extravagance of treatment and of language, which provides an obvious and invigorating counter-balance to the more cautious approach of Howells. This is not necessarily to say that Norris's books are of greater literary value or that they are more accurate and revealing in their presentation of American society: we are simply noting that Norris reflects a new sense of excitement about American society, one which we may perhaps relate to the expansion of American power at that historical moment, and that his novels represent an important transitional stage between the restraint of Howells and the violence of Dreiser.

4
Edith Wharton

I

I f Edith Wharton allowed a faint note of conscious superiority
to creep into her remarks about James's failure to "depict the
American money-maker in action,"[1] she was not entirely without
justification. We might consider, by way of example, what gives
such weight to a book like *The House of Mirth* (1905). Although
only her second novel, and the first to deal with a "modern" scene
and subject, it is an extremely sophisticated work which touches on
many of the themes later to be developed in such novels as *The
Custom of the Country* (1913) and *The Age of Innocence* (1920). In
her autobiography, *A Backward Glance* (1934), Edith Wharton
acknowledges that in choosing New York society as her subject
she was going against the contemporary demand that fiction should
deal with "the man with the dinner pail."[2] This desire for
conformity, she tells us, was one she completely rejected:

> There could be no greater critical ineptitude than to judge a
> novel according to *what it ought to have been about*. The bigger
> the imagination, the more powerful the intellectual equipment,
> the more different subjects will come within the novelist's reach;
> and Balzac spread his net over nearly every class and situation in
> the French social system. As a matter of fact, there are but two
> essential rules: one, that the novelist should deal only with what
> is within his reach, literally or figuratively (in most cases the two
> are synonymous), and the other that the value of a subject depends
> almost wholly on what the author sees in it, and how deeply he is
> able to see *into* it. Almost—but not quite; for there are certain
> subjects too shallow to yield anything to the most searching gaze.
> I had always felt this, and now my problem was how to make use

[1] Edith Wharton, *A Backward Glance*, p. 176. See p. 13 above.
[2] *Op. cit.*, p. 206.

of a subject—fashionable New York—which, of all others, seemed most completely to fall within the condemned category. There it was before me, in all its flatness and futility, asking to be dealt with as the theme most available to my hand, since I had been steeped in it from infancy, and should not have to get it up out of note-books and encyclopaedias—and yet!

The problem was how to extract from such a subject the typical human significance which is the story-teller's reason for telling one story rather than another. In what aspect could a society of irresponsible pleasure-seekers be said to have, on the "old woe of the world", any deeper bearing than the people composing such a society could guess? The answer was that a frivolous society can acquire dramatic significance only through what its frivolity destroys. Its tragic implication lies in its power of debasing people and ideals. The answer, in short, was my heroine, Lily Bart.[3]

The passage has an impressive toughness and clear-headedness. While admiring the achievement of a Balzac, Edith Wharton does not herself attempt to embrace American society as a whole but sees clearly that "the novelist should deal only with what is within his reach." At the same time, she is concerned not merely with the surface aspects of the society she knows but with its deeper and "tragic" implications, and these she explores with remarkable incisiveness in *The House of Mirth*.

Lily Bart, the focal point of Edith Wharton's vision, is the lovely girl, the "rare flower grown for exhibition,"[4] who finds herself "the victim of the civilization which had produced her":[5]

Inherited tendencies had combined with early training to make her the highly specialized product she was: an organism as helpless out of its narrow range as the sea-anemone torn from the rock. She had been fashioned to adorn and delight; to what other end does nature round the rose-leaf and paint the humming-bird's breast? And was it her fault that the purely decorative mission is less easily and harmoniously fulfilled among social beings than in the world of nature? That it is apt to be hampered by material necessities or complicated by moral scruples?[6]

[3] *Op. cit.*, pp. 206-07.
[4] Edith Wharton, *The House of Mirth*, New York 1905, p. 512.
[5] *Op. cit.*, p. 10. [6] *Op. cit.*, pp. 486-7.

Lily's downfall is due largely to the sensitivity of her moral scruples in a world dominated by materialistic values: her progress has certain parallels with that of Howells's Silas Lapham, while it reverses the pattern of Carrie Meeber's career in Dreiser's *Sister Carrie* (1900). As in *Sister Carrie*, where Dreiser counterpoints Hurstwood's fall against Carrie's rise, Edith Wharton counterpoints Lily's decline against the increasing prosperity and power of Rosedale, the Jewish financier. As Rosedale amasses his millions, so society is forced, however grudgingly, to accept him, and Lily Bart finds herself through force of circumstances brought to reconsider his proposal of marriage, which she had earlier, and with some indignation, rejected:

> Much as she disliked Rosedale, she no longer absolutely despised him. For he was gradually attaining his object in life, and that, to Lily, was always less despicable than to miss it. With the slow unalterable persistency which she had always felt in him, he was making his way through the dense mass of social antagonisms. Already his wealth, and the masterly use he had made of it, were giving him an enviable prominence in the world of affairs, and placing Wall Street under obligations which only Fifth Avenue could repay. In response to these claims, his name began to figure on municipal committees and charitable boards; he appeared at banquets to distinguished strangers, and his candidacy at one of the fashionable clubs was discussed with diminishing opposition. He had figured once or twice at the Trenor dinners, and had learned to speak with just the right note of disdain of the big Van Osburgh crushes; and all he now needed was a wife whose affiliations would shorten the last tedious steps of his ascent. It was with that object that, a year earlier, he had fixed his affections on Miss Bart; but in the interval he had mounted nearer to the goal, while she had lost the power to abbreviate the remaining steps of the way.[7]

The crucial reference here is to Rosedale's "placing Wall Street under obligations which only Fifth Avenue could repay." That linking of Wall Street and Fifth Avenue goes to the heart of the matter, and the one phrase is sufficient to suggest that Edith Wharton

[7] *Op. cit.*, pp. 387–8.

already recognises more plainly than Henry James seems ever to have done the economic basis of the society she portrays.

The interpenetration of business and society, the interdependence of success in Wall Street and social recognition in Fifth Avenue, is brought out even more forcefully by the language which Rosedale uses when trying to persuade Lily, a little later in the novel, that she should try to regain her position in society and thus make it possible for him to marry her. Lily reflects:

> Put by Rosedale in terms of business-like give-and-take, this understanding took on the harmless air of a mutual accommodation, like a transfer of property or a revision of boundary lines. It certainly simplified life to view it as a perpetual adjustment, a play of party politics, in which every concession had its recognised equivalent: Lily's tired mind was fascinated by this escape from fluctuating ethical estimates into a region of concrete weights and measures.[8]

Edith Wharton not only recognises the existence of a class-system, she knows exactly how it is constructed, what sanctions maintain it, and what forces can transcend its barriers. Above all, she perceives, as acutely as any American novelist of protest, the subtle and pervasive corruption of values in a society which lives by the single standard of financial success.

Shortly after *The House of Mirth* Edith Wharton wrote *The Fruit of the Tree* (1907), a novel dealing with a specifically economic subject, the ownership and management of a textile mill. It is not a good novel, but it does make explicit an economic awareness which underlies all her work. The action of *The Fruit of the Tree* revolves about the character of Amherst, the manager of the Westmore mills, and about the conflicting demands made upon him by his job and by his marital relationships. He marries his first wife, Bessy Westmore, the owner of the mills, hoping to put into practice his paternalistic schemes for the improvement of working and living conditions. Bessy, however, thinks that business is "vague and tiresome"[9] and that she should not be troubled with it: "it was part of the modern code of chivalry that lovely

[8] *Op. cit.*, p. 417.
[9] Edith Wharton, *The Fruit of the Tree*, New York 1907, p. 182.

woman should not be bothered about ways and means."[10]   When
Amherst persuades her on one point he suffers for it at home: "his
victory at Westmore had been a defeat at Lynbrook."[11]   Amherst's
second wife deliberately sets out to share in his business life as a
preliminary to "evoking the secret unsuspected Amherst out of the
preoccupied business man chained to his task."[12]   At first she seems
to succeed, but Amherst's work remains to the end more important
than his life at home ("it was there, at the mills, that his real life
was led . . .")[13] and we realise that the responsibility for the failure
of his first marriage was not entirely Bessy's.

Edith Wharton makes Amherst himself one of the earliest
idealistic businessmen in American fiction, but she portrays his
fellow businessmen as unconscious of "a moral claim superior to the
obligation of making one's business 'pay'. . . . Business was one
thing, philanthropy another."[14]   Although the latter part of the
book is largely devoted to the relations between Amherst and his
second wife, much as Frank Norris's *The Pit* tends to become more
Laura's story than Jadwin's, the history of the mills remains the
central thread.   At the end, this is made explicit: "However
achieved, at whatever cost of personal misery and error, the work
of awakening and freeing Westmore was done, and that work had
justified itself."[15]   *The Fruit of the Tree*, then, is a committed novel.
What it advocates may be only a mild paternalism, but the criticism
of contemporary business ethics and the contemporary social
structure is firmly made—as, for example, in the description of
Bessy Westmore as the finished product of industrialism:

> Her dress could not have hung in such subtle folds, her white
> chin have nestled in such rich depths of fur, the pearls in her ears
> have given back the light from such pure curves, if thin shoulders
> in shapeless gingham had not bent, day in, day out, above the
> bobbins and carders, and weary ears throbbed even at night with
> the tumult of the looms.[16]

It is this attitude and knowledge which underlies the satirical
superstructure of *The Custom of the Country*, and if the socio-

[10] *Op. cit.*, p. 183.   [11] *Op. cit.*, p. 247.   [12] *Op. cit.*, p. 471.
[13] *Op. cit.*, p. 570.   [14] *Op. cit.*, p. 195.   [15] *Op. cit.*, p. 622.
                    [16] *Op. cit.*, p. 49. See p. 117 below.

economic criticism of this later novel is made by implication rather than by overt statement, it is no less fundamental. The "custom" of the book's title refers to the American dichotomy, mentioned by James, between the businessman at work and the businessman at home. One of the characters remarks on the paradox that American men " 'who make, materially, the biggest sacrifices for their women, should do least for them ideally and romantically.' "[17] Because " 'the average American looks down on his wife,' " he gives her no share in the " 'real business' " of life:[18]

> "Why does the European woman interest herself so much more in what the men are doing? Because she's so important to them that they make it worth her while! She's not a parenthesis, as she is here—she's in the very middle of the picture. . . . Where does the real life of most American men lie? In some woman's drawing-room or in their offices? The answer's obvious, isn't it? The emotional centre of gravity's not the same in the two hemispheres. In the effete societies it's love, in our new one it's business. In America the real *crime passionnel* is a 'big steal'—there's more excitement in wrecking railways than homes."[19]

In the context of the novel, the point about American society is well taken. The businessman's relations with his "womankind" had been a frequent theme of social comedy in James and Howells: the Spragg family bears an unmistakable resemblance to the Ruck family, while in the early scenes of the book we are often reminded of the social aspirations of the Laphams, in *The Rise of Silas Lapham*, and of the Dryfooses, in *A Hazard of New Fortunes*. But *The Custom of the Country* is much more than a comedy of manners. The mutual incomprehension of the businessman and his wife is here the cause of dishonesty, infidelity and divorce, of desperate unhappiness and even of suicide. Business corrupts, we learn, and a condition of the average business life is "the persistent mortification of spirit and flesh."[20] Society is progressively corrupted, for its values are essentially based on the possession of wealth and hence on success in business. Even Mr Spragg, a man of "rigid" domestic morality,

[17] Edith Wharton, *The Custom of the Country*, New York 1913, p. 208.
[18] *Op. cit.*, pp. 205-06.   [19] *Op. cit.*, p. 207.   [20] *Op. cit.*, p. 311.

has "elastic" business principles,[21] and Ralph Marvell's final disaster springs largely from his pursuit of the large, quick profits that reward fortunate speculation.

At the same time, one of the more sympathetic characters in the novel, and certainly one of the most arresting, is Elmer Moffatt, self-made railroad king from the West and first and fourth husband of Undine Spragg. As in her presentation of Rosedale in *The House of Mirth*, Edith Wharton seems to show a greater respect for those who themselves amass money rather than merely inherit it. This is a distinction which Dreiser makes in contrasting Samuel Griffiths and his son in *An American Tragedy* (1925), and Edith Wharton was as well aware as Dreiser of the tendency of money-power to degenerate into exclusive élites in the second and successive generations. Nevertheless, she presents Moffatt somewhat ambiguously. He offends our sensibilities but, like Undine, we sense his power: "he gave her, more than any one she had ever known, the sense of being detached from his life, in control of it, and able, without weakness or uncertainty, to choose which of its calls he should obey."[22] It is not so much that he is a businessman as that business is what he happens to be doing: he could do any number of other things equally well.

Although somewhat reminiscent of Christopher Newman in his "air of placid power,"[23] his western origins, his ownership of railways, his personal magnanimity, Moffatt more closely resembles Adam Verver in his connoisseurship, if in little else. In both Moffatt and Verver this connoisseurship is of an almost predatory nature, but where James leaves us in doubt as to the quality of Verver's taste, failing to specify any of his purchases, Edith Wharton, without entering into great detail, typically takes more risks and persuades us that Moffatt has both genuine sensitivity and good taste: his room contains "a lapis bowl in a Renaissance mounting of enamel and a vase of Phenician glass that was like a bit of rainbow caught in cobwebs. On a table against the window a little Greek marble lifted its pure lines. . . ."[24]

It is true that we sometimes find Edith Wharton indulging in

[21] *Op. cit.*, p. 248.
[23] *Op. cit.*, p. 538.
[22] *Op. cit.*, p. 563.
[24] *Op. cit.*, p. 567.

evasions similar to those which James always adopted when handling businessmen and business settings, but in Edith Wharton's novels we can usually justify such evasions within their contexts, either in terms of characterisation or of some question of technique. We can find an excellent example of this in a revealing interchange between Moffatt and Undine which occurs near the end of the book. Meeting Undine unexpectedly after a long separation, Moffatt recounts the various stages of his rise to affluence and power which has taken place during the intervening years:

> Absorbed in his theme, and forgetting her inability to follow him, Moffatt launched out on an epic recital of plot and counterplot, and she hung, a new Desdemona, on his conflict with the new anthropophagi. It was of no consequence that the details and the technicalities escaped her: she knew their meaningless syllables stood for success, and what that meant was as clear as day to her. Every Wall Street term had its equivalent in the language of Fifth Avenue, and while he talked of building up railways she was building up palaces, and picturing all the multiple lives he would lead in them. To have things had always seemed to her the first essential of existence, and as she listened to him the vision of the things he could have unrolled itself before her like the long triumph of an Asiatic conqueror.
>
> "And what are you going to do next?" she asked, almost breathlessly, when he had ended.
>
> "Oh, there's always a lot to do next. Business never goes to sleep."
>
> "Yes; but I mean besides business."
>
> "Why—everything I can, I guess." He leaned back in his chair with an air of placid power, as if he were so sure of getting what he wanted that there was no longer any use in hurrying, huge as his vistas had become.
>
> She continued to question him, and he began to talk of his growing passion for pictures and furniture, and of his desire to form a collection which should be a great representative assemblage of unmatched specimens. As he spoke she saw his expression change, and his eyes grow younger, almost boyish, with a concentrated look in them that reminded her of long-forgotten things.
>
> "I mean to have the best, you know; not just to get ahead of the

other fellows, but because I know it when I see it. I guess that's the only good reason," he concluded; and he added, looking at her with a smile: "It was what you were always after, wasn't it?"[25]

The style never quite frees itself from the threat of the cliché ("almost breathlessly," "reminded her of long-forgotten things"), but the passage as a whole seems entirely successful and rich in implications, and we see why it may not be completely accurate to speak of Edith Wharton as evading the presentation of business details in the first paragraph. There is great point, after all, in Undine's lack of interest in the business details and in her ignorance of business teminology. What interests her is the money which constitutes the end and outcome of business success; what fascinates her is the image of what that money might represent in the ter-minology of Fifth Avenue. This is the essence of her changed attitude towards Moffatt, and the point is skilfully sustained by the precisely relevant *Othello* metaphor: Moffatt has been earlier presented as a "braver of the Olympians"[26] with "something epic"[27] about him, and there is an eloquent irony in Undine's complete inversion of Desdemona's innocence. In the last sentence there is, of course, irony for Moffatt himself as well as for the reader: Undine's conception of "the best," limited as it is to notions of material acquisition and social prestige, is at once less adventurous and less admirable than Moffatt's own conception.

But Moffatt is not the book's hero. He appears in a better light than most of those who affect to despise him, but his values, no less than theirs, are ultimately money values, and in human relationships he is often insensitive and clumsy: when Undine's son is weeping his heart out for loneliness and lack of love, Moffatt's idea of comforting him is to hold out the hope of his one day becoming "'the richest boy in America.'"[28] The novel perhaps suffers from the fact that none of the major characters engages our sympathies at all deeply: Ralph, though badly used, is ineffective; the Dagonet and De Chelles families are too proud, the Spraggs too pathetic; Undine, in her unqualified materialism, assumes the proportions of a predatory

[25] *Op. cit.*, pp. 537-8.   [26] *Op. cit.*, p. 252.
[27] *Op. cit.*, p. 254.   [28] *Op. cit.*, p. 589.

monster. But if *The Custom of the Country*, though certainly humane and often humorous, strikes us finally as a cold book, that is because the materialism and cynicism at the heart of its society ("Every Wall Street term had its equivalent in the language of Fifth Avenue") appear too clearly for it to be otherwise. Even Moffatt, though he anticipates Jay Gatsby, does not have Gatsby's romantic justifications; for the rest, the world of *The Custom of the Country* remains overwhelmingly a world of Tom and Daisy Buchanans.

2

Fitzgerald's name is invoked here mainly to suggest the special position which *The Custom of the Country* occupies in American literary history. It is not only Edith Wharton's best novel, but one of the great novels of this century. Certainly it is the finest American novel to have appeared between *The Golden Bowl* and *The Great Gatsby*, and in some respects it is a larger achievement than either. Edith Wharton occupies an extremely important intermediary position between James and Fitzgerald: indeed, we might argue that Fitzgerald could hardly have written *The Great Gatsby* without *The Custom of the Country*, and it is beyond argument that *The Custom of the Country* itself could not have been written without the whole body of James's achievement behind it.

In *A Backward Glance* Edith Wharton recalls Henry James's response to *The Custom of the Country* when it first appeared:

after prolonged and really generous praise of my book, he suddenly and irrepressibly burst forth: "But of course you know—as how should you, with your infernal keenness of perception, *not* know? —that in doing your tale you had under your hand a magnificent subject, which ought to have been your main theme, and that you used it as a mere incident and then passed it by?"

He meant by this that for him the chief interest of the book, and its most original theme, was that of a crude young woman such as Undine Spragg entering, all unprepared and unperceiving, into the mysterious labyrinth of family life in the old French aristocracy.[29]

[29] *A Backward Glance*, p. 182.

The presentation of Undine Spragg at Saint Désert (how excellent, in both instances, the choice of names!) is undoubtedly one of the finest things in the novel, and it is the point at which the balance of our sympathies is most delicately maintained, but James's remark seems both a commentary on his own limitations and a tribute to the richness of *The Custom of the Country*. It is the very generosity of Edith Wharton's talent in this book, the fact that she could pick up and develop such a theme only to let it go again almost in passing, that makes it the major work it is. Almost alone among American writers in the early part of this century Edith Wharton here achieves the combination of picaresque variety and amplitude with a controlling artistic intelligence of the Jamesian kind. But if the intelligence at work in the novel is of the Jamesian kind it is not of the Jamesian quality: nothing in Edith Wharton approaches the power or the sensitivity of James at his best. James, on the other hand, could never have committed himself to so extensive an undertaking as *The Custom of the Country*: the social and moral areas involved would have been too great for him to have grasped artistically. At least, he would have felt that they were too great. We sometimes sense in James a kind of temerity, a limiting over-scrupulosity, which prevents him from working on the very largest scale, and the admiration wrung from him by "the coarse, comprehensive, prodigious Zola"[30] suggests that it was a limitation of which he was himself aware.

Edith Wharton is not Zola, but in *The Custom of the Country* she is, if not exactly more prodigious, at least more comprehensive and certainly coarser than James himself. The coarseness is the price paid for the comprehensiveness, but, after the agonising subtleties of *The Golden Bowl*, for all its grace, and the refined obscurities of *The Ivory Tower*, for all its moral intensity, it is possible to feel that the price may be worth the paying. Part of the coarseness consists in the unhesitating rapacity of Edith Wharton's indebtedness to Howells and, above all, to James himself. It would be possible to go through *The Custom of the Country* and refer character after character, situation after situation, back to a possible original in the novels of Howells or James. At the same time James

[30] James, Preface to *The American*, p. xix.

and Howells, singly or together, do not contain Edith Wharton. She is not only more comprehensive than either of them, but in a quite down-to-earth way she also knows more. She is more at home than ever they were in greater and wider worlds. She sees, worldly-wise, how things are done—her Americans are never as innocent as James's; unlike Howells she does not write novels of Utopian propaganda—and it is this combination of intelligence and sanity which gives such an immense assurance to her best work.

3

In the years following the First World War Edith Wharton appeared something of an anachronistic survival. Her style was *démodé*; her social criticism, conservative rather than radical-progressive in temper, seemed no more serious than mere aesthetic revulsion; most of the younger novelists seem to have found nothing in her work that they could "use." This was perhaps because, for all the strength of her individual vision, her technique remained fundamentally Jamesian. It was to the early and middle rather than the later James that she was mainly indebted, and, like a minor nation buying up the discarded weapons of a great power, she found herself well-equipped but already a little outdated.

It is the great interest of Edith Wharton's work, however, that unrestricted by the Jamesian inhibitions, she is able to bring the Jamesian techniques to bear upon social areas and socio-economic questions which James himself touches upon very lightly or not at all. At the same time she does not have the devouring energy which Frank Norris displays in *The Octopus* and in those sections of *The Pit* which deal with the business side of Jadwin's life. *The Custom of the Country* can be seen as standing midway between the crude force of Norris and the sensitive intelligence of James, though it still falls short of James's vision, in "The Question of the Opportunities," of what the American business novel might be. Elmer Moffatt, Mr Spragg, and even Ralph Marvell show more signs than do James's own businessmen of being "seamed all over with the wounds of the market," but Edith Wharton still does not depict either here or in *The Fruit of the Tree* "the immensity and complexity of the general struggle, a boundless ferocity of battle."

Yet she represents society both accurately and powerfully, and she succeeds in her characterisation of Moffatt and Rosedale at precisely the point where we shall see Dreiser failing in the presentation of Frank Cowperwood, his major attempt at a portrait of a big businessman. Dreiser knew much better than Edith Wharton how such men made their money, although she understood these matters much better than James had done, but he had little idea of what they did with their money when they had it or of how they actually behaved in the presence of their social "betters." Here Edith Wharton is absolutely at home, and not snobbishly so: her treatment of Rosedale and Moffatt is not unsympathetic, and she shows herself to be rather better at imagining unknown depths than is Dreiser at imagining unknown heights. Dreiser's *The Stoic*, for example, is a dismal failure, whereas in *The House of Mirth* the scenes of Lily Bart's degradation are convincing and only slightly sentimentalised.

The achievement of Edith Wharton still remains insufficiently recognised, mainly because from our viewpoint she appears always in the shadow of Henry James. But to the American writer in the nineteen-twenties she must have seemed a far more immediate presence than James himself—she was, after all, still alive and still publishing. Even so, for reasons already suggested, few writers proved susceptible to her influence and example. For those few, however, and notably for Scott Fitzgerald, she seems to have had an importance which at once rivalled and complemented that of Dreiser.

5

Theodore Dreiser

James, writing as a critic in "The Question of the Opportunities," saw that the businessman might be "often an obscure, but not less often an epic, hero." As a novelist, however, James was almost exclusively concerned with the businessman in epic or near-epic roles. This, at least, he had in common not only with Edith Wharton and Frank Norris, but also with most other novelists of business in the late nineteenth and early twentieth centuries. Before considering the work of some of those other novelists, notably that of Theodore Dreiser, we should perhaps recognise just how important, how illustrious a figure the businessman has sometimes seemed in American eyes. Van Wyck Brooks, by no means a propagandist for American commercial civilisation, could say in 1915 that

the idealization of business has, in America, a certain validity which elsewhere it could not have. For business in America is not merely more engaging than elsewhere, it is even perhaps the most engaging activity in American life. One cannot compare the American commercial type with the commercial type that England has evolved without feeling in the latter a certain fatty degeneration, a solemn, sanctified, legalized self-satisfaction, which our agile, free, open, though sometimes indefinitely more unholy type is quite without; for even in his unholiness the unholy business man in America is engagingly crooked rather than ponderously corrupt. Beside the English business man . . . the American business man is a gay, sprightly, child-like being, moved and movable, the player of a game, a sportsman essentially, though with a frequently dim perception of the rules. One has only to compare the Bank of England, that squat impregnable mass which grips a score of London acres, with, for example, the Woolworth Tower, which has in it so much of the impulse that has built cathedrals, to feel this divergence in the quality of English and American business.

What is the natural history of this divergence? Why, precisely that the world of trade in England has always been an underworld, precisely that everything which is light, gay, disinterested, personal, artistic has held aloof from it, has been able to form a self-subsisting world that lies beyond it, while trade itself is only a dull residuum. The cream has risen to the top, and the world of business is perfectly conscious that it is only skimmed milk; and if the aldermen wax fat it is in a spirit that Americans would call defiance and despair. For in America there has been no such separation of the cream and the milk. Business has traditionally absorbed the best elements of the American character, it has been cowed by no sense of sub-jection, it has thriven in a free air, it has received all the leaven, it has occupied the centre of the field. Just those elements which in other countries produce art and literature, formulate the ideals and methods of philosophy and sociology, think and act for those disinterested ends which make up the meaning of life; just that free, disinterested, athletic sense of play which is precisely the same in dialectic, in art, in religion, in sociology, in sport—just these, relatively speaking, have in America been absorbed in trade. It is not remarkable that, on the one hand, our thought and literature are so perfunctory, while, on the other, American business is so seductive, so charming, so gay an adventure . . .[1]

We do not necessarily have to accept this analysis in its entirety in order to acknowledge its force. It is, after all, largely an elaboration of James's statement that "Business plays a part in the United States that other interests dispute much less showily than they sometimes dispute it in the life of European countries."

Surprisingly enough it is Upton Sinclair, in his portrait of J. Arnold Ross in *Oil!* (1927), who comes as near as anybody to embodying Van Wyck Brooks's conception of the businessman. In Sinclair's early novels businessmen appear either as shadowy abstractions, as in *The Jungle* (1906), or as monster-like caricatures, as in *The Metropolis* (1908). In *Oil!*, no less than in these early books, Sinclair remains uncompromisingly committed against all that Ross, the oil-man, represents; nevertheless he deliberately

[1] Van Wyck Brooks, *America's Coming-of-Age*, New York 1958, pp. 69-70.

presents Ross as possessing qualities of personal attractiveness which emerge the more strongly from this context of economic hostility. Even the communists, we learn, respect businessmen of Ross's kind: they have power and do not hesitate to use it; they play the game for all they are worth. Paul Watkins, fighting to take away the power of the oil-men, does not in the least blame them for fighting to hold on to it.

The deliberate duality which we find in *Oil!*, and which re-appears in varying degrees in Ernest Poole's *The Harbor* (1915) and in Abraham Cahan's *The Rise of David Levinsky* (1917), seems a good deal more satisfactory, from both a political and a literary standpoint, than the fundamental and often unconscious ambiguity that we find in the work of Tarkington, Winston Churchill, and the many other writers who, whatever their political attitudes, have failed to escape from the literary attitudes of the "genteel tradition." The hero of Tarkington's *The Midlander* (1923), for example, is undoubtedly Dan Oliphant, the forceful businessman and speculative builder, but we see him always from a distance, through the admiring eyes of Martha Shelby, who loves him, or the critical eyes of his brother Harlan, who has an invincible distaste for the disruptive and often ugly results of Dan's enterprises. As a character Dan himself scarcely exists; even in the discussions between Martha and Harlan he remains a kind of debater's abstraction, a convenient personification of the "conqueror, called Progress, being the growth of the city."[2] Despite the feeble gentility of Harlan, it seems likely that many of his attitudes are Tarkington's own, and that Harlan's grudging conversion to a half-hearted admiration of his brother reflects Tarkington's own faltering attempt to come to terms with the new America he is describing. The novel ends on a note of unconvincing compromise, with the assurance that Dan's building development is beautiful after all and the possibility, voiced by Martha, that Dan (now dead) may even have seen beauty in the plume of factory smoke appearing through the trees:

"I think he felt something in it that neither you nor I can under-stand."

[2] Booth Tarkington, *The Midlander*, Garden City, New York 1924, pp. 1-2.

"I think maybe he did," Harlan agreed. "Then why couldn't he at least have lived to see the fruition of what he planted, since he loved it and it was beautiful to him? Why should he be 'dead and forgotten?'"

"Listen!" Martha said. She was still looking up at the smoke against the sky, so far above the long masses of flowering bridal-wreath that bordered the terrace where she and her husband stood. "Listen! That murmur of the city down yonder—why, it's almost his voice!"[3]

It is a very hesitant and half-hearted peace-offering to the "conqueror called Progress," and a very unsatisfactory conclusion to the novel.

We find a similar dichotomy in Tarkington's *The Plutocrat* (1927), but here it arises from a conflict between the author's intentions and the recalcitrance of his material; his own deeper instincts may have proved recalcitrant as well. Laurence Ogle, the smart, supercilious young playwright, gradually learns to admire Earl Tinker, the self-made and excessively extraverted businessman, and at the end of the book, Ogle, now engaged to Tinker's daughter, watches his future father-in-law being driven off, with a colourful escort, to visit the Bey of Tunis:

Tinker's whole course across Barbary had been like this, a jocose kind of pageantry, Laurence thought. And, in the end, what *was* the man? "Barbarian," "Carthaginian," "Goth," he had been called; but with qualifications: a barbarian, but a great one; a Carthaginian, but a great one; —a Goth, the little old English lady had just said; but she called him a magnificent one.

"Wave to him, Mother!" Olivia cried. "Look at him! He's still showing off for us—to make us laugh. Wave to him, Mother!"

As she said, Tinker was still standing up in the car, and gloriously waving his shining hat. The sun was behind him, outlining him in dusty fire; and his figure, now at a distance, seemed to rise above the tossing heads of the chargers about him and beyond him like that of some mockingly triumphant charioteer riding home to glory in the arena of the Circus Maximus. After all, it was Medjila who had been right, Laurence thought; —here was neither Carthaginian nor barbaric Goth, or if he was, he was above all

[3] *Op. cit.*, pp. 492-3.

other things, the New Roman. Then, all at once, that problem for the future appeared less difficult, and the young man felt it might not be so important, after all, to conceal Tinker from the Macklyns and Albert Joneses [his "intellectual" friends].

For, in the cloud of dust against the sun, the powerful and humorous figure, still standing and waving as it rode on toward long-conquered Carthage, seemed to have become gigantic.[4]

This is the apotheosis of the businessman in the American novel. Yet Tinker remains in many ways a dismaying character. He has many admirable qualities of frankness, kindness and courage, but he is a philistine, and very nearly a boor, and in his intimate relationships he seems wholly insensitive. Above all, he seems entirely lacking in ideas and ideals. Standing by the tomb of St Augustine, he states his personal creed to an uncomprehending courier. Insisting that " 'the human race has got to make progress,' " he declares " 'The only hell we worry about nowadays is slippin' back in our progress; we got to show a bigger and better business this year than we did last year.' "[5] There is humour here, but it is of an uneasy kind.

Tarkington was too deeply rooted in the social attitudes and literary manners of the genteel tradition ever to abandon them or even to subject them to stringent critical review. This, of course, largely explains why his treatment of the business hero is so compromised by doubts and hesitations. Like Churchill, Tarkington seems to have been greatly attracted to men of power, but to have doubted all the time the propriety of such an attraction. Churchill, adopting the stance of a reformer, nevertheless gives Jethro Bass, the political boss of *Coniston* (1906) and *Mr. Crewe's Career* (1908), a heart of gold, and makes Hugh Paret, the corporation lawyer of *A Far Country* (1915), undergo a political and moral conversion as sudden as it is inadequately explained. Tarkington, taking more and more the side of the businessman, eventually makes Earl Tinker a lord of the earth without for a moment making him an attractive or even a credible human being. In place of the deliberate duality of *Oil!* we find an ambiguity which not only flaws the whole

[4] Booth Tarkington, *The Plutocrat*, Garden City, New York 1927, pp. 542-3.
[5] *Op. cit.*, p. 480.

pattern of the novels but almost suggests a moral shiftiness, an attempt to be on both sides at once. Tarkington and Churchill were drawn again and again to the epic hero, but, perhaps because of a lingering distaste for business itself, they could never be entirely at ease with him.

Dreiser is the first important novelist to break completely with the genteel tradition in treating the business theme. Even Frank Norris, by giving such prominence to Laura's story in *The Pit*, shows that he has not entirely freed himself from the tradition's compromises and reticences. Although in Dreiser's letters we find him praising books like *With the Procession* (1894),[6] we discover in turning to this and other novels of Henry Blake Fuller, such as *The Cliff-Dwellers* (1893), essentially the same world of social climbing and domestic drama, with just the occasional hint of violence, as we can find in the poorer novels of Howells or in a book like Tarkington's *The Gentleman from Indiana* (1899). Cornelia McNabb, in *The Cliff-Dwellers*, may perhaps be a direct literary predecessor of Carrie Meeber, the heroine of Dreiser's first novel, but the importance of Carrie lies precisely in the much greater directness with which her history is told.

2

A passage from *Sister Carrie* will serve to reflect not only Dreiser's interest in the world of business but also his attitude towards it:

> Into this important commercial region the timid Carrie went. . . . She walked bravely forward, led by an honest desire to find employment and delayed at every step by the interest of the unfolding scene, and a sense of helplessness amid so much evidence of power and force which she did not understand. These vast buildings, what were they? These strange energies and huge interests, for what purposes were they there? She could have understood the meaning of a little stone-cutter's yard at Columbia City, carving little pieces of marble for individual use, but when the yards of some huge stone corporation came into view, filled

[6] *Letters of Theodore Dreiser*, ed. Robert H. Elias, Philadelphia 1959, pp. 121 and 612.

with spur tracks and flat cars, transpierced by docks from the river and traversed overhead by immense trundling cranes of wood and steel, it lost all significance in her little world.[7]

The autobiographical *A Book About Myself* (1922) and *Dawn* (1931), show that Carrie's awe at "so much evidence of power and force which she did not understand" is a direct counterpart to Dreiser's own youthful feelings about Chicago. The fascination of Chicago remained with Dreiser all his life: so did the fascination of business, bolstered as it was by his professional interest as a journalist in the careers of men who had made good, and by his personal obsession with wealth, power and success. This intense interest in business affects almost all of Dreiser's novels: much of *The "Genius"* (1915) is devoted to Eugene Witla's advertising and managerial work, much of *Jennie Gerhardt* (1911) to the business affairs of the Kane family, while Samuel Griffiths's collar-factory plays an important part in the action of *An American Tragedy* (1925). *The Bulwark* (1946) could also justifiably be classified as a business novel, although this is not really its central theme. But when considering Dreiser as a business novelist the books that spring to mind are the three which describe the career of Frank Cowperwood: *The Financier* (1912), *The Titan* (1914), and *The Stoic* (1947). *The Financier* is "prodigiously got up," to use James's phrase, but badly put together. *The Stoic* Dreiser could never finish, and it was published after his death in its incomplete form. *The Titan*, the middle volume, and the best of the three, has many of the qualities of the ideal business novel without being a great novel itself.

In *The Titan*, Dreiser presents Frank Cowperwood as intensely "individual," a kind of land-locked Captain Ahab: "Rushing like a great comet to the zenith, his path a blazing trail, Cowperwood did for the hour illuminate the terrors and wonders of individuality."[8] Indeed, we see Cowperwood almost as a superman; Dreiser bestows the title on him in the chapter heading "Man and Superman," and so Berenice imagines him: "As she thought of him—waging his terrific contests, hurrying to and fro between New York and Chicago, building his splendid mansion, collecting

[7] Theodore Dreiser, *Sister Carrie*, New York 1900, pp. 17–8.
[8] Theodore Dreiser, *The Titan*, New York 1914, p. 551.

his pictures, quarreling with Aileen—he came by degrees to take on the outlines of a superman, a half-god or demi-gorgon. How could the ordinary rules of life or the accustomed paths of men be expected to control him? They could not and did not."[9] Cowperwood thinks of himself as a man of destiny: "He could, should, and would rule alone. No man must ever again have the least claim on him save that of a suppliant. . . . By right of financial intellect and courage he was first, and would so prove it. Men must swing around him as planets around the sun."[10] Ruthless, individualistic, determined to be the master of his own destiny, Cowperwood carries Emerson's doctrine of self-reliance to its logical and terrifying conclusion.

Yet Cowperwood by no means appears wholly self-reliant. On another occasion he seems to Berenice "a kind of superman, and yet also a bad boy—handsome, powerful, hopeful, not so very much older than herself now, impelled by some blazing internal force which harried him on and on."[11] Apparently, a maternal emotion rather than any other takes Berenice to him on the night of his defeat: " 'I thought . . . that you might really need me now.' "[12] An even greater modification of his independence is his insatiable sexual appetite. Such an appetite may have seemed to Dreiser a sign of the vigour proper to a merchant-prince, but it could equally betray emotional inadequacy. With Cowperwood it is a matter not merely of appetite but of addiction; he has all the addict's desperation and lack of control, and this seriously handicaps him in his business affairs: his defeat in the crucial matter of the fifty year franchises is due very largely to the implacable silent hatred of Hosmer Hand, aroused by Cowperwood's seduction of his wife. Dreiser makes it quite clear that the growing opposition to Cowperwood stems mainly from his sexual adventures: "It was not until the incidents relating to Cowperwood and Mrs. Hand had come to light that things financial and otherwise began to darken up."[13] In short, Cowperwood behaves stupidly, especially as, apart from their availability, these wives of his business colleagues do not particularly attract him.

[9] *Op. cit.*, p. 527.   [10] *Op. cit.*, p. 27.   [11] *Op. cit.*, p. 468.
[12] *Op. cit.*, p. 550.   [13] *Op. cit.*, p. 285.

Cowperwood also acts unwisely in alienating on other grounds such people as Purdy and MacDonald. But Dreiser deliberately placed Cowperwood in tight corners, for what he wanted to celebrate was not so much Cowperwood's wisdom as his courage, his tenacity in the face of heavy odds, his bold handling of millions of dollars, his undauntedness in a political atmosphere in which, however deceptive the surface appearance, "a jungle-like complexity was present, a dark, rank growth of horrific but avid life—life at the full, life knife in hand, life blazing with courage and dripping at the jaws with hunger."[14]   While Dreiser succeeds in conveying much of his sense of Cowperwood's grandeur, he fails either to make him wholly credible or to convey the full excitement of the great affairs in which he is involved: Norris managed this better in *The Pit* by concentrating on Jadwin's own activities in the hurly-burly of the exchange. In *The Titan* this kind of interest is too much diluted; Dreiser's documentary passion, more controlled here than in *The Financier*, still leads him to lose Cowperwood in his surroundings. So much is done by others on Cowperwood's behalf, and attention is so often shifted to them for whole chapters at a time, that we never get a sufficient sense of Cowperwood sitting competent, cool and omniscient at the centre of an enormous web of his own spinning. Yet something of that kind was needed to hold all the multifarious political and business activities together.

We also notice a certain dull repetitiousness about Cowperwood's business affairs, as about his love affairs: the operations in which he is successively involved tend to differ from each other in degree rather than in kind. This repetition points in turn to a more fundamental inadequacy in the book, the failure of Cowperwood to develop as a character. Dreiser does not use these ever vaster business dealings in order to bring out some new facet of Cowperwood's character or to throw a brighter light on what we already know of him: they simply happen. In fact, Cowperwood scarcely grows at all. He springs fully-armed into the opening pages of *The Financier* and, watching the lobster eat the squid, he learns at once the single principle that will guide all his future conduct: "Things

[14] *Op. cit.*, p. 516.

lived on each other—that was it."[15]   In *The Stoic*, Dreiser attempts to give a new direction to Cowperwood's character, but without success; he eventually kills Cowperwood off, in a rather abrupt manner, and turns his attention to Berenice as a more satisfactory vehicle for his changed ideas.

3

Dreiser modelled Cowperwood in detail upon a real-life figure, Charles A. Yerkes, the Chicago traction magnate, in whom he seems to have perceived almost mythic possibilities. In a later article he wrote:

> Some tales are too great to be told, or they need retelling. Certain I am of one thing, the age that produced at once the mechanical perfection of the world and its most colossal fortunes is classic. From that period certainly some Croesus, Lepidus or Maecenas is sure to show forth in fable, song, or story. In my limited search and with my selective tendencies none seemed of so great import, socially, sociologically, financially, philosophically as the individual whom I have selected. A rebellious Lucifer this, glorious in his somber conception of the value of power. A night-black pool his world will seem to some, played over by fulgurous gleams of his own individualistic and truly titanic mind. To the illuminate it will have a very different meaning, I am sure, a clear suggestion of the inscrutable forces of life, as they shift and play— marring what they do not glorify—pagan, fortuitous, inalienably artistic.[16]

That Dreiser's achievement fell short of his conception was due to nothing so much as to his attempt, hinted at in the phrase "inalienably artistic," to present Cowperwood as a kind of artist. Stephanie Platow "conceived of him as a very great artist in his realm rather than as a business man, and he grasped this fact after a very little while and appreciated it."[17]   Whereas Frank Norris actually showed some tendency to elevate the businessman

---

[15] Theodore Dreiser, *The Financier*, Cleveland and New York [n.d.], p. 5.

[16] Quoted in F. O. Matthiessen, *Theodore Dreiser*, London 1951, p. 135.

[17] *The Titan*, pp. 215-6.

above the artist,[18] Dreiser inclines to place them on an equal footing:

> Cowperwood was innately and primarily an egoist and intellectual, though blended strongly therewith was a humane and democratic spirit. We think of egoism and intellectualism as closely confined to the arts. Finance is an art. And it presents the operations of the subtlest of the intellectuals and of the egoists. Cowperwood was a financier.[19]

"Finance is an art": Dreiser always carefully discriminates between the operations of finance, which may be on the level of art, and those of commerce, which are unworthy of serious attention. This insistence on the superior creativeness of financial speculation and manipulation as contrasted with the dull sordidness of mere trade may be a little difficult to accept, but it is central to Dreiser's conception of Cowperwood. Governor Archer, we learn, "was by nature materially and commercially minded—therefore without basic appeal to the higher ranks of intelligence."[20] It is true that Dreiser, with his carelessness about individual phrases, says at one point that Cowperwood "wanted fame and reputation, but he wanted money even more"[21]; nevertheless we are clearly meant to regard him as essentially free from crudely materialistic motives. His secretary, Antoinette Nowak, thinks of him as utterly different from "the men of the business world, crazy over money, and with no understanding of anything save some few facts about Chicago and its momentary possibilities. In Cowperwood's office . . . she had learned more of life than she had ever dreamed existed. He was like a vast open window out of which she was looking upon an almost illimitable landscape."[22] At such moments Dreiser's conception of the businessman approaches that of Van Wyck Brooks.

When Dreiser tries to define this special, artistic quality of Cowperwood's mind he can do no more than make large but

---

[18] See, for example, Norris, *The Responsibilities of the Novelist*, p. 133: "One does not claim that the artist is above the business man. Far from it."

[19] *The Financier*, p. 134.   [20] *The Titan*, p. 512.
[21] *Op. cit.*, p. 185.   [22] *Op. cit.*, p. 131.

ineffectual gestures. He makes his most sustained attempt through the thoughts of Aileen, for whom Cowperwood has

> a mind and spirit far greater than any other she had ever known. Neither honor, virtue, consistent charity nor sympathy was there, but only a gay, foamy, unterrified sufficiency and a creative, constructive sense of beauty that, like sunlit spray, glowing with all the irradiative glories of the morning, danced and fled, spun driftwise over a heavy sea of circumstance. Life, however dark and somber, could never apparently cloud his soul. Brooding and idling in the wonder palace of his construction, Aileen could see what he was like. The silver fountain in the court of orchids, the peach-like glow of the pink marble chamber, with its birds and flowers, the serried brilliance of his amazing art-collections were all like him, were really the color of his soul.[23]

This is especially interesting in that it describes Cowperwood in terms of the "palace of art" of his own conception and construction, the outward expression of his own artistic nature. Unfortunately, we cannot take the palace itself at all seriously, nor—for we know what they comprise—the "amazing art-collections."

As F. O. Matthiessen points out,[24] Dreiser had very uncertain artistic taste and very little notion of what it meant to be an artist. Indeed, when we see how Dreiser characterises the true artist, as Eugene Witla is supposed to be in *The "Genius"*, we find it less surprising that he can equate the businessman and the artist. In the course of the book Witla moves quite easily from art to advertising, to the management of advertising and publishing concerns, and back again to art. Indeed, he makes a great success as a businessman, only returning to his art after losing his job because of a Cowperwoodian passion for a young girl. Dreiser always insists that Witla is "primarily an artist"[25] and has "the artistic temperament,"[26] but the unconvincingness of Witla as an artist is perhaps sufficiently

[23] *Op. cit.*, p. 493.
[24] Matthiessen, *Theodore Dreiser*, p. 147.
[25] Theodore Dreiser, *The "Genius"*, New York 1915, p. 467.
[26] *Op. cit.*, p. 430.

suggested by his reflections upon being appointed advertising manager to the Kalvin Publishing Company:

> Eight thousand a year! Was he eventually going to become a great business man instead of an artist? . . . He foresaw an apartment on Riverside Drive in New York, a house in the country perhaps, for he fancied he would not always want to live in the city. An automobile of his own, perhaps; a grand piano for Angela; Sheraton or Chippendale furniture; friends, fame— what artist's career could compare to this? Did any artist he knew enjoy what he was enjoying now, even? Why should he worry about being an artist? Did they ever get anywhere? Would the approval of posterity let him ride in an automobile now? He smiled as he recalled Dula's talk about class superiority—the distinction of being an artist, even though poor. Poverty be hanged! Posterity could go to the devil! He wanted to live now—not in the approval of posterity.[27]

4

Dreiser shows little understanding of art or of the artist's vocation; indeed, he seems isolated from virtually all cultural movements and traditions. Moral and social traditions are the only ones with which we can confidently identify him. In all his completed novels he demonstrates the drive towards the top inherent in the American ideology of success, although, in later years his attitudes, like those of many other Americans, underwent a violent change, and in *Tragic America* (1931) he violently attacks those American capitalists whom—in *The Financier* and *The Titan*, in the portrait of old Archibald Kane in *Jennie Gerhardt*, and in the essay on "The American Financier" in *Hey, Rub-A-Dub-Dub* (1920)—he had previously portrayed as representing the most dynamic and productive forces in American society. In *The Bulwark*, which, with *The Stoic*, Dreiser was finishing at the time of his death, Solon Barnes seeks spiritual peace by renouncing his business interests and Freeborn K. Baker, a character strongly reminiscent of Cowperwood, is unsympathetically portrayed. This change seems to date from the

[27] *Op. cit.*, p. 440.

shock of the stock-market crash of 1929 and the subsequent depression, but the first hint of it perhaps appears in *An American Tragedy*, the story of Clyde Griffiths, the American failure, in aspiration almost identical with Frank Cowperwood but in achievement his very antithesis.

As a writer Dreiser is *sui generis*. He had not read Zola before writing *Sister Carrie*, nor even, according to Mencken,[28] Frank Norris. Right to the end he continued along his own individual path, cutting out his own footholds step by step as he went. Among American novelists not even Norris or Sinclair Lewis offer anything quite comparable to the almost grotesque passages of ecstatic "romancing" that occur in many of his novels—passages such as the apostrophe to Chicago near the beginning of *The Titan*:

> The city of Chicago, with whose development the personality of Frank Algernon Cowperwood was soon to be definitely linked! To whom may the laurels as laureate of this Florence of the West yet fall? This singing flame of a city, this all America, this poet in chaps and buckskin, this rude, raw Titan, this Burns of a city! By its shimmering lake it lay, a king of shreds and patches, a maundering yokel with an epic in its mouth, a tramp, a hobo among cities, with the grip of Caesar in its mind, the dramatic force of Euripides in its soul. A very bard of a city this, singing of high deeds and high hopes, its heavy brogans buried deep in the mire of circumstance. Take Athens, oh, Greece! Italy, do you keep Rome! This was the Babylon, the Troy, the Nineveh of a younger day. Here came the gaping West and the hopeful East to see. Here hungry men, raw from the shops and fields, idyls and romances in their minds, builded them an empire crying glory in the mud.[29]

Dreiser's manner, however, is too pedestrian and documentary to sustain the kind of sweeping "romantic" excitement that Norris is capable of at his best, and the most remarkable feature of *The Financier* and *The Titan* is not the quality of the writing but Dreiser's supreme effort, comparable only to Zola's and far beyond what

[28] H. L. Mencken, "Theodore Dreiser," in *The Shock of Recognition*, ed. Edmund Wilson, London 1956, p. 1162.
[29] *The Titan*, p. 6.

any other American novelist had attempted, to conquer the occultness of business by means of exhaustive research. In large measure
he succeeded: the financial and political world of Chicago is amply
and convincingly bodied forth in his pages. But the body lacks a
heart, remains inert. There is a failure not of documentation but
of imagination. Like his Carrie, Dreiser understood very well the
lower levels of business—the hierarchical structure of the collar-
factory in *An American Tragedy*, for example—but he never entirely
grasped what went on at the peaks of power and success. Those
"strange energies and huge interests" of Chicago which appeared
to the young Dreiser as such fascinating enigmas never ceased
to fascinate him throughout his life, nor did they cease to be
enigmas.

This imaginative limitation appears throughout Dreiser's work,
apart from those all too rare occasions—parts of *Sister Carrie* and
Jennie Gerhardt, for example, and a few sections of *An American
Tragedy*—when it is transcended by the sheer strength of Dreiser's
humanity. Characteristically, Dreiser takes the great mass of his
material either directly from his own experiences or from fully
documented accounts of other people's lives. Unfortunately, he
rarely succeeds in achieving artistic detachment from his own
experiences, and his most nearly autobiographical novel, *The
"Genius"*, is also his worst, immensely long, sprawling and chaotic.
He tends to be at his best when he can use something outside himself—someone else's career, an actual case-history—as a core to
which his material can accrete in orderly fashion. Thus Dreiser's
sister was the original of Carrie, the Cowperwood novels are based
on the life of Yerkes, and *An American Tragedy* closely follows the
records of an historical murder trial. By basing his novels firmly
on fact Dreiser felt that he was getting closer to reality, and, after all,
it is Dreiser's realism, in its sociological as much as in its artistic
aspects, which now provides the chief interest of his work.

As an artist, Dreiser presents considerable difficulties. F. O.
Matthiessen, by turning from Hawthorne and Melville, from
James and Eliot, to write of Dreiser in his last book, has, in effect,
made the appreciation of Dreiser a crucial test of a full response to
American literature. Yet it is almost impossible for the reader to

reconcile himself to the sheer badness of Dreiser's writing: few writers have been so insensitive to language, so ignorant of the possibilities of their craft. Nor is it simply that Dreiser has no ear for colloquial speech, that his grammar is faulty, his rhetoric ludicrously high-flown, his image-making power almost non-existent. Much more serious is his frequent inability to say clearly what he means, the sheer imprecision and inconsistency of much of his writing. The presentation of character is often slipshod and shifting. On page 385 of *The Titan* Aileen says of Cowperwood: "He was never brutal to me." She is speaking to Lynde, to whom, on page 267, she had first been drawn because "He would be winsome and coaxing, but at the same time strong, direct, deliciously brutal, like her Frank." We are thus left in doubt about so central a question as Cowperwood's relationship with his wife. Even more glaring inconsistencies appear. On page 197 of *The Titan* we learn of Cowperwood that "His greatest weakness, if he had one, was that he could but ill brook opposition of any kind." On pages 218-9 we read: "Cowperwood, individual, reliant, utterly indifferent to opposition of any kind. . . ."

Dreiser's admirers do not deny that he has faults, but they claim that he rises superior to them. The case is well put by Alfred Kazin in *On Native Grounds*:

> It is because he has spoken for Americans with an emotion equi-valent to their own emotion, in a speech as broken and blindly searching as common speech, that we have responded to him with the dawning realization that he is stronger than all the others of his time, and at the same time more poignant; greater than the world he has described, but as significant as the people in it. To have accepted America as he has accepted it, to immerse oneself in something one can neither escape nor relinquish, to yield to what has been true and to yearn over what has seemed inexorable, has been Dreiser's fate and the secret of his victory.[30]

This is persuasive, but not sufficiently persuasive to convince us that Dreiser's faults are in fact his virtues. In his second sentence, however, Kazin touches upon the one quality in Dreiser which demands and receives a positive response. Dreiser identified

[30] Alfred Kazin, *On Native Grounds*, New York 1942, pp. 89-90.

himself more completely than any other writer has done with the deepest motivations and aspirations of contemporary American life, and he did so not as a conscious act of will, but because he could not do otherwise, because he was himself the perfect embodiment of the forces charted in his books.

In the closing paragraphs of the autobiographical *A Hoosier Holiday* (1916), Dreiser, returning to New York after a visit to his native Middle West, has a vision of America as a whole and of the "great dreams" Americans have dreamed since the nation was founded. He sees the faults and limitations of the democratic experiment but, "for the dream's sake," he would like to see America survive:

> And for these reasons I would have this tremendous, bubbling Republic live on, as a protest perhaps against the apparently too unbreakable rule that democracy, equality, or the illusion of it, is destined to end in disaster. It cannot survive ultimately, I think. In the vast, universal sea of motion, where change and decay are laws, and individual power is almost always uppermost, it must go under—but until then—
>
> We are all such pathetic victims of chance, anyhow. We are born, we struggle, we plan, and chance blows all our dreams away. If, therefore, one country, one state dares to dream the impossible, why cast it down before its ultimate hour? Why not dream with it? It is so gloriously, so truly a poetic land. We were conceived in ecstasy and born in dreams.
>
> And so, were I one of sufficient import to be able to speak to my native land, the galaxy of states of which it is composed, I would say: Dream on. Believe. Perhaps it is unwise, foolish, childlike, but dream anyhow. Disillusionment is destined to appear. You may vanish as have other great dreams, but even so, what a glorious, an imperishable memory!
>
> "Once," will say those historians of far distant nations of times yet unborn, perchance, "once there was a great republic. And its domain lay between a sea and sea—a great continent. In its youth and strength it dared assert that all men were free and equal, endowed with certain inalienable rights. Then came the black storms of life—individual passions and envies, treasons, stratagems, spoils. The very gods, seeing it young, dreamful, of great cheer,

were filled with envy. They smote and it fell. But, oh, the wondrous memory of it! For in those days men were free, because *they imagined they were free—"*

Of dreams and the memory of them is life compounded.[31]

Dreiser himself had dreamed the American dream. Thus for Dreiser the novelist, as Kenneth S. Lynn has shown,[32] the American "success" story was not merely a usable theme; it was, imperatively and inescapably, the only possible theme. Dreiser's preoccupation with success in his novels directly reflected the major preoccupation of his own early life: he himself had longed for success, with all its implications of wealth, luxury, freedom and fame, and his interest in business sprang primarily from his understanding that business, in one form or another, was the route by which success was most often and most rapidly achieved.

In reading Dreiser we must be aware of his biography; only thus can we fully appreciate him, only thus can we begin to excuse his faults. Moreover, Dreiser has an historical importance out of all proportion to the actual quality of his achievement. When we see Dreiser in his role of literary pioneer, opening up new territory and making it available for later development and civilisation, then we find it easier to understand his ruggedness, if not wholly to condone it. Dreiser has, too, a somewhat incoherent but none-theless powerful sense of humanity, evident in *Tragic America* as much as in *An American Tragedy*, and his novels, though clumsy, ponderous and contradictory, have a weightiness, compounded of passionate sincerity and deeply felt experience, which becomes finally impressive.

5

Sherwood Anderson has left a memorable image of Dreiser:

Theodore Dreiser is old—he is very, very old. I do not know how many years he has lived, perhaps forty, perhaps fifty, but he is very old. Something gray and bleak and hurtful, that has been in the world perhaps forever, is personified in him.

[31] Theodore Dreiser, *A Hoosier Holiday*, London [1932], pp. 512-3.
[32] Kenneth S. Lynn, *The Dream of Success*, Boston and Toronto 1955, pp. 13-74.

When Dreiser is gone men shall write books, many of them, and in the books they shall write there will be so many of the qualities Dreiser lacks. The new, the younger men shall have a sense of humor, and everyone knows Dreiser has no sense of humor. More than that, American prose writers shall have grace, lightness of touch, a dream of beauty breaking through the husks of life.

O, those who follow him shall have many things that Dreiser does not have. That is a part of the wonder and beauty of Theodore Dreiser, the things that others shall have, because of him.

Long ago, when he was editor of the *Delineator*, Dreiser went one day, with a woman friend, to visit an orphan asylum. The woman once told me the story of that afternoon in the big, ugly gray building, with Dreiser, looking heavy and lumpy and old, sitting on a platform, folding and refolding his pocket-handkerchief and watching the children—all in their little uniforms, trooping in.

"The tears ran down his cheeks and he shook his head," the woman said, and that is a real picture of Theodore Dreiser. He is old in spirit and he does not know what to do with life, so he tells about it as he sees it, simply and honestly. The tears run down his cheeks and he folds and refolds the pocket-handerkchief and shakes his head.[33]

The helpless honesty of Dreiser is what moves us and compels us, however unwillingly, to read him. He sees the tears of things, and weeps himself, but his tragedy, as man and as writer, lies in his inability to see the human condition whole. In his vast and repetitious novels he cannot seize firmly upon his own most significant experiences, or upon those of other people, but must put everything down: the moments of true insight remain imbedded in a mass of turgid prose and lifeless documentation. At the same time, his human sympathy is too comprehensive for him to imagine that the sufferings he so painfully observes can find an easy political cure, and he never shapes his novels in response to the demands of a narrow political commitment. This does not mean, unfortunately, that Dreiser is responding sensitively and flexibly to the demands of his material: it is simply that the material itself has taken charge.

[33] Sherwood Anderson, "Dreiser," in *The Portable Sherwood Anderson*, ed. Horace Gregory, New York 1949, pp. 557-8.

Dreiser remains an enigmatic figure who will not be formulated in a phrase. He hardly achieved his ambition to be the American Balzac, but he is, after all, the nearest American counterpart to Zola. Frank Norris was more directly influenced by Zola and much more familiar with his work, but where *The Pit* remains a literary response to Zola, showing clear signs of its indebtedness to a particular work, *The Financier* and *The Titan* represent wholly and authentically a direct response to the actual conditions of American life: although less well written than *The Pit*, and more clumsily constructed, they constitute an altogether bigger achievement. Dreiser emerges less impressively from comparisons with writers more accomplished than Norris. Placed by the side of, say, *The Custom of the Country*, the novels of the Cowperwood series and even *An American Tragedy* begin to look like the raw material of the art of fiction rather than the art itself. If it is difficult to like Dreiser, it is impossible not to admire him: it is equally impossible, however, to think of him as a major novelist.

6

Sherwood Anderson and Sinclair Lewis

Sherwood Anderson's passage on Dreiser reveals a good deal of Anderson himself, in its generosity, in its earnest but rather naïve optimism, in the self-consciousness of the style. It is a pleasing piece, and Anderson in his best work is an attractive writer. More obviously than Dreiser he lacks major stature, but whereas Dreiser strikes us as admirable without being attractive, Anderson often seems attractive without being particularly admirable. Anderson's early life, like Dreiser's, was rich in experiences—of small-town life, of manual labour, of factories, of cities, of advertising and business—which would seem to have offered an ideal preparation for the writing of social novels. Many of his early aspirations, like Dreiser's, were towards conventional American standards of success. In the America of his youth, he writes in the autobiographical *A Story Teller's Story* (1924), there seemed "but one direction, one channel, into which all such young fellows as myself could pour their energies. All must give themselves wholeheartedly to material and industrial progress."[1] He recalls the resolution he made at that time:

> "I will become a man of action, in the mood of the American of my day. I will build railroads, conquer empires, become rich and powerful. Why should I not do something of the sort as well as all the other men who have done it so brilliantly? America is the land of opportunity. I must keep that thought ever in my mind."[2]

[1] Sherwood Anderson, *A Story Teller's Story*, New York 1924, p. 219.
[2] *Op. cit.*, p. 218.

Anderson differs from Dreiser in that throughout the greater part of his work, he fails to exploit these peculiarly American experiences and aspirations in any interesting way.

Despite Anderson's great gifts and opportunities as a social novelist, none of his novels seems entirely satisfying as a whole; he is only intermittently at his best, in an occasional short story or in certain sections of a novel—for example, the sensitive description of Sam McPherson's relations with his braggart father at the beginning of *Windy McPherson's Son* (1916). The remainder of this book deals with Sam's rise to wealth and "success," his subsequent abandonment of his position and his wife in order to search for the "Truth," and his final return with three adopted children and a vague message of hope. These later episodes have a kind of muddled earnestness, as in this passage of explicit economic criticism:

> There may be businessmen in America who do not get what they can, who simply love power. One sees men here and there in banks, at the heads of great industrial trusts, in factories and in great mercantile houses of whom one would like to think thus. They are the men who one dreams have had an awakening, who have found themselves; they are the men hopeful thinkers try to recall again and again to the mind.
>
> To these men America is looking. It is asking them to keep the faith, to stand themselves up against the force of the brute trader, the dollar man, the man who with his one cunning wolf quality of acquisitiveness has too long ruled the business of the nation.[3]

Anderson is much given to gusty generalisations of this kind, and they become increasingly frequent in subsequent novels; again and again, he foregoes concrete presentations of men in society in favour of vague statements about man and his search for truth. Yet his real strength appears not in such all-embracing formulations but in narrowly particularised images which carry, despite their almost primitive simplicity, a rich freight of human and social relevance. The best known of these images, of course, are those in

[3] Sherwood Anderson, *Windy McPherson's Son*, London and New York 1916, p. 139.

Winesburg, Ohio (1919), in which Anderson works out his theory of the "grotesque": "the moment one of the people took one of the truths to himself, called it his truth, and tried to live his life by it, he became a grotesque and the truth he embraced became a falsehood."[4]

More impressive in many ways, however, despite its serious structural faults, is the novel *Poor White* (1920). Anderson himself called this "a novel of the coming of industrialism,"[5] and it offers, above all, a series of vivid, sometimes violent, images of the impact of industrialism upon the agrarian society of the Middle West. Hugh McVey, the huge, inarticulate poor white boy from Missouri, comes north to Ohio and discovers in himself a marvellously creative mechanical inventiveness. His inventions are taken up by a local manufacturer, he becomes successful, wealthy and even famous, but he remains, in his days of "success," as isolated and as inarticulate as he has ever been; towards the end of the novel he gradually awakens, finally reaching the point where he rejects the mechanised industrial world he has helped to create. Other characters are almost equally memorable: Tom Butterworth, for example, who turns from farming to business and, like Howells's Dryfoos, grows hard and insensitive in the process, and Ben Peeler, the carpenter, who in abandoning craftsmanship for commerce loses much of the savour of living:

> He had no time now to stop for a half-hour's gossip with a prospective builder of a barn, and did not come to loaf in Birdie Spinks' drug-store at the end of the day. In the evening he went to the lumber office and Gordon Hart came over from the Bank ... Ben and Gordon sometimes worked in the lumber office until midnight. On warm still nights the sweet smell of new-cut boards filled the air of the yard and crept in through the open windows, but the two men, intent on their figures, did not notice.[6]

Richest of all in its implications, however, is the story of Joe Wainsworth, the harness-maker. Wainsworth, pathetic in his

[4] Sherwood Anderson, *Winesburg, Ohio*, New York [1919], p. 5.
[5] *Letters of Sherwood Anderson*, ed. Howard Mumford Jones, Boston [1953], p. 281.
[6] Sherwood Anderson, *Poor White*, New York 1920, pp. 204-5.

inability to comprehend or come to terms with the new industrial society that is making him obsolete, nevertheless approaches heroic stature by murdering his assistant Jim Gibson, a prototype of the slick modern salesman, whose final treachery had been to order factory-made harness for the shop. Wainsworth's actions following the murder make the significance of his act abundantly clear:

> For an hour Joe stayed in the shop with the dead man. The eighteen sets of harness shipped from a Cleveland factory had been received that morning, and Jim had insisted they be unpacked and hung on hooks along the shop walls. He had bullied Joe into helping hang the harnesses, and now Joe took them down alone. One by one they were laid on the floor and with Jim's knife the old man cut each strap into little pieces that made a pile of litter on the floor reaching to his waist. When that was done he went again to the rear of the shop, again stepping almost carelessly over the dead man, and took the revolver out of the pocket of an over-coat that hung by the door.[7]

This fanatical Luddite passion is not unprecedented in American fiction: it possesses Denton in Howells's *The World of Chance*. Nor, it would seem, has it become entirely anachronistic: the hero of Allan Seager's recent novel *Amos Berry* (1953) shoots the president of the corporation for which he works on the grounds that he represents "the organization." But no presentation of this theme, so fundamental to the whole American experience of violent transition from an agrarian to an urban-industrial society, is so vivid, so moving or so quintessential as the episode in *Poor White*.

The novel which perhaps comes closest to *Poor White* in theme, while excelling it in energy and forcefulness, is D. H. Lawrence's *The Rainbow* (1915). Lawrence takes as one of his central themes the impact of industrialisation upon an agricultural community in the English Midlands, underlining his point by such symbolism as the drowning of Tom Brangwen, the farmer, by the flooding of the canal which serves the nearby coal-mines. It is curious that *The Rainbow* should end, like *Poor White*, on a note of optimism for which the book itself offers little justification, but it seems even

[7] *Op. cit.*, pp. 342-3.

more curious that in *Poor White* Anderson should be nearer in spirit, and in achievement, to Lawrence, whom he had not then read, than he would ever be in the consciously Lawrentian novels of a few years later. *Many Marriages* (1922-3) and *Dark Laughter* (1925), the most important of these, are very bad novels indeed. Anderson portrays John Webster, the hero of *Many Marriages*, as a washing-machine manufacturer, but he is interested in Webster, as in Sam McPherson and, for the most part, Hugh McVey, not as a businessman but as a "truth-seeker." Bruce Dudley, the hero of *Dark Laughter*, is a newspaperman, not a businessman, but he too seeks truth. In all of these novels Anderson is returning to the central event of his own life, reviewing it, mulling it over in fictional terms.

At the age of forty-five Anderson abandoned his career in business and became a writer. The break, as Irving Howe has pointed out,[8] was neither so abrupt nor so deliberate as is often believed, and it was, perhaps, a sense of dissatisfaction, even of insecurity, deriving from the manner of his escape which brought Anderson back to the theme in novel after novel. He dwells on the escape much as Bunyan in *Grace Abounding* dwells on the moment of his conversion. For him, as for Bunyan, the step was a momentous one, yet we may feel that he makes too much of it, and that he has falsified the evidence a little. Just as Bunyan might have been a more rewarding writer if he had been a little less strict in his theology, so Anderson might have been a better novelist if he had taken himself less seriously as an artist. On the other hand, without the theology, without the ambition to be an artist, neither of them might have written a word. *The Pilgrim's Progress* of course, is one of the great books of the language, while nothing of Anderson's approaches the first rank; Bunyan's strength is the triumphant assurance of his faith, while Anderson's great weakness is precisely the lack of any such assurance. Yet both are fundamentally simple men, and what we retain most vividly from their books are simple, almost archetypal images of basic human emotions and perennial human situations.

Anderson's images are intuitive rather than intellectual

<hr/>

[8] Irving Howe, *Sherwood Anderson*, [New York 1951], p. 49.

formulations. He adopts towards his material an attitude of innocence, which he learned—or thought he had learned—from Mark Twain, whom he passionately admired. Anderson believed, so he wrote to Van Wyck Brooks, that when Twain came East "he began to think of himself as a writer and lost something of his innocence":[9]

> Well, now, you see I'm coming around. The cultural fellows got hold of Mark. They couldn't hold him. He was too big and too strong. He brushed their hands aside.
> But their words got into his mind. In the effort to get out beyond that he became a pessimist.
> Now, Brooks, you know a man cannot be a pessimist who lives near a brook or a cornfield. When the brook chatters or at night when the moon comes up and the wind plays in the corn, a man hears the whispering of the gods.
> Mark got to that once—when he wrote *Huck Finn*. He forgot Howells and the good wife and everyone. Again he was the half-savage, tender, god-worshipping, believing boy. He had proud, conscious innocence.
> I believe he wrote that book in a little hut on a hill on his farm. It poured out of him. I fancy that at night he came down from his hill stepping like a king, a splendid playboy playing with rivers and men, riding on the Mississippi, on the broad river that is the great artery flowing out of the heart of the land.
> Well, Brooks, I'm alone in a boat on that stream sometimes. The rhythm and swing of it is in some of my songs that are to be published next month. It sometimes gets into some of the Winesburg things. I'll ride it some more, perhaps. It depends on whether or not I can avoid taking myself serious[ly]. Whom the gods wish to destroy they first make drunk with the notion of being a writer.[10]

The passage suggests just how dangerous the influence and example of Twain could be. Twain is the supreme American example of the "natural" writer, extremely prolific, apparently careless in matters of form. But Twain was careless about form only in the larger sense of structure and pattern, in matters of language and style he was usually painstaking. Hemingway's attempt to build

---

[9] *Letters of Sherwood Anderson*, p. 31.   [10] *Op. cit.*, p. 33.

on Twain ended triumphantly, Anderson's in comparative failure, and largely because Hemingway looked to the self-conscious stylist in Twain, Anderson to the "natural" storyteller. Hemingway, himself an extremely self-conscious artist, "stylised" Twain's style, and brought it within an artfully contrived novel structure. Anderson tried to put himself in an attitude of receptivity towards experience in the hope that creativity would flow out of him as he believed it had out of Twain. Unfortunately, because of his personal history and of the kind of artistic commitment he had made, Anderson could not hope to be a natural, spontaneous writer of this kind, and he seems to have lacked the initiative, or perhaps the intelligence, to set about the task of assessing realistically his own gifts and limitations, of constructing his art upon a firm foundation of self-knowledge. As it is, despite his great natural gifts as a story-teller, he never wrote a satisfactory novel. The facts of Anderson's biography and the evidence of *Poor White* and *Winesburg, Ohio* amply attest to the excellence of his equipment as a social novelist, yet he chose instead to turn his writing to the service of obscure quasi-mystical intuitions which he seems never to have grasped and which he was incapable of presenting.

2

In *Poor White*, Anderson wrote a novel of the coming of industrialism; in *Babbitt* (1922) Sinclair Lewis produced the first American novel of any importance to regard industrialism not as a monstrous encroaching force to be hailed or resisted but simply as an enveloping all-pervasive condition of modern life. The contemporary impact of the opening chapters of *Babbitt* derived not from any satirical intention they might have but from their unstrenuous presentation of scenes and manners that were immediately familiar to a wide public. *Babbitt* clearly belongs not to the crests but to the ground-swell of American life. Lewis has marked out a different territory from Dreiser, and even from Tarkington, and American folk-lore has absorbed George F. Babbitt as one of the earliest and certainly the most vigorous of the obscure business heroes.

The novel deals very largely with selling, rather than with the wider aspects of business; Babbitt himself sells real-estate, and he joins his friends of the smoking-compartment in a discussion of the subject:

> They went profoundly into the science of business, and indicated that the purpose of manufacturing a plow or a brick was so that it might be sold. To them, the Romantic Hero was no longer the knight, the wandering poet, the cowpuncher, the aviator, nor the brave young district attorney, but the great sales-manager, who had an Analysis of Merchandizing Problems on his glass-topped desk, whose title of nobility was "Go-getter", and who devoted himself and all his young samurai to the cosmic purpose of Selling—not of selling anything in particular, for or to anybody in particular, but pure Selling.[11]

In passages such as this *Babbitt* has some claim to be regarded as a guide to the folkways of America's commercial civilisation. Lewis, indeed, seems to have had some such aim in view; in a sketch for a projected introduction to *Babbit* he wrote:

> Though this is the individual romance of one G. T. Pumphrey [subsequently George F. Babbitt] and not the breviary of his community, that community enters his every moment, for it is himself, created in his varnished image. Monarch City is every "progressive, go-ahead, forward-looking, live, up-to-date" city of more than eighty thousand in the United States and Western Canada, with 8 or 10 venerable exceptions.[12]

Babbitt undoubtedly does have a fundamental fidelity to its material, or it would not have so caught the popular imagination. At the same time we find throughout the novel a persistent heightening of contrasts, an exaggeration tending to caricature, that stamps it as finally unserious. Because of Lewis's stylistic extravagances, his carelessness, his willingness to jeopardise overall strategy for the sake of scoring a minor tactical point—a verbal joke, for example, or an irrelevant sideswipe at some revered institution—we are often

[11] Sinclair Lewis, *Babbitt*, New York 1922, p. 143.
[12] *The Man from Main Street*, edd. Harry E. Maule and Melville H. Cane, London 1954, p. 24.

left uncertain as to whether he intends to satirise or not. Here, for example, he gives us Babbitt's views on business ethics:

> He serenely believed that the one purpose of the real-estate business was to make money for George F. Babbitt. True, it was a good advertisement at Boosters' Club lunches, and all the varieties of Annual Banquets to which Good Fellows were invited, to speak sonorously of Unselfish Public Service, the Broker's Obligation to Keep Inviolate the Trust of His Clients, and a thing called Ethics, whose nature was confusing but if you had it you were a High-class Realtor and if you hadn't you were a shyster, a piker, and a fly-by-night. These virtues awakened Confidence, and enabled you to handle Bigger Propositions. But they didn't imply that you were to be impractical and refuse to take twice the value of a house if a buyer was such an idiot that he didn't jew you down on the asking-price.[13]

We remain vaguely uneasy with this largely because Lewis has nowhere made clear against what standards Babbitt should be measured. Scott Fitzgerald was perhaps thinking of passages such as this when he wrote in 1926, in "How to Waste Material": "Finally the novel of business will be cudgeled into being satire by the questionable but constantly reiterated implication that the author and his readers don't partake of the American commercial instinct and aren't a little jealous."[14]

There can be little doubt about Lewis's intentions in *Dodsworth* (1929), his other major portrait of a businessman. Henry Steele Commager, in picking out Sam Dodsworth and Tarkington's Earl Tinker as "after Silas Lapham, almost the only respectable businessmen in American fiction," finds them both "dubious" characters.[15] Earl Tinker, as we have seen, is certainly "dubious," but Sam Dodsworth does not so clearly merit the description. *Dodsworth* is a long and repetitious book, but its meanderings finally converge in reasonably coherent fashion, and Sam Dodsworth emerges, as Lewis plainly intended, as a sympathetic figure. *Dodsworth* sometimes suggests a recantation of *Babbitt*, but a recantation

---

[13] *Babbitt*, p. 42.
[14] F. Scott Fitzgerald, "How to Waste Material: A Note on My Generation," (1926), in *Afternoon of an Author*, ed. Arthur Mizener, Princeton 1957, p. 118.
[15] Henry Steele Commager, *The American Mind*, New Haven 1950, p. 274.

with an important difference: we are no longer in the petty-business world but in a world of big business, with a hero who is primarily an inventor, a creator, and only secondarily, a business-man. The theme of the "creative" businessman appears again in the person of Myron Weagle, the "artist" of hotel-keeping, in *Work of Art* (1934): in that inept novel, the theme becomes merely ludicrous, but in *Dodsworth* it compels a certain respect. When Sam Dodsworth consoles himself for not being a "savant" the term may strike us as unfairly "loaded," but our sympathy must still, to some extent, be with him:

> Suddenly he felt better about it. Was it possible that in some involved, unelucidated way, he himself was a savant in fields not admitted by the academicians as scholarship? He told himself that in the American motor-world he was certainly not known merely as a pedler and as a financial acrobat, but as the authority on auto-mobile-designing, as the first man to advocate four-wheel brakes. Hm. *Did* that constitute him a scholar, or—
>
> Or possibly an artist? He had created something! He had no pictures in the academies, no books to be bound in levant, no arias nor flimsy furniture named after him, but every one of the twenty million motors on the roads of America had been influenced by his vision, a quarter of a century ago, of long, clean streamlines!"[16]

Similarly we find him regretting his son's decision to sell bonds because it is not a way to "build things," to be creative.[17] Sam Dodsworth, as both a sympathetic character and, in material terms, a successful businessman, constitutes the obvious exception to the generalisations that might otherwise be made about Lewis's treat-ment of the American "success" theme, which, although not an obsession with him as with Dreiser, remains a constant preoccupa-tion. Even Dodsworth, however, realises that his success is largely to blame for the failure of his marriage and that it has impoverished him in other ways. Early in the book he pleads for time in which to grow accustomed to the idea of having leisure: "I'm a good citizen. I've learned that Life is real and Life is earnest and the

---

[16] Sinclair Lewis, *Dodsworth*, New York 1929, pp. 246-7.
[17] *Op. cit.*, p. 176.

presidency of a corporation is its goal. What would I be doing with anything so degenerate as enjoying myself?"[18]

In most of Lewis's novels "success" is rejected; he affirms instead individualism and personal integrity. In the world of these novels success can only be achieved at the cost of integrity: this, in effect, is the "statement" of *Elmer Gantry* (1927), of *Gideon Planish* (1943), and of *Arrowsmith* (1925). In *Arrowsmith* we find constantly reiterated the idea that the scientist, in order to remain a true scientist, a dedicated man, must actually be protected against success. Dr Gottlieb tells Martin Arrowsmith:

> "But once again always remember that not all the men who work at science are scientists. So few! The rest—secretaries, press-agents, camp-followers! To be a scientist is like being a Goethe: it is born in you. Sometimes I t'ink you have a liddle of it born in you. If you haf, there is only one t'ing—no, there is two t'ings you must do: work twice as hard as you can, and keep people from using you. I will try to protect you from Success. It is all I can do."[19]

In *Elmer Gantry* Lewis reserves his most scathing passages for the careerists of religion, as in this description of Gantry himself at the Methodist Annual Conference:

> But moving through these masses, easily noticeable, the inevitable successes: the district superintendents, the pastors of large city congregations, the conceivable candidates for college presidencies, mission-boards, boards of publication, bishoprics. . . .
>
> Most notable among the aristocrats were a certain number of large, suave, deep-voiced, inescapably cordial clerical gentlemen who would have looked well in Shakespearean productions or as floor-walkers. And with them was presently to be found the Reverend Elmer Gantry.
>
> He was a new-comer, he was merely hoping to have the Conference recognize his credentials and accept him as a member, and he had only a tiny church, yet from somewhere crept the rumour that he was a man to be watched, to be enrolled in one's

[18] *Op. cit.*, p. 32.
[19] Sinclair Lewis, *Arrowsmith*, New York [1958], p. 291.

own political machine; and he was called "Brother" by a pastor whose sacred rating was said to be not less than ten thousand a year. They observed him; they conversed with him not only on the sacraments but on automobiles and the use of pledge envelopes; and as they felt the warmth of his handshake, as they heard the amiable bim-bom of his voice, saw his manly eyes, untroubled by doubts or scruples, and noted that he wore his morning clothes as well as any spiritual magnate among them, they greeted him and sought him out and recognized him as a future captain of the hosts of the Almighty.[20]

The organisation, through the temptation of the wealth and power it represents, inevitably corrupts. As Frank Shallard discovers, it can also oppress. Even in such an early novel as *Our Mr. Wrenn* (1914), Lewis presents the organisation as something to be escaped from, and in *The Job* (1917) he gives the first of several more or less frightening portraits of organisations at work. Una Golden, the heroine of *The Job*, is often mentioned by sociologists: her distinction, in their eyes, lies in her historical importance as the first full-length portrait of an office-girl in American fiction. Office-girls and "typewriters" had appeared as minor characters from the time of Howells's *The Rise of Silas Lapham*, but before Una Golden none of them had taken a central role. Indeed, from the sociologists' point of view, the whole novel has great interest. Here, for example, Lewis carefully defines the exact place which Una occupies in the office hierarchy of Pemberton's, "the greatest manufactory of drugs and toilet articles in the world":[21]

> Una's caste, made up of private secretaries to the chiefs, was not above the buzzer. She had to leap to the rattle-snake tattoo, when Mr. Ross summoned her, as quickly as did the newest Jewish stenographer. But hers was a staff corps, small and exclusive and out of the regular line. On the one hand she could not associate with the chiefs; on the other, it was expected of her in her capacity as daily confidante to one of the gods, that she should not be friendly, in coat-room or rest-room or elevator, with the un-recognized horde of girls who merely copied or took the bright young men's dictation of letters to drug-stores. These girls of the

[20] Sinclair Lewis, *Elmer Gantry*, London 1927, pp. 335-6.
[21] Sinclair Lewis, *The Job*, New York 1917, p. 218.

common herd were expected to call the secretaries, 'Miss', no matter what street-corner impertinences they used to one another.[22]

"Caste at Pemberton's," writes Lewis, "was as clearly defined as ranks in an army."[23]   Lewis's meticulous analysis of each rank of this business bureaucracy represents social observation of a most valuable and original kind.   In *The Job*, however, as in so many of his novels, he at once diversifies and compromises this observation by allowing a persistent intrusion of "romance."   In rhetorical vein, and in words directly reminiscent of Frank Norris, Lewis exclaims:

> Not as priest or soldier or judge does youth seek honor to-day, but as a man of offices.   The business subaltern, charming and gallant as the jungle-gallopers of Kipling, drills files, not of troops, but of correspondence.   The artist plays the keys, not of pianos, but of typewriters.   Desks, not decks; courts of office-buildings, not of palaces—these are the stuff of our latter-day drama.   Not through wolf-haunted forests nor purple cañons, but through tiled hallways and elevators move our heroes of to-day.
>
> And our heroine is important not because she is an Amazon or a Ramona, but because she is representative of some millions of women in business, and because, in a vague but undiscouraged way, she keeps on inquiring what women in business can do to make human their existence of loveless routine.[24]

The explicitness of the passage suggests how artificially Lewis has imposed the "romance" upon the observation, and in fact *The Job* cannot be called a good novel.   But it looks forward to later and better novels of Lewis's which pursue this central theme of the "obscure" hero in an organisational setting.   Lewis appears at his best in portraying the anxieties and frustrations of the "small man" who feels himself borne down by forces too powerful for him to resist and too shadowy for him fully to comprehend.   The way in which Babbitt is brought to heel after his brief flirtation with "liberal" ideas provides perhaps the most striking example of this, but in many of the novels the pressures are brought to bear not by a social group or class but by a specific organisation.   Lewis repeatedly uses the word "factory" to describe the mechanical, inhuman character of great institutions: he applies it to both a

[22] *Op. cit.*, pp. 232.   [23] *Op. cit.*, p. 230.   [24] *Op. cit.*, pp. 46-7.

medical clinic[25] and a state university[26] in *Arrowsmith*, and in *Babbitt*
he refers to " that great department-store, the State University."[27]
In *Arrowsmith*, *Elmer Gantry*, *Gideon Planish*, and *It Can't Happen
Here* (1935), the organisation becomes quite specifically something
to be fought.

No doubt such opposition was of great emotional importance
to Lewis, but apart from the special case of *It Can't Happen Here*,
it seems unlikely that he thought deeply in a political context or
even that he had any clear conception of the possible social effects
of increasing institutionalisation. In this respect, his attitude remains
essentially the attitude of Carol Kennicott towards the end of *Main
Street* (1920):

> And why, she began to ask, did she rage at individuals? Not
> individuals but institutions are the enemies, and they most afflict
> the disciples who the most generously serve them. They insinuate
> their tyranny under a hundred guises and pompous names, such as
> Polite Society, the Family, the Church, Sound Business, the Party,
> the Country, the Superior White Race; and the only defence against
> them, Carol beheld, is unembittered laughter.[28]

In *Main Street* we are by no means entirely on Carol Kennicott's
side, but in many ways she speaks for Lewis himself. Her whole
career gives expression to Lewis's view at that time that "the
ghetto-like confinement of small towns could be—not always was,
but so easily could be—a respectable form of hell."[29]   Carol's
realisation that "institutions are the enemies" indicates that her
personality and her role of village rebel in some measure reflect
Lewis's own persistent restlessness and discontent: it certainly
cannot be taken as an indication that Lewis was deeply concerned
with institutions as such, or with the fundamental predicaments
of American society.

3

The most surprising thing about *Babbitt* is its dedication to Edith
Wharton, for whatever literary tradition Sinclair Lewis may belong

---

[25] *Arrowsmith*, p. 281.   [26] *Op. cit.*, p. 9.   [27] *Babbitt*, p. 69.
[28] Sinclair Lewis, *Main Street*, London 1923, p. 427.
[29] *The Man from Main Street*, p. 202

to, it seems unlikely to be one that will embrace Edith Wharton as well. However profoundly she may have treated of American material in certain of her novels, Edith Wharton remains by temperament and training unmistakably a "paleface"—to use Philip Rahv's terminology[30]—while Lewis stands out as an uncompromising "redskin." In fact, it is hard to detect any direct literary influences upon Lewis, but Twain and Dreiser stand firmly behind him. The influence of Dreiser resists precise identification, since it is of that fundamental and pervasive kind to which Lewis himself referred in his Nobel Prize address:

> Now to me, as to many other American writers, Dreiser more than any other man, marching alone, usually unappreciated, often hated, has cleared the trail from Victorian and Howellsian timidity and gentility in American fiction to honesty and boldness and passion of life. Without his pioneering, I doubt if any of us could, unless we liked to be sent to jail, seek to express life and beauty and terror.
>
> My great colleague Sherwood Anderson has proclaimed this leadership of Dreiser. I am delighted to join him. Dreiser's great first novel, *Sister Carrie*, which he dared to publish thirty long years ago and which I read twenty-five years ago, came to housebound and airless America like a great free Western wind, and to our stuffy domesticity gave us the first fresh air since Mark Twain and Whitman.[31]

We may find it especially interesting that Lewis should link Dreiser with Twain and Whitman as one of those writers who had made new areas of the American experience available to his successors; as Lewis says, Sherwood Anderson had earlier paid Dreiser a precisely similar tribute.

The influence of Twain on Lewis resembled in certain respects the influence of Twain on Anderson, and it involved much the same dangers. George Jean Nathan once observed that Sinclair Lewis's novels originated in his "gift of protracted and inane oratory":

> One could always tell a new novel coming on when the oratorical mood in any one, single, thematic direction assailed our

[30] Philip Rahv, "Paleface and Redskin," in *Image and Idea*, Norfolk, Conn. 1957, pp. 1-6.
[31] *The Man from Main Street*, p. 8.

friend. *The Man Who Knew Coolidge* was nothing more than a series of such orations gathered together, with not a word changed. . . . *Dodsworth*, a year later, was heralded both before and directly after our friend's European material-seeking trip by innumerable vaudeville performances in the British dialect, aided and abetted by a monocle that Red had purchased for the further embellishment of his histrionic talents.[32]

We have plenty of evidence that Twain was given to just this kind of brilliant spontaneous creation in speech, and we may set against Nathan's description of Lewis's orations the reasons which Twain once gave for choosing to dictate his *Autobiography*:

> Within the last eight or ten years I have made several attempts to do the autobiography in one way or another with a pen, but the result was not satisfactory; it was too literary. With the pen in one's hand, narrative is a difficult art; narrative should flow as flows the brook down through the hills and the leafy woodlands, its course changed by every bowlder it comes across and by every grass-clad gravelly spur that projects into its path; its surface broken, but its course not stayed by rocks and gravel on the bottom in the shoal places; a brook that never goes straight for a minute, but *goes*, and goes briskly, sometimes ungrammatically, and sometimes fetching a horseshoe three-quarters of a mile around, and at the end of the circuit flowing within a yard of the path it traversed an hour before; but always *going*, and always following at least one law, always loyal to that law, the law of *narrative*, which *has no law*. Nothing to do but make the trip; the how of it is not important, so that the trip is made.[33]

We hardly need to compare this with Anderson's letter to Van Wyck Brooks, quoted earlier in this Chapter, to see just where Twain's example could lead. It would, of course, be foolish to condemn the method itself, since the pattern of *Huckleberry Finn* is clearly reflected in Twain's remarks, but the disastrous results of Anderson's attempts to achieve "spontaneity" make it abundantly clear that for a writer to sustain such a method through many books

[32] George Jean Nathan, "Memories of Fitzgerald, Lewis and Dreiser," *Esquire*, L (Oct. 1958), pp. [150-1].

[33] Quoted in *The Complete Short Stories of Mark Twain*, ed. Charles Neider, Garden City, New York 1957, p. xiv.

calls for almost instinctive mastery of a wide range of fully absorbed material. And this Lewis does not have. Although, as a fully professional writer, he is extremely adept at working up a new subject, a new area of material, we find him returning again and again to a small group of themes, characters and scenes. In *Gideon Planish*, for example, he attempts to re-work the theme of *Elmer Gantry* in a slightly different setting. In *Dodsworth* he returns, at a more sophisticated level, to the basic idea of *Our Mr. Wrenn*, and the theme appears again in *The Prodigal Parents* (1938). Characters from one book frequently turn up in another: for example, George F. Babbitt makes appearances in *Arrowsmith* and in *Elmer Gantry*, and the name of Elmer Gantry often crops up in *Gideon Planish*.

In almost every Lewis novel at least one character, often the hero, acts and talks exactly like George F. Babbitt, or, what is almost the same thing, like Lowell Schmaltz of *The Man Who Knew Coolidge* (1928). The leading citizens of Gopher Prairie speak in much that way, so do Elmer Gantry, Gideon Planish, and Mr Edward Schwartz in *The Job*, while the hero of *Our Mr. Wrenn* speaks a scarcely distinguishable New York version. What Lewis puts into the mouths of these characters, it seems clear, is a caricature of Middle Western "booster" speech; it is not the accurate rendering of actual speech-patterns such as we find in Ring Lardner or in Twain himself. Often, no doubt, Lewis simply indulges on paper his "gift of protracted and inane oratory." Interestingly enough, Nathan says that *The Man Who Knew Coolidge* was a direct transcription of such orations: the first section of that book represents Lewis's most sustained and most successful passage of speech caricature, and it might be argued that almost everything stylistically original and interesting in his work appears in essence in those few pages.

Oh, I guess I'm an old crank. But Del is so young, and she thinks she knows everything but she's innocent as a baby, but— Oh, I'm a regular fusser. But anyway, we certainly did have one large round time that evening—evening, huh! Say, we certainly were high-rollers for once! I'll bet it was three o'clock before we hit the hay. I remember—
It was kind o' comic! Here was Mame—that's my wife—

supposed to be a good respectable dame, and me, a deacon in the church, and us coming down Broadway at three G.M. singing "We Won't Go Home Until Morning!"

You see, Sam—he's got the nerve of the devil—he picked up a couple from Fort Worth, Texas (and maybe she wasn't some baby; say, she had all the regular New York dames there beat a mile), and somehow, I don't exactly remember how, we got acquainted with another couple from San José, California, a gentleman that was in the fruitranching business and his wife and son, he took a shine to Delmerine; and up in the bar I got talking to a gentleman and lady from Kansas City, Missouri—or it may have been Kansas City, Kansas: I can't exactly remember, at this late date—and the whole lot of us carried on like we'd always known each other, dancing and laughing and drinking toasts and singing and drinking and cutting up—Say! But I hate to think of what it cost me. But as I told my wife, that's the way of it, in New York.[34]

Here we have the basic theme on which most of the other novels enact variations.

Apart from the influence on Lewis of Twain and Dreiser, we also detected earlier some signs of a possible affinity between Lewis and Frank Norris. Norris, although a far more self-conscious writer than Lewis, has a similar appetite for the excitement and romance of the American experience. Lewis would surely have endorsed almost every word of *The Responsibilities of the Novelist.* Indeed, his novels exemplify many of its precepts more faithfully than Norris's own, and his observations on writing often read like Norris brought up-to-date:

And industrialism itself—more dramatic than the universities, more impressive and more terrible than any army with banners, a topic for a Shakespeare and a Zola combined, single organisations with 200,000 employees engaged in the most active and cunning war with half a dozen like armies—who of our young people longing for Greenwich Village or Paris so that they may "find something to write about" has been able to see, or has dared to attempt, this authentically epic theme? Is Waterloo a more gigantic

[34] Sinclair Lewis, *The Man Who Knew Coolidge*, New York 1928, pp. 69-70.

spectacle than the Ford plant at River Rouge? Is the conquest of an Indian kingdom by an English proconsul more adventurous than the General Motors' invasion of the German motor world? He that hath eyes to see, let him see![35]

This is strongly reminiscent of Norris's enthusiastic outbursts about the romance of commerce and of his attempt in *The Octopus* to write the "neglected epic" of the West. Lewis and Norris differ, however, in that Lewis nowhere attempts a comprehensive treatment of society. Each novel presents a fragment of society, usually in terms of a single dominating character—as Lewis's fondness for using characters' names for titles suggests—and of a single thematic idea. His general habit, especially in the later novels, is to take an idea, work it up, and then write it out: in the process, more often than not, he first inflates and then exhausts it. The "idea" of *Work of Art* is simply that a dedicated businessman may be more of an "artist" than an insincere writer; the "idea" of *The Prodigal Parents* is sufficiently summarised in its title; *The Man Who Knew Coolidge*, though an amusing *tour de force*, scarcely has an "idea" at all. These are weak foundations on which to venture the erection of full-length novels.

Yet we must acknowledge Lewis's success in capitalising on what were apparently his most crippling limitations both of talent and of experience. In an autobiographical essay, "Breaking into Print," Lewis writes:

And how did a Harry Sinclair Lewis, son of an average doctor in a Mid-Western prairie village who never—but never!—heard at table any conversation except "Is Mrs. Harmon feeling any better?" and "Butter's gone up again" and "Mrs. Whipple told me that Mrs. Simonton told her that the Kellses have got a cousin from Minneapolis staying with them"—a youth who till he was ready to enter university had never seen any professional writer except the local country editors—how came it that at eleven he had already decided to become a short-story writer (an ambition, incidentally, that he never adequately carried out), and that at fourteen he sent off to *Harper's Magazine* what he believed to be a poem?[36]

[35] *The Man from Main Street*, p. 124.   [36] *Op. cit.*, pp. 77-8.

Neither he, nor we, can answer that question. But, given Lewis's impulse to write, we can easily see where most of his early material came from. Lewis both mirrored and spoke to the American middle-class because he was so intimately and thoroughly of that class himself. Therein lay his great strength, the source of an assurance such as Anderson always lacked. On the other hand, it was his great limitation that he never genuinely transcended the limits of his class and of his early background: his stylistic equipment was inadequate, and he lacked deep resources of imagination and sympathy. Although he sometimes achieved considerable vigour of expression, it was always within an extremely narrow range; his observations of American society were often incisive, but they were made in terms of a very restricted point of view. By 1927 he had virtually exhausted his natural, "given" material in *Main Street* and *Babbitt* and then gone on to write, in *Arrowsmith* and *Elmer Gantry*, his two basic versions of the American "success" theme. Only these books hold promise of lasting value.

We earlier saw Sherwood Anderson as an outstanding example of a gifted writer who seemed to lose his way as an artist, rejecting the kind of social fiction in which he might have excelled in order to pursue literary aims which were outside the range of his particular gifts. Sinclair Lewis, on the other hand, exemplifies the less gifted writer who, having once discovered the kind of thing he can do well, continues to do it, with little significant variation, to the end of his career. This contrast between the two writers has been largely responsible for the present situation in which Anderson's reputation is almost non-existent while Lewis's remains considerably higher than his limited achievement would seem to warrant.

7

F. Scott Fitzgerald

Dreiser's presentation of Frank Cowperwood involves a crude celebration of business with which we cannot always sympathise. Tarkington wavers between the opposing poles of "bigness" and dignity and his novels peter out in indecision. Part of Fitzgerald's distinction as a social novelist derives from his perception that by presenting an "epic hero" whose business acumen, exceptional as it is, forms only one aspect of his total personality, he could at once increase the stature of the hero and decrease the importance of business: herein lies the special interest of Jay Gatsby and Monroe Stahr. In his first novel, *This Side of Paradise* (1920), Fitzgerald explicitly rejects the business theme through the mouth of Amory Blaine:

> "And I wish American novelists would give up trying to make business romantically interesting. Nobody wants to read about it, unless it's crooked business. If it was an entertaining subject they'd buy the life of James J. Hill and not one of these long office tragedies that harp along on the significance of smoke—"[1]

However, *The Beautiful and Damned* (1922), Fitzgerald's second novel, though very far from being exclusively concerned with business, does present a shadowy caricature of a millionaire philanthropist in Adam J. Patch, and its hero, Anthony Patch, Adam's grandson, does find himself temporarily involved in the business world. Indeed, in this rather ponderous and self-conscious book the brief descriptions of business life provide, perhaps because Fitzgerald has for once reasonably solid ground under his feet, some of the most lively moments. When Anthony goes to work for

---

[1] F. Scott Fitzgerald, *This Side of Paradise*, New York 1920, p. 234. Fitzgerald may have been thinking especially of Booth Tarkington's *The Turmoil* (1915).

Wilson, Heimer and Hardy as a bond salesman he discovers that the discussions in the employees' lunchroom all circle round "success stories":

> During the preceding year one of the assistant secretaries had invested all his savings in Bethlehem Steel. The story of his spectacular magnificence, of his haughty resignation in January, and of the triumphal palace he was now building in California, was the favorite office subject. The man's very name had acquired a magic significance, symbolizing as he did the aspirations of all good Americans. Anecdotes were told about him—how one of the vice-presidents had advised him to sell, by golly, but he had hung on, even bought on margin, "and *now* look where he is!"
>
> Such, obviously, was the stuff of life—a dizzy triumph dazzling the eyes of all of them, a gypsy siren to content them with meagre wage and with the arithmetical improbability of their eventual success.
>
> To Anthony the notion became appalling. He felt that to succeed here the idea of success must grasp and limit his mind. It seemed to him that the essential element in these men at the top was their faith that their affairs were the very core of life. All other things being equal, self-assurance and opportunism won out over technical knowledge; it was obvious that the more expert work went on near the bottom—so, with appropriate efficiency, the technical experts were kept there.[2]

Although not especially good writing, this exceeds the general level of *The Beautiful and Damned*. Above all it demonstrates, if not great knowledge, considerable shrewdness, and the tone, especially in the last paragraph, is firm enough to persuade us of the accuracy of the observation. Perhaps we may regard it as a minor example of the kind of confidence trick Fitzgerald performs so superbly in *The Great Gatsby* (1925). Gatsby's business affairs are revealed only in brief and ambiguous glimpses, and we learn little more of his background than we do of Christopher Newman's. This is less disturbing in *The Great Gatsby* than in *The American*, largely because Fitzgerald, without necessarily being more informative than James, at least supplies more food for the imagination: " 'Well, he's no

---

[2] F. Scott Fitzgerald, *The Beautiful and Damned*, New York 1922, pp. 230-1.

use to us if Detroit is his idea of a small town,' " says Gatsby into the telephone,[3] and though we do not fully understand the remark we are ready to be convinced that Gatsby is involved in large, and possibly dubious, operations. No more is necessary for Fitzgerald's purposes: indeed the very vagueness of Gatsby's background actually enhances his almost mythic stature.

The precise methods by which Gatsby makes his money are irrelevant. Highly relevant, however, is the element of illegality involved: indeed, this is why Fitzgerald makes such use of an otherwise peripheral character, Meyer Wolfsheim, with his talk of a "business gonnegtion"[4] and his distinction of being, as Gatsby explains, "the man who fixed the World's Series back in 1919."[5] In stressing the corruption at the heart of Gatsby's dream, as well as exposing, through the presentation of Daisy, the tawdriness of what the dream aspires to, Fitzgerald clearly intended a fundamental criticism of the "American Dream" itself and of the business society to which, in the twentieth century, it had become indissolubly wedded. So, in *Tender is the Night* (1934), Gatsby's crooked business has its symbolic counterpart in Nicole's violation by her business-man father, and Fitzgerald's view of American society finds its most explicit expression in the comment on Nicole's shopping orgy:

Nicole was the product of much ingenuity and toil. For her sake trains began their run at Chicago and traversed the round belly of the continent to California; chicle factories fumed and link belts grew link by link in factories; men mixed toothpaste in vats and drew mouthwash out of copper hogsheads; girls canned tomatoes quickly in August or worked rudely at the Five-and-Tens on Christmas Eve; half-breed Indians toiled on Brazilian coffee plantations and dreamers were muscled out of patent rights in new tractors—these were some of the people who gave a tithe to Nicole, and as the whole system swayed and thundered onward it lent a feverish bloom to such processes of hers as wholesale buying, like the flush of a fireman's face holding his post before a spreading blaze. She illustrated very simple principles, containing in herself her own doom, but illustrated them so accurately that there was

[3] F. Scott Fitzgerald, *The Great Gatsby*, in *Three Novels of F. Scott Fitzgerald*, New York [1953], p. 71.
[4] *Op. cit.*, p. 54.   [5] *Op. cit.*, p. 56.

grace in the procedure, and presently Rosemary would try to imitate it.[6]

To speak of Fitzgerald's "confidence trick" in *The Great Gatsby* is to describe his technique, not decry it. Angus Wilson, after all, has said that all fiction depends upon a confidence trick,[7] and Coleridge spoke long ago of the willing suspension of disbelief that constitutes poetic faith. It is, perhaps, only saying the same thing in a different way to suggest that *The Great Gatsby* persuades us poetically rather than logically. At the end of Fitzgerald's brilliant display of advocacy we stand, despite all the evidence, with Gatsby—like Nick, for whom Gatsby represented everything for which he had "an unaffected scorn."[8] And we do not merely find him "Not Guilty": vindication merges into acclamation. The method works primarily through the imagery. It is almost a cinematic technique, achieving economy, speed and tautness by building up the narrative through the scene rather than the chapter unit, cutting abruptly from one scene to another, using the flashback, creating a total pattern through recurrent phrases, scenes, situations, images—images such as Gatsby's yellow car, Daisy's white roadster, the blue lawns of Gatsby's house, and the green light at the end of Daisy's dock. We might examine, for the sake of example, the way in which Daisy's representativeness is defined by the images which cluster round her. After the famous moment when Gatsby describes Daisy's voice as "full of money,"[9] Nick, as narrator, goes on:

> That was it. I'd never understood before. It was full of money—that was the inexhaustible charm that rose and fell in it, the jingle of it, the cymbals' song of it . . . High in a white palace the king's daughter, the golden girl . . .[10]

This paragraph forms the climax of the two strands of imagery which also come together in Daisy's name: the daisy flower is white with a golden centre ("in a white palace . . . the golden

---

[6] F. Scott Fitzgerald, *Tender is the Night*, New York 1934, pp. 71-2.
[7] Interview, in *Writers at Work*, ed. Malcolm Cowley, New York 1958, p. 257.
[8] *The Great Gatsby*, p. 3.   [9] *Op. cit.*, p. 91.   [10] *Ibid.*

girl"). We see Daisy herself as always associated with whiteness: in Chapter I and again in Chapter VII Daisy and Jordan Baker sit together on the couch "like silver idols weighing down their own white dresses,"[11] Daisy speaks of their "white girlhood" together,[12] and Jordan tells Nick that Daisy as a girl "dressed in white, and had a little white roadster."[13] This whiteness obviously carries suggestions of innocence, remoteness and inaccessibility (the "white palace"), but in the first chapter it already becomes clear that something more is in question:

> Sometimes she and Miss Baker talked at once, unobtrusively and with a bantering inconsequence that was never quite chatter, that was as cool as their white dresses and their impersonal eyes in the absence of all desire. They were here, and they accepted Tom and me, making only a polite pleasant effort to entertain or to be entertained. They knew that presently dinner would be over and a little later the evening, too, would be over and casually put away.[14]

Thus the whiteness goes with the life-denying "absence of all desire" and links up with Nick's final dismissal of Tom and Daisy as "careless people" who "smashed up things and creatures and then retreated back into their money or their vast carelessness."[15] The "innocence" is destructive, like that of Graham Greene's "quiet American"; the inaccessibility represents a withdrawal from those "promises of life" to which Gatsby himself displays such sensitivity.[16]

The associations of the other strand of imagery, culminating in "the golden girl," are with ideas of wealth. At the very beginning of the novel Nick speaks of his first actions on coming East to live: "I bought a dozen volumes on banking and credit and investment securities, and they stood on my shelf in red and gold like new money from the mint, promising to unfold the shining secrets that only Midas and Morgan and Mæcenas knew."[17] To this sentence we must refer back the description of the Buchanans' house: Fitzgerald describes it as "red-and-white" outside, surrounded by roses, and with windows "glowing now with reflected gold";[18]

---

[11] *Op. cit.*, p. 88   [12] *Op. cit.*, p. 10.   [13] *Op. cit.*, p. 57.
[14] *Op. cit.*, p. 11.   [15] *Op. cit.*, p. 136.   [16] *Op. cit.*, p. 4.
[17] *Op. cit.*, p. 5.   [18] *Op. cit.*, p. 7.

inside Daisy and Jordan wait in a "crimson," "rosy-colored" room with a "wine-colored rug" below "the frosted wedding-cake of the ceiling."[19]   Daisy herself is associated again and again with gold; she has a gold pencil; in Gatsby's bedroom she sees his "toilet set of pure dull gold" and "took up the brush with delight, and smoothed her hair";[20] her youth, like that of Judy Jones in "Winter Dreams,"[21] is recalled in terms of "golden and silver slippers" and faces "like rose petals."[22]

Many other examples could be quoted—for instance, Gatsby dresses for his first reunion with Daisy in "a white flannel suit, silver shirt, and gold-colored tie"[23]—but enough has probably been said to indicate the characteristic features of the technique.[24] We can perhaps define it more closely by means of a brief comparison between Fitzgerald and his English contemporary E. M. Forster.[25]   Forster's *Howards End* (1910) has a famous passage in which Margaret and Helen watch the tide come into Poole Harbour:

> There was a long silence, during which the tide returned into Poole Harbour. "One would lose something," murmured Helen, apparently to herself. The water crept over the mud-flats towards the gorse and the blackened heather. Branksea Island lost its immense foreshores, and became a sombre episode of trees. Frome was forced inward towards Dorchester, Stour against Wimborne, Avon towards Salisbury, and over the immense displacement the sun presided, leading it to triumph ere he sank to rest. England was alive, throbbing through all her estuaries, crying for joy through the mouths of all her gulls, and the north wind, with contrary motion, blew stronger against her rising seas. What did it mean? For what end are her fair complexities, her changes of soil, her sinuous coast? Does she belong to those who have moulded

[19] *Op. cit.*, p. 8.   [20] *Op. cit.*, p. 70.
[21] F. Scott Fitzgerald, "Winter Dreams," in *The Stories of F. Scott Fitzgerald*, ed. Malcolm Cowley, New York [1956], pp. 127-45. See especially p. 140. See also Malcolm Cowley, "The Romance of Money," Introduction to *The Great Gatsby*, in *Three Novels of F. Scott Fitzgerald*, pp. ix-xx.
[22] *The Great Gatsby*, p. 115.   [23] *Op. cit.*, p. 64.
[24] For an illuminating analysis along somewhat similar lines see W. J. Harvey, "Theme and Texture in *The Great Gatsby*," *English Studies*, XXXVIII (1957), 12-20.
[25] Cp. the comparison between Forster and Sherwood Anderson in Lionel Trilling, *E. M. Forster*, Norfolk, Conn. [1943], pp. 20-2.

her and made her feared by other lands, or to those who have added nothing to her power, but have somehow seen her, seen the whole island at once, lying as a jewel in a silver sea, smiling as a ship of souls, with all the brave world's fleet accompanying her towards eternity?[26]

We may set against this the equally famous conclusion of *The Great Gatsby*:

> Most of the big shore places were closed now and there were hardly any lights except the shadowy, moving glow of a ferryboat across the Sound. And as the moon rose higher the inessential houses began to melt away until gradually I became aware of the old island here that flowered once for Dutch sailors' eyes—a fresh, green breast of the new world. Its vanished trees, the trees that had made way for Gatsby's house, had once pandered in whispers to the last and greatest of all human dreams; for a transitory enchanted moment man must have held his breath in the presence of this continent, compelled into an æsthetic contemplation he neither understood nor desired, face to face for the last time in history with something commensurate to his capacity for wonder.
>
> And as I sat there brooding on the old, unknown world, I thought of Gatsby's wonder when he first picked out the green light at the end of Daisy's dock. He had come a long way to this blue lawn, and his dream must have seemed so close that he could hardly fail to grasp it. He did not know that it was already behind him, somewhere back in that vast obscurity beyond the city, where the dark fields of the republic rolled on under the night.
>
> Gatsby believed in the green light, the orgiastic future that year by year recedes before us. It eluded us then, but that's no matter—tomorrow we will run faster, stretch out our arms farther. . . . And one fine morning—
>
> So we beat on, boats against the current, borne back ceaselessly into the past.[27]

We may immediately note how alike the two authors seem to be in their imagery, in their use of symbols, in their gift of rhetoric, in their feeling for the native land that lies beneath and beyond the human dramas enacted upon it. In *Howards End* and *The Great*

---

[26] E. M. Forster, *Howards End*, London 1947, pp. 185-6.
[27] *The Great Gatsby*, p. 137.

Gatsby they are dealing with the same basic theme, which each sees as a national theme: the conflict between the outer life and the inner life, between, to put it crudely, those who do and those who feel. Forster conducts an intensive exploration of this conflict, which is not for him a clash of black and white, and the novel moves towards resolution and reconciliation. He perceives and faces the difficulty of persuading us to accept the Wilcox-Schlegel marriage, but we never do accept it entirely.

The conclusion of *The Great Gatsby* leaves us with no such feeling of dissatisfaction, largely because the movement of the book is circular; the action and the symbolism are designed to illustrate, emphasise and justify Nick Carraway's opening distinction between Gatsby, with his "heightened sensitivity to the promises of life," and, on the other hand, the "foul dust [which] floated in the wake of his dreams."[28] When in the final paragraphs, in the course of Nick's funeral oration, Fitzgerald suddenly expands Gatsby's story into a parable of man's fate, the splendour of the rhetoric blinds us to the fact that the previous action of the novel has not completely prepared us for such a development. Fitzgerald has not presented Gatsby heretofore in quite these ambitious terms, nor has he provided us with the evidence on which to judge Gatsby's qualifications for such a role. In retrospect, this may give rise to certain intellectual doubts about *The Great Gatsby*, but as we read the book Fitzgerald's stylistic brilliance carries us resistlessly through. The mode of *The Great Gatsby* is essentially poetic, and on that level Fitzgerald achieves a wholly satisfying resolution.

2

It seems likely that this sustained use of imagery was the quality in *The Great Gatsby* to which T. S. Eliot responded so generously; it has obvious affinities with his own method in *The Waste Land*. His letter to Fitzgerald about *The Great Gatsby* speaks of its being "the first step that American fiction has taken since Henry James. . . ."[29] This linking of Fitzgerald with James has fascinated

[28] *Op. cit.*, p. 4.
[29] T. S. Eliot to F. Scott Fitzgerald, 31 Dec. 1925, in F. Scott Fitzgerald, *The Crack-Up*, ed. Edmund Wilson, New York [1945], p. 310.

critics ever since. Certain features of *The Great Gatsby* seem reminiscent of James, yet it seems unlikely that Fitzgerald had read much, if any, of James's work at this time. James E. Miller, Jr, in his study of Fitzgerald's early novels, concludes: "Although Fitzgerald, at the time of writing *The Great Gatsby*, was apparently not under the direct influence of James, he could have felt an immense indirect attraction through any number of writers who themselves had gone to school to the master."[30]

Curiously enough, Miller does not go on to mention Edith Wharton, although her name appears elsewhere in his study. Gilbert Seldes, who, as Mizener notes,[31] had talked with Fitzgerald about the book, said when reviewing *The Great Gatsby* for *The Dial* that Fitzgerald had derived the scenic method "from Henry James through Mrs. Wharton."[32] She was, in any case, by far the most important, and the best known, of James's followers; and Fitzgerald certainly knew and admired her work. He sent her a copy of *The Great Gatsby* when it first appeared; her letter of thanks, though warm and appreciative, contains one rather curious criticism:

> My present quarrel with you is only this: that to make Gatsby really Great, you ought to have given us his early career (not from the cradle—but from his visit to the yacht, if not before) instead of a short résumé of it. That would have situated him, & made his final tragedy a tragedy instead of a "fait divers" for the morning papers.[33]

It is a little surprising that Edith Wharton should criticise Fitzgerald for something which he might well have derived from her own method in, say, the presentation of Elmer Moffatt in *The Custom of the Country*. Moffatt's background is very lightly sketched in, but he is seen in action, or on the brink of action, sufficiently often to convince us, as Christopher Newman probably does not, that he is capable of the achievements attributed to him. As we have seen, Fitzgerald followed a very similar method in presenting

[30] James E. Miller, Jr, *The Fictional Technique of Scott Fitzgerald*, The Hague 1957, p. 72.
[31] Arthur Mizener, *The Far Side of Paradise*, London 1951, p. 170.
[32] Gilbert Seldes, "Spring Flight," *The Dial*, LXXIX (1925), 163.
[33] Edith Wharton to F. Scott Fitzgerald, 8 Jun. 1925, in *The Crack-up*, p. 309.

Gatsby, whose history, situation, and aspirations resemble Moffatt's in several important respects. Indeed, we may think of *The Great Gatsby* as in certain ways bringing up-to-date the American sections of *The Custom of the Country*. Certain important themes occur in both novels: the conflict between West and East within America itself; the relationship between the possession of wealth, social success and "getting the best girl"; and, above all, the presentation of the money-society of New York, both at its amusements and in its domestic settings, and of the corruption at the heart of that society. Daisy, with her voice "full of money," bears an obvious resemblance to Undine Spragg; Tom Buchanan recalls Peter Van Degen. Gatsby himself resembles Moffatt in many ways, but in others he resembles Ralph Marvell: he imagines his "golden girl" to be much finer than she really is, and he ends by dying on her account.

We need not conclude that Fitzgerald, in writing *The Great Gatsby*, was directly indebted to *The Custom of the Country*, though he may well have been influenced by the narrative techniques which Edith Wharton had used in *Ethan Frome*.[34] But Fitzgerald, as a social novelist, is certainly much closer to Edith Wharton than to any of his other predecessors or contemporaries: he works in the same social area, uses similar characters, and views society from much the same standpoint.[35] Both Fitzgerald and Edith Wharton clearly perceive the existence of an American class system dominated by the money-power, but although they adopt a critical attitude towards this society they are not primarily concerned with satirising it. They recognise the corruption, but they are drawn irresistibly as novelists to the fascinating coruscation of the social surface.

When Fitzgerald speaks of Nicole as the product of capitalistic

[34] Some of Edith Wharton's remarks in the Introduction to *Ethan Frome* (New York [1939], pp. v-x) seem relevant to a consideration of Nick Carraway's role in *The Great Gatsby*: "Each of my chroniclers contributes to the narrative *just so much as he or she is capable of understanding* of what, to them, is a complicated and mysterious case; and only the narrator of the tale has scope enough to see it all, to resolve it back into simplicity, and to put it in its rightful place among his larger categories." (p. ix).

[35] On this point see Frederick J. Hoffman, "Points of Moral Reference: a Comparative Study of Edith Wharton and F. Scott Fitzgerald," *English Institute Essays*, 1949, New York 1950, pp. 147-76.

exploitation we may again recall Edith Wharton's description of Mrs Westmore in *The Fruit of the Tree*:

> Her dress could not have hung in such subtle folds, her white chin have nestled in such rich depths of fur, the pearls in her ears have given back the light from such pure curves, if thin shoulders in shapeless gingham had not bent, day in, day out, above the bobbins and carders, and weary ears throbbed even at night with the tumult of the looms.[36]

The central idea here, of course, is something of a cliché of nineteenth-century romanticism, going back at least as far as Keats's "Isabella".[37] At the same time, we can speak of the two passages as remarkably similar in content, in tone and even in cadence. Moreover, in both passages the author appears in what we may think of as an uncharacteristic mood, for neither Edith Wharton nor Fitzgerald habitually makes explicit statements on questions of politics, economics, or social justice. The two passages may in fact represent the emergence of basic attitudes normally unexpressed, but we must also recognise that while Fitzgerald and Edith Wharton are alike in not taking American society at its own valuation, they are also alike in their frank enjoyment of that society's practical and material advantages.

Fitzgerald also greatly admired Theodore Dreiser, and Dreiser's influence can sometimes be detected in Fitzgerald's early work. For example, we may think of Hurstwood as a possible ancestor of Dick Diver, and of Dorothy Raycroft, in *The Beautiful and Damned*, as owing a good deal to Jennie Gerhardt. Critics have suggested a possible original for Jay Gatsby in "X," the hero of Dreiser's story " 'Vanity, Vanity,' Saith the Preacher,"[38] while the principal theme of *The Great Gatsby* as a whole is anticipated towards the end of *The Titan*, when Cowperwood tells Berenice:

> I have done whatever I have done in connection with you and your mother because I have been in love with you and because I

[36] Edith Wharton, *The Fruit of the Tree*, p. 49. See p. 58 above.

[37] John Keats, "Isabella, or the Pot of Basil," stanzas XIV and XV, in *The Poetical Works of John Keats*, ed. H. W. Garrod, Oxford 1939, pp. 219-20.

[38] See Maxwell Geismar, *Rebels and Ancestors*, Boston [1953], p. 342 n., and Eric Solomon, "A Source for Fitzgerald's *The Great Gatsby*," *Modern Language Notes*, LXXIII (1958), 186-8.

wanted you to become the splendid thing I thought you ought to become. You have not known it, but you are the cause of my building the house on Fifth Avenue—the principal reason. I wanted to build something worthy of you. A dream? Certainly. Everything we do seems to have something of that quality. Its beauty, if there is any, is due to you. I made it beautiful thinking of you.[39]

After all, it should not especially surprise us that Fitzgerald should have found himself in sympathy with Dreiser, a fellow Mid-Westerner who was similarly obsessed with the theme of success. Indeed, for a writer so much interested in the idea of success, Fitzgerald must perhaps be reckoned unlucky in achieving his own success so quickly and so easily, so that he never really knew the experience of being on the way up; and we may wonder, thinking of his protest in "How to Waste Material,"[40] how far he was personally conscious not so much of a shortage of material as of a narrowness of range, of a life certainly not devoid of experience but lacking in real diversity. Even in such a persuasive passage as the end of The Great Gatsby, which simply as a piece of writing was completely out of Dreiser's reach, the impression remains—impossible to substantiate—of Fitzgerald leaning on Dreiser, finding strength in Dreiser's massiveness, learning a sense of proportion from the older man's more comprehensive social knowledge and social vision.[41]

We spoke earlier of the importance of Edith Wharton and Theodore Dreiser as contrasting and complementary influences on

[39] Theodore Dreiser, The Titan, pp. 466-7.

[40] F. Scott Fitzgerald, "How to Waste Material: a Note on My Generation," in Afternoon of an Author, ed. Arthur Mizener, Princeton 1957, pp. 117-8. Fitzgerald comments on contemporary American social novelists and their "insincere compulsion to write 'significantly' about America" (p. 117), and he observes: "In any case we are running through our material like spend-thrifts—just as we have done before. In the Nineties there began a feverish search for any period of American history that hadn't been 'used,' and once found it was immediately debauched into a pretty and romantic story. These past seven years have seen the same sort of literary gold rush; and for all our boasted sincerity and sophistication, the material is being turned out raw and undigested in much the same way." (p. 118).

[41] Compare, for example, the end of The Great Gatsby, quoted on p. 113, with the conclusion of Dreiser's A Hoosier Holiday (1916), quoted on pp. 83-84.

the American social novel. In the best work of Fitzgerald we can perhaps recognise the amalgamation of some of the most valuable elements in the work of his two predecessors, both of whom he greatly admired. The establishment of the social environment of *The Beautiful and Damned* is too laborious and too overloaded with explicit detail, but *The Great Gatsby* seems to combine the comprehensive social awareness and social knowledge of Dreiser with the technical skill of Edith Wharton. This combination of influences supports Fitzgerald in his audacious and magnificently successful attempt to create a novel of manners within a social context whose extreme instability Fitzgerald himself best indicated when analysing the nineteen-twenties in "Echoes of the Jazz Age."[42] Fitzgerald creates by his poetic techniques a world arrested at a particular moment in time, grasped and known in all its complexity, measured in its evanescence, looked at from all sides as if it were itself an artifact, an object susceptible of aesthetic and moral contemplation. It might conceivably be argued that Fitzgerald *cannot* have known this world as deeply as Dreiser knew it or as deeply as the novel suggests, but the very convincingness of *The Great Gatsby* makes such arguments irrelevant.

3

We have seen that in most of Fitzgerald's novels business does not play a greater part than in the typical Edith Wharton novel. Both treat it as the invisible seven-eighths of the iceberg, the indispensable, often unacknowledged basis of the whole social world, the "given" quantity to which no reference need be made except in times of personal or general disaster: so business intrudes into *The Age of Innocence* only because of the social repercussions of Beaufort's "failure." Business plays just such a role in *The Great Gatsby*. In *The Beautiful and Damned* Fitzgerald deals less with business than with money-power and, like James in *The Ivory Tower*, with the corrupting effects of inherited wealth. *Tender is the Night*, considered as the story of the Warren sisters, is a novel of the businessman's womankind with the businessman himself almost entirely

[42] F. Scott Fitzgerald, "Echoes of the Jazz Age," in *The Crack-Up*, pp. 13-22.

excluded. But, if Fitzgerald had lived to complete *The Last Tycoon* (1941), we might have had a business novel of considerable comprehensiveness and power, and of quite a different kind from *The Great Gatsby*.

On 29 September, 1939, Fitzgerald wrote to his publisher that his new novel, *The Last Tycoon*, had been set "safely in a period of five years ago to obtain detachment."[43] A year later, in September 1940, we find him telling Gerald Murphy that the novel is "as detached from me as *Gatsby* was, in intent anyhow."[44] That final qualifying phrase raises doubts which the letterhead reinforces (Twentieth Century-Fox Film Corporation Studios, Beverley Hills, California),[45] and in fact the detachment seems to have proved elusive: *The Last Tycoon* lacks the distanced, curiously "classical" air of *The Great Gatsby*. The volume as we have it contains a collection of brilliant and powerful scenes; these hardly begin to cohere into a novel, and not only for the reason that the book was unfinished.

Indeed, we may doubt whether Fitzgerald could have finished *The Last Tycoon* according to his original conception. Many of Fitzgerald's difficulties derived from the fact that he was, in effect, writing two novels in one: a "psychological" novel about Monroe Stahr, and a "social" novel about Hollywood. In his letter to Edmund Wilson of 25 November, 1940, the emphasis appears to be on the latter: "I honestly hoped somebody else would write it [the novel] but nobody seems to be going to."[46] However, the starting-point of the book seems clearly to have been the genius of Stahr himself, "the last tycoon," just as the central interest of *The Great Gatsby* had been in Gatsby himself. The "social" interest in *The Great Gatsby*, though considerable, serves primarily to display and explain the human relationships: it never takes control. In *The Last Tycoon*, as far as it had gone, the "social" content also remains reasonably functional, but we may judge from Fitzgerald's plans for the conclusion of the novel that had he tried to work out the plot of *The Last Tycoon* along the lines he proposed, his growing

---

[43] F. Scott Fitzgerald, Notes to *The Last Tycoon*, in *Three Novels of F. Scott Fitzgerald*, p. 141.
[44] *The Crack-Up*, p. 282.   [45] *Op. cit.*, p. 281.   [46] *Op. cit.*, p. 285.

interest in the intrigue, corruption and violence of Hollywood might well have taken control and swamped the rest.

Fitzgerald does not seem fully to have realised that in *The Last Tycoon* he faced a problem of construction quite different from the one he had so brilliantly solved in *The Great Gatsby*; otherwise he would surely not have tried to cast his new book so completely in the *Gatsby* mould. Since he planned *The Last Tycoon* as a short novel of about fifty-one thousand words, he turned naturally to *The Great Gatsby* for a usable pattern, and the frequent references to *The Great Gatsby* in Fitzgerald's notes for *The Last Tycoon* and in his letters at this time make it clear that while he was planning and writing the new book he had the earlier one very much in mind. In any case, this would have been sufficiently plain from a comparison of the two. Each tells the story of a man who, from humble beginnings, has risen to a position of great power. In each we first come to know of the man not in person but by reputation and by the attitude of others towards him. Then we see the man himself in the centre of his world, his position and his greatness defined by the nature of that world which revolves upon him as its axis: Fitzgerald's outline for *The Last Tycoon* says explicitly that he intends the chapters describing Stahr's day to be "equal to guest list and Gatsby's party,"[47] namely, to Chapter Three and the first two pages of Chapter Four of *The Great Gatsby*. We watch in each the failure of the man in his personal life, in an all-important relationship with a woman; then his violent, senseless death; and finally his funeral, so strongly contrasted with his life (in notes for the end of *The Last Tycoon* Cecilia imagines Stahr present at the funeral and saying "Trash!").[48]

The most important and perhaps the most questionable of *The Last Tycoon*'s debts to *The Great Gatsby* is the half-involved first-person narrator. Fitzgerald describes Cecilia as "*of* the movies but not *in* them";[49] a very similar comment could have been made about Nick Carraway's place in the world of *The Great Gatsby*. But Nick, as a piece of structural machinery, is a superb invention: he remains on stage almost throughout the novel, and we are never

[47] Notes to *The Last Tycoon*, p. 142.   [48] *Op. cit.*, p. 132.
[49] *Op. cit.*, p. 138.

in doubt about the sources of his information. Nick as narrator never strains our credulity; Cecilia as narrator worries us from the start. Fitzgerald clearly intended her to play a Nick Carraway role, but because of her own limited participation in the action she cannot fulfil Nick's narrative function. Nick's other major role is to act as a vehicle for moral judgments, and here again Cecilia falls short. Fitzgerald planned a final scene in a sanatorium, intending to invest Cecilia, through her illness, with greater portentousness, but she lacks weight in the story as we have it. She seems too immature, and too involved emotionally with the people and actions she describes to be able to make worthwhile judgments or to help us to judge.

The correspondences between *The Last Tycoon* and *The Great Gatsby* are not accidental, and they may have helped to twist *The Last Tycoon* out of its proper path, whatever that may have been. Gatsby's violent death has ironic appropriateness, but the violent death proposed for Stahr seems unmotivated and relatively without point, except in so far as Fitzgerald was planning a reference back to the airliner episode in Chapter One. The unsatisfactory love-affair forms the core of *The Great Gatsby* and indeed of Gatsby himself, but, although Fitzgerald told his publisher that he wanted Stahr's affair with Kathleen to be "the meat of the book,"[50] he seems not too have had a completely clear conception of their relationship. In fact, Stahr the lover remains a somewhat shadowy figure in the chapters that we have, and it is certainly Stahr the producer and businessman who emerges the more vividly.

4

Because the making of motion-pictures involves questions of artistic judgment, it seems, as Fitzgerald noted, rather an odd kind of business. But it unquestionably is a business: as Cecilia Brady tells us on the first page, "My father was in the picture business as another man might be in cotton or steel."[51] The enmity between Stahr and Brady derives largely from the latter's exclusively business approach to film-making, but Stahr himself, though he must

[50] *Op. cit.*, p. 139.   [51] *The Last Tycoon*, p. 3.

pronounce on matters of taste, remains inevitably a businessman as well. When Wylie White challenges Stahr's description of himself as a "merchant," Stahr sticks to the word and suggests that Charles Francis Adams, when he criticised "Gould, Vanderbilt, Carnegie, Astor," was " 'probably a sourbelly' . . . . ' He wanted to be head man himself, but he didn't have the judgment or else the character.' "[52]

Stahr thus seems to align himself with the great American capitalists. But the tone of his answer works together with Wylie White's admiration to prevent our thinking of him entirely in these terms, and when we see him at lunch with the financiers we quickly realise his isolation among them. As a young man he had been "more than now . . . a money man among money men. Then he had been able to figure costs in his head with a speed and accuracy that dazzled them."[53] Since then, we learn, Stahr "had grown away from that particular gift, though it was always there."[54] Stahr remains a brilliant businessman, but he has become something more. Fitzgerald's grand conception of Stahr both includes his business ability and transcends it:

> He spoke and waved back as the people streamed by in the darkness, looking, I suppose, a little like the Emperor and the Old Guard. There is no world so but it has its heroes, and Stahr was the hero. Most of these men had been here a long time—through the beginnings and the great upset, when sound came, and the three years of depression, he had seen that no harm came to them. The old loyalties were trembling now, there were clay feet everywhere; but still he was their man, the last of the princes. And their greeting was a sort of low cheer as they went by.[55]

The kind of representative importance with which Fitzgerald intended to invest Stahr does not wholly emerge in the novel as we have it. But it becomes sufficiently plain that if Stahr is an embodiment of heroic individualism he has—despite his paternalism, his dislike of unions, and his fight with Brimmer—nothing of the Fascist about him. Indeed, one of the major themes of *The Last Tycoon* seems to be a partial identification of Stahr with Abraham

[52] *Op. cit.*, pp. 16-17.
[53] *Op. cit.*, p. 45.
[54] *Ibid.*
[55] *Op. cit.*, p. 27.

Lincoln. Arthur Mizener has pointed out the importance of the Lincoln motif in Fitzgerald's presentation of Stahr: he relates it, with the reference to Andrew Jackson in the episode at The Hermitage in the opening chapter, to the "political fable" Fitzgerald seems to have been developing in the book.[56] It may be, however, that the identification of Stahr with Lincoln, though never complete, goes further than this, affecting other sides of Stahr's character and other aspects of the book.

Boxley, the English novelist, finds Stahr irritating, but "he had been reading Lord Charnwood and he recognized that Stahr like Lincoln was a leader carrying on a long war on many fronts . . . . Stahr was an artist only, as Mr. Lincoln was a general, perforce and as a layman."[57] Going to Lord Charnwood's biography, *Abraham Lincoln*, it is interesting to discover Charnwood quoting contemporary references to Lincoln as "the Tycoon"[58] and as "King Abraham I."[59] The coincidence with Fitzgerald's title is striking, and usefully reminds us that Fitzgerald intended Stahr as a "tycoon" in the original sense of that word quite as much as in the modern sense. There seems a possible hint here, too, of Fitzgerald's description of Stahr as "the last of the princes" and of the moment when Kathleen assures Stahr that her real king was not nearly so king-like as Stahr himself.[60]

There are other points of similarity between Charnwood's Lincoln and Fitzgerald's Stahr: both are men of humble origins and little education but of great ability and vision; both practice in their relations with subordinates complete accessibility and an unforced personal democracy; both accept without hesitation the full responsibility of their position while disliking many of the duties involved. As Fitzgerald saw, an obvious analogy can be drawn between Stahr's position and Lincoln's: Stahr can be seen as the the commander-in-chief, receiving reports from the battleline, issuing orders to his generals (the directors), overseeing work which has to be done in detail by others. In a smaller way, Lincoln's

---

[56] Arthur Mizener, *The Far Side of Paradise*, pp. 295-6.
[57] *The Last Tycoon*, p. 106.
[58] Lord Charnwood, *Abraham Lincoln*, London 1917, p. 234.
[59] *Op. cit.*, p. 377.   [60] *The Last Tycoon*, p. 112.

habit of telling a little story when a reproof had to be administered somewhat resembles Stahr's method of handling Boxley, while it is surely in terms of the Lincoln analogy that the curious scene with the Negro on the beach at Malibu begins to take on fuller meaning: like Lincoln, but unlike Wylie White earlier in *The Last Tycoon*, Stahr will transform his kingdom for the Negro's sake.

Above all, Stahr resembles Lincoln in responding supremely to to the demands of power. Writers, he tells Brimmer,

> ". . . are not equipped for authority. . . There is no substitute for will. Sometimes you have to fake will when you don't feel it at all."
> "I've had that experience."
> "You have to say, 'It's got to be like this—no other way'— even if you're not sure. A dozen times a week that happens to me. Situations where there is no real reason for anything. You pretend there is."
> "All leaders have felt that," said Brimmer. "Labor leaders, and certainly military leaders."[61]

Stahr stands as the centre, the keystone of his world: in Fitzgerald's imagery, he is "the king,"[62] "the helmsman,"[63] "the oracle."[64] He himself constitutes the "unity."[65] When he delivers a judgment: "The oracle had spoken. There was nothing to question or argue. Stahr must be right always, not most of the time, but always— or the structure would melt down like gradual butter."[66] If the power of decision is, as many people would maintain, the essence of business success, then Stahr is one of the very few businessmen in fiction in whom we see the process of decision actually at work. His method, hinted at in the exchange with Brimmer, is magnificently expounded in his conversation with the pilot of the aircraft in the opening chapter:

> He was looking down at the mountains.
> "Suppose you were a railroad man," he said. "You have to send a train through there somewhere. Well, you get your surveyors' reports, and you find there's three or four or half a dozen gaps, and not one is better than the other. You've got to

[61] *Op. cit.*, p. 121.   [62] *Op. cit.*, p. 112.   [63] *Op. cit.*, p. 105.
[64] *Op. cit.*, p. 56.   [65] *Op. cit.*, p. 58.   [66] *Op. cit.*, p. 56.

decide—on what basis? You can't test the best way—except by doing it. So you just do it."

The pilot thought he had missed something.

"How do you mean?"

"You choose some one way for no reason at all—because that mountain's pink or the blueprint is a better blue. You see?"

The pilot considered that this was very valuable advice. But he doubted if he'd ever be in a position to apply it.

"What I wanted to know," he told me ruefully, "is how he ever got to be Mr. Stahr."[67]

We know that Fitzgerald took this passage from an actual conversation, but that scarcely detracts from its impressiveness: indeed, we may see it as a mark of Fitzgerald's shrewdness, which we have already seen guiding him to a convincing presentation of worlds other than his own, that he should have recognised, despite the almost absurd simplicity of the remark, its revealing accuracy. Fitzgerald records that, listening to the speaker, he was impressed by "something more than shrewdness—by the largeness of what he thought."[68] It might be argued that the characterisation of Stahr betrays traces of Fitzgerald's old tendency to uncritical hero-worship; certainly his attempt to invest Stahr with "largeness" in the last two paragraphs of Chapter One, whatever its rhetorical success, is not altogether substantiated by what we see of Stahr in action. The very solidity and concreteness of Fitzgerald's presentation of Stahr, the very convincingness of the scenes in what Cecilia calls "A Producer's Day," work against an acceptance of Stahr as a larger-than-life figure. However impressive his omnicompetence, few of Stahr's individual decisions seem especially remarkable —apart, perhaps, from his insistence on making a picture that will lose money. The shadowiness with which Jay Gatsby is presented may raise occasional questions in the reader's mind but it has undoubted artistic advantages.

5

If he had lived, Fitzgerald's completion and revision of *The Last Tycoon* might well have made this criticism irrelevant. There can be

[67] *Op. cit.*, pp. 19-20.   [68] Notes to *The Last Tycoon*, p. 135.

no question of the seriousness and thoroughness of Fitzgerald's attempt in this novel to present a detailed portrait of a specific industry and of a dominating figure in that industry. His portrayal of Stahr and of Stahr's world is scarcely less deliberate as social documentary than Dreiser's portrayal of Cowperwood. This is made clear by such notes as: "[Brady] is the monopolist at his worst— Stahr, in spite of the inevitable conservatism of the self-made man, is a paternalistic employer."[69] In his paternalism, indeed, Stahr, seems rather reminiscent of Amherst in *The Fruit of the Tree*, but Fitzgerald has here an advantage over both Edith Wharton and Dreiser, and even over the author of his own earlier books, in his comprehensive knowledge of the world he presents and in his understanding, both as moralist and as novelist of manners, of all sides of his hero's personality.

Completed, *The Last Tycoon* would have been triumphant evidence of Fitzgerald's ability to write a social novel radically different from *The Great Gatsby* in both aim and method. Instead of relying on the brilliant poetic techniques which had enabled him to create the earlier novel's wholly convincing yet somewhat insubstantial world of manners, Fitzgerald in *The Last Tycoon* was attempting to reflect, through accretion of carefully selected detail, the whole fabric of the film industry as he knew it. *The Last Tycoon* would not necessarily have been a better book than *The Great Gatsby* nor more ambitious in scope than *Tender is the Night*, but we may suspect that the Hollywood setting would have been not merely evoked, as the Long Island and New York settings are so skilfully evoked in *The Great Gatsby*, but recreated with complete solidity and understanding; while Monroe Stahr, for his part, would have become not only, with the possible exception of Dick Diver, the most fully drawn of Fitzgerald's characters, but one of the outstanding portraits of a businessman in the history of American fiction.

[69] *Op. cit.*, p. 140.

8

John Dos Passos

I

James had seen that the businessman might be an obscure as
well as an epic hero, but before the nineteen-twenties American
novelists had rarely presented him in such a role. E. W.
Howe's *The Story of a Country Town* (1883) and Hamlin Garland's
Main-Travelled Roads (1891), using a rural setting, anticipate the
inversion of the success theme found in *An American Tragedy*, while
the anonymity and powerlessness of the employee are touched upon
in the work of Henry Blake Fuller, especially in *The Cliff-Dwellers*
(1893), and of William Dean Howells, as in the scene in *A Hazard
of New Fortunes* (1890) when March, about to be visited in his
office by his employer, has "a disgreeable feeling of being owned
and of being about to be inspected by his proprietor."[1] These,
however, are the exceptions, and in general American social
novelists at the turn of the century neglected the theme. In the
nineteen-twenties, however, there was *Babbitt*, in the nineteen-
thirties there were the "proletarian" novelists, and by 1943 J. P.
Marquand, in his novel *So Little Time*, has this comment on the
fading of the epic hero in the popular imagination:

> In the past twenty years, the United States has been most
> fickle in its selection of types for hero-worship. It is difficult to
> realize, in the light of the present, that Bankers and Business
> Executives once were heroes, in the 'twenties. Jeffrey Wilson could
> remember when the circulation of periodicals such as the *American
> Magazine* was built largely on the heroic backlog of Big Business.
> Pages were filled with photographs of bankers at play, and with
> inspiring interviews with men like the late Messrs. Schwab and
> Vanderlip, telling the youth of America how they, too, could

[1] Howells, *A Hazard of New Fortunes*, I. 284.

succeed. This, of course, was before Bankers and Executives were swept away into the Limbo of disrepute when the dam of the depression broke, and before some wag at the Senate hearing placed that midget on the knee of Mr. Morgan.[2]

Marquand goes on to describe the new type of hero as first "the Man in White . . . that quiet, nerveless soldier fighting his lonely battle on the murky frontier of Science, strangling microbes, manufacturing artificial hearts, so that America might live," and then, in the mid-nineteen-thirties, the foreign correspondent.[3]

If these last observations represent only part of the truth, Marquand seems substantially accurate in his comment on the disappearing bankers and business executives. The authors of a study into "Values in Mass Periodical Fiction, 1921-1940" show convincingly that in magazine fiction, at least, a marked decrease in the number of business heroes did occur between the nineteen-twenties and the nineteen-thirties. After a study of changing success themes in the *Saturday Evening Post*, one of the most important vehicles of popular image-making, they conclude that during the nineteen-thirties there was "a shift in emphasis away from the 'titan' success theme, in which the hero is exalted for his own genius over and above other group values, to the 'little man' success theme, in which the reward symbol is due to the hero as the bearer of specific group virtues."[4]

The trends of mass-periodical fiction do not necessarily coincide with those of serious fiction; indeed, the evidence is rather to the contrary. There seems little doubt, however, that the American social novelists of the nineteen-twenties and nineteen-thirties differed increasingly from those of the two previous decades: they depicted a different society, they had new social and political attitudes, and they naturally inclined to other types of hero. Certainly the big businessman appeared less and less, either as hero or as villain; instead, novelists tended to present either the small

[2] J. P. Marquand, *So Little Time*, Boston 1943, pp. 24-5.
[3] *Op. cit.*, p. 25.
[4] Patricke Johns-Heine and Hans H. Gerth, "Values in Mass Periodical Fiction, 1921-1940," in *Mass Culture*, edd. Bernard Rosenberg and David Manning White, Glencoe, Ill. [1957], p. 230.

businessman, nominally his own master but in fact hedged about by all kinds of economic and social pressures, or the minor employee of a large organisation, nominally a free individual but in fact subtly shaped and conditioned by the circumstances of his job. One of the earliest and most famous instances of this transition is Dreiser's analysis of the American failure in *An American Tragedy* ten years after his presentation of the American success in *The Financier* and *The Titan*.

2

The fullest exploration and documentation of the transition appears in the novels of John Dos Passos. His trilogy *U.S.A.*, first published in a complete edition in 1938, was one of the outstanding novels of its decade. Twenty-five years later it is widely regarded as merely an exposition of discredited political ideas in terms of an out-moded literary convention, of some interest as a "document" but certainly of minor importance as a novel. It is often spoken of as a "monumental" work, with the clear inference that it is not only a period piece but a particularly long and tedious one. Dos Passos cannot be so lightly dismissed. No American writer has attempted more, and few writers anywhere have brought to succesful completion novels of the size and scope of *U.S.A.* Dos Passos's ambition was impossibly grandiose, and as an attempt to present in fictional terms the development of American society from 1900 to 1929, *U.S.A.* was doomed to at least partial failure. Yet it remains, for all its faults, the fullest and most impressive fictional treatment of that period, and it firmly establishes Dos Passos's claim to be considered the most important social novelist since Dreiser.

U.S.A. is an extremely long book: its three parts, *The 42nd Parallel* (1930), *1919* (1932), and *The Big Money* (1936), were originally published as separate novels, and each alone made a sizable volume. However, Dos Passos immediately impresses us with the ease, swiftness, and flexibility of his narrative: "mostly *U.S.A.* is the speech of the people,"[5] says the prefatory sketch, and the writing displays above all the forceful and colourful raciness of colloquial speech. Unfortunately it also displays the faults of colloquial speech,

[5] John Dos Passos, *U.S.A.*, New York [1938], p. vii.

and there is a certain lack both of variety and tension. This lack, of course, is in part deliberate, arising from the fact that Dos Passos creates a documentary effect by reporting everything in the same tone of voice: the humour is deadpan, the tragedy is viewed with apparent detachment. "Tragedy," indeed, is hardly the word to use in this context, for tragedy demands a personal responsibility and freedom to choose that Dos Passos's characters do not have: this is a "naturalistic" novel, and the characters are in the grip of forces they are powerless to control. The lack of emphasis, the absence of peaks, is thus unavoidable, but it does cast a certain greyness and tonelessness over the narrative sections of the book. The flow is smooth and steady, but no individual moment stays long in the mind.

To some extent, Dos Passos needs this effect. None of the characters must become so important, or even so interesting, that they obscure the view of America as a whole. It was in an attempt to give his portrait of a nation the fullest possible depth and scope that Dos Passos introduced the devices of the Biography, the Newsreel, and the Camera Eye. Of these, the Biographies now seem easily the most successful: they are sharply edged, hard-hitting, economical. Dos Passos uses the Newsreels to pinpoint the actual historical moment, to catch and preserve its unique flavour, but he frequently mars such an effect by including too much unspecific and undatable material and by indulging in rather mechanical ironic effects. Such well-known Camera Eye passages as the childhood memories in *The 42nd Parallel*[6] or the evocation in *The Big Money*[7] of the night of Saccho and Vanzetti's execution are extraordinarily vivid, but these interludes in general are rather obscurely related to the rest of the book and the less successful of them look forward only too clearly to the windy prose poems of *District of Columbia* (1952).

While we may note the considerable interest and importance of Dos Passos's experiments with these techniques, it is extremely unlikely that any writer would now consider directly repeating them. Even Norman Mailer, who owes much to Dos Passos,

[6] John Dos Passos, *The 42nd Parallel*, in *U.S.A.*, pp. 5-6, 24-5, etc.
[7] John Dos Passos, *The Big Money*, in *U.S.A.*, pp. 461-4.

approaches them only rather unambitiously in the interludes in
The Naked and the Dead, and in *U.S.A.* itself they, more than anything else, date the book for the contemporary reader. Yet the
Biographies and, for all their weaknesses, the Newsreels and the
Camera Eye interludes do broaden the impression of America,
whereas the ultimate effect of the narrative is rather to narrow that
impression: the book is, after all, a novel and necessarily the lives
of the characters tend to criss-cross, intermingle, and run in the
same channels—as business contacts of J. Ward Moorhouse, for
instance, or as guests at Eveline's parties. As has often been noted,
the picture of America that emerges from the book has serious
limitations. Important sections of society are not represented and
the characters tend to be rather the same sort of people, of similar
class backgrounds, leading desperate and unsettled lives full of
arrivals and departures and casual love affairs. What is absent is
the sense of the heavy underswell of American life, of the great
mass of ordinary, relatively static, politically indifferent working-
and middle-classes: scarcely anyone in *U.S.A.* has a home and family.

It would be too much to expect that Dos Passos or any other
writer could capture America alive and whole. *U.S.A.* gives us a
thoroughgoing account of Dos Passos's America, but that is only a
segment, though a large and important one, of the whole, and a
segment, moreover, which has been decisively shaped by the
pressure of the political views which Dos Passos held at the time.
Throughout the novel, despite its "documentary" effect, its air of
objectivity, we can readily detect the author's voice: most clearly
present in the Camera Eye passages, it is also audible in the ironical
juxtapositions of the Newsreels and in the dexterous slanting of the
Biographies. In the narrative itself key words and associations
quickly differentiate between the "good" ("unionist," "wobbly,"[8]
"working-man") and the "bad" ("Wilsonian," "patriotism,"
"stockmarket"). Eventually we come to feel that politics must
have been much simpler then, the issues more clear-cut, friend more
easily told from foe.

[8] A "wobbly" was a member of the I.W.W. (Industrial Workers of the World),
a revolutionary socialist organisation active in the United States at the beginning
of this century.

Business and businessmen in *U.S.A.* fall especially under Dos Passos's levelling condemnation: both are "bad," contemptible, and villainous. This holds not only for J. Ward Moorhouse, the public relations counsel in the novel, but also for several men whose lives are recalled in the Biographies: Andrew Carnegie, for example, and Minor C. Keith, founder of the United Fruit Company, in *The 42nd Parallel*; John Pierpont Morgan and his son in *1919*; Henry Ford and Samuel Insull in *The Big Money*. Dos Passos writes, of one of them: "Why that uneasy look under the eyes, in the picture of Minor C. Keith the pioneer of the fruit trade, the railroad builder, in all the pictures the newspapers carried of him when he died?"[9] However, inverting Dreiser's earlier admiration for finance as an "art," he reserves his fiercest language for the purely financial manipulators like the Morgans:

> (War and panics on the stock exchange,
> machinegunfire and arson,
> bankruptcies, warloans,
> starvation, lice, cholera and typhus:
> good growing weather for the House of Morgan.)[10]

As political polemic this is extremely effective. The sketch of Morgan too, is quite masterly in its economy:

> J. Pierpont Morgan was a bullnecked irascible man with small black magpie's eyes and a growth on his nose; he let his partners work themselves to death over the detailed routine of banking, and sat in his back office smoking black cigars; when there was something to be decided he said Yes or No or just turned his back and went back to his solitaire.[11]

These passages succeed largely because the first over-simplifies while the second uses caricature. Neither, of course, is without some basis in truth, but essentially their success depends upon exaggeration and the elimination of qualifications. They do not persuade us that Dos Passos has any real understanding of Morgan or of the power he wields. They reveal the voice of moral anger rather

---

[9] *The 42nd Parallel*, p. 244.
[10] John Dos Passos, *1919*, in *U.S.A.*, p. 340.
[11] *Op. cit.*, p. 338.

than of rational analysis. Dos Passos at this time may have thought of himself as a twentieth-century radical, but his tone and attitude are closely akin to those of a medieval moralist.

The career of Charley Anderson, beginning at the end of *The 42nd Parallel* and occupying a large part of *The Big Money*, clearly brings out the essentially moralistic nature of Dos Passos's preoccupations. Charley Anderson has marvellous gifts as a mechanic. The most valuable friendship of his life is with another mechanic, Bill Cermak, who is later killed in an accident to an aircraft piloted by Charley: "You and me, Bill, the mechanics against the world,"[12] says Charley, at one of his best moments. But money and success destroy Charley. He deserts his original friend and partner, sets himself up in an expensive apartment, and exhausts his money and energy in the fruitless courtship of a self-centred society woman who feels no affection for him. He gambles on Wall Street and loses heavily. In fact, Charley Anderson's destruction as a man proceeds step by step with his achievement of material wealth and conventional success: as he moves further from the workbench and becomes more involved in the stock market so he goes more swiftly and irrevocably downhill. He finally dies as the result of a car crash that is not so much an accident as the natural outcome of a drunken bravado so extreme as to amount to a deathwish.

It is almost a "morality," an *exemplum* of the kind which was so popular with English preachers in the late Middle Ages, and which continued to appear after the Reformation in the work of Puritan moralists like Bunyan. It recalls, more recently, the rather simple moral patterns which, in Chapter Two, we discovered in a number of novels by Howells, notably *The Rise of Silas Lapham* and *A Hazard of New Fortunes*. It recalls, too, the stridencies of Upton Sinclair and the earnest simplicities of Sherwood Anderson. Dos Passos's attack on the power and corruption of business is essentially based on moral indignation. So, for that matter, is his whole presentation of American society in *U.S.A.* His rationale may have been economic and political, but his impetus, however closely identified with the rationale, was moral and emotional.

---

[12] *The Big Money*, p. 229.

This, though his limitation as a sociologist, is his strength as a novelist. The crash of 1929 defeated Dreiser as an artist by the violence with which it overturned his most fundamental assumptions: he abandoned fiction for economic discussion, as in *Tragic America*. For Dos Passos, however, a much younger man, the crash was a kind of liberation: by confirming him in a single-minded purpose that was intensely moral as well as political and economic it gave his work an entirely new forcefulness and strength. The advantage that the Dos Passos of *U.S.A.* has over the Dos Passos of *Manhattan Transfer* (1925) is not simply in the increased scope offered by taking a whole nation rather than one city as subject: it is rather in the greater sustaining and unifying power that comes from a direct, unhesitating moral vision. The portrait of America in *U.S.A.* is incomplete in many ways, but it is the more clearly drawn, the outlines are bolder, because it is seen from a single, and single-minded, point of view.

3

In order to gain some insight into the nature of this moral impetus it may be helpful to look for a moment outside the body of Dos Passos's own work. For instance, Thorstein Veblen's influence undoubtedly pervades Dos Passos's antipathy towards the financier, and the description of Veblen in *The Big Money*,[13] in the longest Biography of the whole *U.S.A.* trilogy, is perhaps the best existing short introduction to Veblen's personality and ideas. To Dos Passos and other radical writers, however, Veblen's work seems to have been less valuable as a tight system of economic and social theory than as a rich quarry from which to mine whatever suited their particular purposes. From their point of view one of the most important things about Veblen, as Max Lerner points out, was that he "peopled his intellectual world with well-defined symbolic types"[14]—among them the Captain of Industry, who later degenerates into the Captain of Finance or, in a different social context, into the Captain of Education; the Modern Scientist and his near

---

[13] "The Bitter Drink," *op. cit.*, pp. 93-105.
[14] Max Lerner, Introduction to *The Portable Veblen*, New York 1948, p. 46.

relation the Engineer, in whom Veblen placed most of his hopes for the future; and the Heroic Freeholder, a type of the "peaceful, sturdy farmer-craftsman-citizen" who has a good deal in common with Jefferson's yeoman-farmer.[15]

Several of Veblen's type-figures were undoubtedly seized upon by contemporary writers. Apart from Veblen's influence on Dos Passos, Kenneth S. Lynn has described Robert Herrick's attempt to dramatise Veblen's heroic engineer in *The Web of Life*,[16] and there seem to be clear suggestions of Veblen's influence in Anderson's *Poor White*. Similar suggestions appear in the characters of Eugene Morgan, the builder of motor-cars, and Dan Oliphant, the builder of houses, in Tarkington's *The Magnificent Ambersons* and *The Midlander*, and in such Sinclair Lewis characters as Dodsworth, the creative engineer, and Martin Arrowsmith, the dedicated scientist who, rather like Veblen himself, rejects institutions and wealth and retires to a hut in the woods. But it is hard to be sure, in any particular instance, that Veblen's influence has been decisive. Many of his type-figures, such as the Captain of Industry and the Captain of Finance, were already firmly rooted in the popular imagination long before Veblen began to write, and if Charley Anderson's fate is a Veblenian parable it also resembles in its outlines and in its implications the pre-Veblenian career of Howells's Dryfoos. Emphasis on the importance of the engineer or the scientist offers perhaps the surest sign of Veblen's influence, but even the end of *Arrowsmith* reminds us of Thoreau rather than of Veblen.

Indeed, we can best see Veblen's work as a reinforcement of an already long-established tradition of agrarian protest. He was much more concerned with the future than most Populists, and he was less antagonistic to the machine, but, as Henry Steele Commager observes, "he can be understood better in terms of agrarian radicalism than of eastern progressivism or of the revolutionary economics of central Europe."[17] Thus John Steinbeck's description, in *The Grapes of Wrath* (1939), of fruit rotting while children die may be regarded as a direct illustration of Veblen's doctrine of business

[15] *Op. cit.*, p. 47.
[16] Kenneth S. Lynn, *The Dream of Success*, pp. 223-8.
[17] Henry Steele Commager, *The American Mind*, p. 238.

sabotage, but its emotional overtones seem to reach back past
Veblen to the language of Populist protest:

> There is a crime here that goes beyond denunciation. There is
> a sorrow here that weeping cannot symbolize. There is a failure
> here that topples all our success. The fertile earth, the straight tree
> rows, the sturdy trunks, and the ripe fruit. And children dying of
> pellagra must die because a profit cannot be taken from an orange.
> And coroners must fill in the certificates—died of malnutrition—
> because the food must rot, must be forced to rot.[18]

Dos Passos is a more subtle writer than Steinbeck, but we can
recognise something of the same attitude—individualistic, agrarian,
fundamentally conservative—throughout his work. In almost all
his novels there is an underlying emotional commitment, closely
akin to Veblen's and not unlike that in such novels as Howells's
A Hazard of New Fortunes and Anderson's *Poor White*, which finds
its most nearly explicit statement in one of the later books, *The
Grand Design* (1949), the final section of the *District of Columbia*
trilogy. The novel obviously attacks the incompetence of Washington bureaucracy during the New Deal period: what should be
noticed, however, are the values by which bureaucracy is judged.
Mr Hodgins, the Southern farmer who is carrying out his own
resettlement programme without government help, laughs when
Paul Graves suggests that the government co-operative might
undercut his milk prices:

> "You try," he said. "Why, if you gave it away, I'll still have a
> better product and a market for it."
> "Why?" asked Paul.
> "Because everybody's business is nobody's business," said
> Hodgins dryly.[19]

Similarly Nat Kubik, who runs a highly efficient and up-to-date
farm in Iowa, maintains: "You can't manage a farm by
committee."[20] Both these individualistic farmers are presented

[18] John Steinbeck, *The Grapes of Wrath*, p. 477.
[19] John Dos Passos, *The Grand Design*, in *District of Columbia*, Boston 1952,
p. 157.
[20] *Op. cit.*, p. 250.

affirmatively and the "lesson" of the book is that reform, to be effective, must start from the bottom rather than from the top. The emphasis on individualism takes added colour from the opening section of the book, "Daniel Boone Country." Dos Passos uses Millard O. Carroll's journey to Washington to take up a post in the Department of Agriculture to establish firmly in our minds both the beauty of the land which the bureaucrats discuss in terms of "selfliquidating projects" and the old American values which survive in the countryside but are forgotten in government offices:

> Soon the highway left the river and headed up through dense bare thickets into the hills full of lengthening shadows. At a signpost that read Hot Springs Millard turned off over a broad loosely gravelled road. Small stones rattled under the mudguards. The fields were becoming irregularly shaped and cramped between vinegrown hedgerows. Occasionally they passed a cabin open in the middle with a stone chimney at the end from which blue smoke streaked out in the chill wind giving them a taste of fat pine and coaloil lamps as they passed.
> "It seems so far away," said Millard between clenched teeth. "It all seems a hundred years ago. . . . God I love this continent."[21]

The old woman whose son fixes a flat tyre for the Carrolls grieves to hear of the object of their journey: "So you-all's goin' to Washington to jine the government. . . . Us folks don't have no truck with no government."[22] In the car again Carroll's wife says, "It was like talking to Dan'l Boone's mommer," and Carroll adds, "I feel as if we were seeing it the way he saw it."[23] Once in bureaucratic Washington, however, Carroll will no longer see the countryside with the eyes of Daniel Boone. Dos Passos agrees with the old woman: government and the fiercely individualistic spirit of Boone are irreconcilable.

The commitment is agrarian; more specifically, it is Jeffersonian. Thus "Mr. Lecturer" of *The Prospect Before Us* (1950) invokes the name of Jefferson and pleads for decentralisation, for less social stratification, for more personal liberty and self-government; *The Head and Heart of Thomas Jefferson* (1954) is a highly sympathetic

[21] *Op. cit.*, pp. 17-18.   [22] *Op. cit.*, p. 20.   [23] *Ibid.*

account of Jefferson's life and thought up to the time he became President; and early in World War II Dos Passos wrote *The Ground We Stand On* (1941), recounting the story of Roger Williams and, again, of Jefferson's early career, as a declaration of faith in America and in the strength of American democracy: "I believe that somewhere in the individual sturdiness of plain people there is ground for a firm political conviction,"[24] he declares in the Preface to the English edition. The "somewhere" perhaps betrays a certain lack of intellectual clarity and certainty; the language of the rest of the sentence immediately recalls the terms in which Jefferson and many American agrarians after him had expressed their admiration for the yeoman farmer. Jefferson, says Dos Passos,

> was a frontiersman, first, and always felt the great continent, stretching ridge after ridge to the west, opening out into the grasslands, rivers, plains, a boundless store for the generations growing up, the promise of a future that like a great convex mirror magnified every act and gesture of the men working their fields and building their farms in the tiny settlements along the eastern seaboard.[25]

The lyrical expansiveness of the language suggests not only Dos Passos's deep admiration for the man he is describing but also his personal commitment to this image of America.

This commitment profoundly affects almost the whole of Dos Passos's work. Although he does not always explicitly affirm the values of agrarian democracy, they are always present, and throughout the novels the emotional and moralistic overtones of the social criticism suggest that Dos Passos, like Howells, may not always have been fully conscious of the deeper motivations of his writing. In the early novels, above all in *U.S.A.*, these motivations are overlaid by an explicit dedication to specific political programmes, but progressive disillusionment with such programmes, an erosive process, has brought Dos Passos's fundamental attitudes and beliefs much nearer to the surface. It is clearly not in the least fortuitous that the aspect of the New Deal treated in *The Grand Design* should

[24] John Dos Passos, *The Ground We Stand On*, London 1942, [Preface].
[25] *Op. cit.*, p. 14.

be the Department of Agriculture, but it is no more fortuitous that in *U.S.A.*—where we have already noted the "exemplary" career of Charley Anderson and the attack on the "non-productive" financiers—the sense of the beauty and spaciousness of the American continent should be consistently counterpointed against the squalor of contemporary society and the restrictiveness of modern social organisations. Dos Passos achieves similar effects in *Three Soldiers* (1921), his novel about World War I, when he sets the brutal inhumanity of war and of military life against a background of rural peace and beauty, and in the final pages of *Manhattan Transfer* Jimmy Herf, joyfully leaving the city at last, encounters on his way a little horse-drawn wagon "loaded with flowers" and exuding a "rich smell of maytime earth."[26]

Dos Passos's novels of recent years have been disappointing; as essentially political novels, however, often containing acute social insights, they do have some value. For example, a certain sociological interest attaches to the three attacks on radical attitudes in *Chosen Country* (1951), despite the fact that they have been loosely linked to a story which is both sentimental and undistinguished. In this late work the moral fervour of the early novels has been succeeded by a passionate anti-Communism, an obsessional anger which seems to have been the one powerful emotion left to Dos Passos after his bitter disillusionment with the New Deal. This anti-Communist theme first appears as a minor motif in *The Big Money*, where the rigid organisation of the Communist party is seen as destructive of individual integrity. A little later it becomes the central preoccupation of *Adventures of a Young Man* (1939), the first section of *District of Columbia*: Glenn Spotswood, a well-meaning political innocent, becomes involved in Communist chicanery at the time of a miner's strike and later volunteers for Spain, where he is first imprisoned as a Trotskyite and later sent out to a futile death. The theme appears again in *The Great Days* (1958) and completely dominates *Most Likely to Succeed* (1954), which becomes at times almost hysterical in its denunciation of Communist activities in the theatre and in Hollywood.

It is not on these late novels, however, but on his earlier work

[26] John Dos Passos, *Manhattan Transfer*, New York and London 1925, p. 403.

that Dos Passos's reputation must ultimately rest, and in *Three Soldiers, Manhattan Transfer* and, supremely, *U.S.A.*, he has a body of work which no serious student of modern American fiction can possibly ignore. At different times Dos Passos has directed his social criticism at widely contrasting targets—from the inhuman military organisation in *Three Soldiers* and the senseless chaos of the monstrous city in *Manhattan Transfer* to the corrupt "power superpower" of monopoly capitalism, the stifling bureaucracy of the New Deal, and the monolithic rigidity of the Communist Party—and his political position has seemed to undergo violent shifts from the extreme left to the extreme right. Dos Passos has been writing over a long period, and the shifts in his political attitudes are partly the reflexion of profound changes in the whole political situation, both at home and abroad; moreover, the very generosity and impetuousness of his protests against injustice and inhumanity, whenever and wherever they may occur, have sometimes led him into intellectual inconsistencies. All of his work, however, is informed by a deep attachment to a conception of America which it seems fair to call both agrarian and Jeffersonian, and in all his books the institution or the aggregation is the enemy, bigness is evil, and the destruction or erosion of individual integrity and dignity is tragic—and not less so because this is seen to be the fate of Everyman in a modern urban-industrial society.

9

Institutions in Fiction

I

In November 1950, speaking of such "reportage" as *The Prospect Before Us* (1950), Dos Passos told an interviewer: " 'I've been trying a big-term experiment. . . . I've been trying to get a series of written photographs of institutions as they develop. These various trips I take, I sort of keep one question in mind: what sort of institutions are appearing and how do they affect people?' "[1] Dos Passos has always been preoccupied with institutions and in his non-fictional works he has made quite clear the essentially Jeffersonian and agrarian basis of his attitude towards them. In his novels, from the army world of *Three Soldiers* to the bureaucratic Washington of *The Grand Design*, he has continually depicted man in his relation to the institutions which alter, condition, and control his life, especially those institutions to which he stands in the relation of employee. Other modern novelists share this interest in institutions and there is now a long list of American novels in which the action and moral intention devolve upon the way in which the individuals relate themselves to their particular institution. We shall consider these as "institutional" novels, although it is important to recognise that such categories are in no sense formal: they indicate no more than that the novels mentioned have similar settings and, on occasion, similar themes.

Institutional settings, of course, have been chosen by modern novelists with widely differing interests and preoccupations: Carson McCuller's *Reflections in a Golden Eye* (1941) is set in a Southern army base, Calder Willingham's *End as a Man* (1947) in a military academy, John Updike's *The Poorhouse Fair* (1959) in

[1] Harvey Breit, *The Writer Observed*, Cleveland and New York [1956], p. 144.

a poor-law institution, David Karp's *Leave Me Alone* (1957) in a publishing house, and much of John Cheever's *The Wapshott Chronicle* (1957) in government jobs of various kinds. More relevant to our present discussion are several distinguishable groups of essentially social novels which can be regarded as specifically "institutional" in theme. One such group deals with business and includes, for example, Cameron Hawley's *Executive Suite* (1952) and *Cash McCall* (1955), Sloan Wilson's *The Man in the Gray Flannel Suit* (1955), Carl Jonas's *Jefferson Selleck* (1952) and John Brooks's *The Man Who Broke Things* (1958). Another group is made up of such "*exposé*" novels as Budd Schulberg's *The Harder They Fall* (1947) and *Waterfront* (1955), Herman Wouk's *Aurora Dawn* (1947), Frederic Wakeman's *The Hucksters* (1946), and Al Morgan's *The Great Man* (1955). In this chapter and the next we shall deal especially with novels about military organisations, about Hollywood and the motion-picture business, and about universities and colleges.

The reasons for the present importance of the institutional theme are not difficult to discover. It is a direct response to the growth of vast bureaucratic institutions in every area of American life—in government, business, entertainment, the armed services, even in philanthropic foundations and universities—and it represents a further stage of that movement away from the epic hero in favour of the obscure hero which we noted earlier. We now see the obscure hero as not simply a man without fame but as one who lives and works within an organisation which overshadows his life and which, because he is dependent upon it, can restrict his freedom of action and even of moral choice. In earlier novels the organisation often did not have a formal structure—it might be a social class, as in *The Age of Innocence*, or a group of local interests, as in *Babbitt*—but in more recent novels it is more likely to have an immediately recognisable institutional structure—a business organisation, for example, as in J. P. Marquand's *Point of No Return* (1949), a religious body, as in James Gould Cozzens's *Men and Brethern* (1936), or a military organisation, as in Norman Mailer's *The Naked and the Dead* (1948).

To a greater or a lesser degree, such institutional novels all deal with

the problems that confront men working within large organisations
based upon hierarchies of promotion and command—problems
concerning the sources of effective power and the moral responsibility with which it is wielded; problems of success or failure in
terms of "personal politics," to use a phrase of C. P. Snow's;[2]
above all, problems which arise when the organisation demands
unhesitating loyalty from the individuals who must execute its
policies whether they find them morally repugnant or not. William
H. Whyte, Jr, in *The Organization Man*, regards these problems as
essentially "bureaucratic," but the more comprehensive term
"institutional" seems to describe more accurately the kind of
situation presented in the novels we are now discussing. Indeed,
in many of these novels the institution dominates the story so
effectively that without too much exaggeration we may speak
of the institution itself as hero. In *U.S.A.* there is a real sense
in which the central character is the nation itself, while
in Wessel Smitter's *F.O.B. Detroit* (1938), to choose a very
minor example from the same period, the factory with its
assembly-line looms over the story like the mine in Zola's
Germinal.

As the reference to Zola may suggest, this is not in itself a new
conception: in American fiction it appears as early as 1893 in
H. B. Fuller's *The Cliff-Dwellers*, in which the great office-block
overshadows the lives of all those who work within its walls.
Institutionalism and bureaucracy, in America as elsewhere, have
had a longer history than is often realised. Lewis Mumford, in
The Culture of Cities, describes the vast growth of "tentacular
bureaucracy" throughout the western world during the nineteenth
century,[3] and of the American situation William Miller observes:
"First among the railroads, but by the turn of the century in many
other lines as well, the characteristic big business firm had become
a big bureaucracy. Functions at each level of operation, supervision,
and policy making had become more or less strict and specific,
channels of authority and communication had been set up, and
hierarchies of ascent had become articulated."[4] The whole trend

[2] C. P. Snow, *The Masters*, London 1951, p. 275.
[3] Lewis Mumford, *The Culture of Cities*, London 1940, pp. 226-7.

of recent historical and sociological research into American business has been to discredit the "success" myth, the "rags-to-riches" saga, the notion of the typical business leader as a self-made man, and to show that even in the late nineteenth and early twentieth centuries a very large proportion of leading businessmen reached their positions by bureaucratic routes, by regular promotion within an hierarchical organisation. Miller particularly mentions a new type emerging at this period, the "captive professional," usually a lawyer, who was "no longer free to have clients or reject them, but tied to the service of a single business interest that could move him about like an ordinary employee."[5]

It is interesting that one of the first American novels that can usefully be described as institutional in theme, Winston Churchill's *A Far Country*, published in 1915, has in Hugh Paret, the corporation lawyer, a central character of precisely this type. As the title suggests, the book has the structure of a parable: Paret, after a journey into the far country of financial and political corruption, returns at last to the honest values for which his father had stood. Also published in 1915 was Ernest Poole's *The Harbor*, in which the hero, after an initial attraction to big business and the god "Efficiency," becomes gradually converted to the cause of the workers. In both novels, as in Sinclair Lewis's *The Job* (1917), the heroes respond to the institutional situation by escaping from it. As we have seen, similar themes appear in the novels of Dreiser and Dos Passos, and they also appear, although less seriously, in some of Booth Tarkington's work and in Christopher Morley's *Human Being* (1932) and *Kitty Foyle* (1939). Like institutionalism itself, the institutional theme in American fiction already has something of a history, but, these earlier examples notwithstanding, only since the end of World War II has it really been possible to speak of bureaucracy and institutionalism both as permeating features of American life and as recurrent themes of American social novels.

[4] William Miller, "The Business Elite in Business Bureaucracies," in *Men in Business*, ed. William Miller, Cambridge, Mass. 1952, p. 287.
[5] *Op. cit.*, p. 288.

2

In his chapter on "The Organization Man in Fiction,"[6] William H. Whyte, Jr, makes the centrepiece of his discussion Herman Wouk's *The Caine Mutiny* (1951), which is one of many novels dealing with the army, navy, or air force primarily as institutions which have appeared in America since the end of the war. Apart from *The Caine Mutiny*, the most important of these novels are Marquand's *Melville Goodwin, U.S.A.* (1951) and Cozzens's *Guard of Honor* (1948), both discussed in Chapter Eleven, James Jones's *From Here to Eternity* (1951), Irwin Shaw's *The Young Lions* (1948), and Norman Mailer's *The Naked and the Dead* (1948). Although these novels may present men fighting, they differ from such combat novels as Harry Brown's *A Walk in the Sun* (1944) in that they deal more especially with struggles within the military hierarchy itself—with relationships between officers and enlisted men, between superior officers and their inferiors, between regular officers and ex-civilians, between the power moralists and the passionate individualists.

In discussing *The Caine Mutiny* Whyte exaggerates the irrelevance of the book's conclusion and the monstrosity of its moral, but seems not to notice that it often hints at a mystique of command:

Even at anchor, on an idle, forgotten old ship, Willie experienced the strange sensations of the first days of a new captain: a shrinking of his personal identity, and a stretching out of his nerve ends to all the spaces and machinery of his ship. He was less free than before. He developed the apprehensive listening ears of a young mother; the ears listened in his sleep; he never quite slept, not the way he had before. He had the sense of having been reduced from an individual to a sort of brain of a composite animal, the crew and ship combined. The reward for these disturbing sensations came when he walked the decks. Power seemed to flow out of the plates into his body. The respectful demeanor of the officers and crew thrust him into a loneliness he had never known, but it wasn't a frigid loneliness. Through the transparent barrier

---

[6] William H. Whyte Jr, *The Organization Man*, New York 1956, pp. 243-8. See also H. J. Friedsam, "Bureaucrats as Heroes," *Social Forces*, XXXII (1954), 269-74.

of manners came the warming unspoken word that his men liked him and believed in him.[7]

Even Lieutenant Keefer, the despised, trouble-making "intellectual" who is the villain of the piece, comes finally to learn that "You can't understand command until you've had it."[8]

It is interesting to set against this a passage from *The Naked and the Dead* in which General Cummings first discovers the intoxication of command: "To command all that. He is choked with the intensity of his emotion, the rage, the exaltation, the undefined and mighty hunger."[9] No doubt it is his personal moral revulsion which leads Mailer to exaggerate his presentation of Cummings, yet the comparison does suggest the main intellectual—and perhaps moral—criticism that can be levelled at Wouk: that he does not draw the political conclusions which his "message" implies, and that he thus obscures the deadly irony involved in fighting Fascism with a military instrument which, perhaps necessarily, but none the less actually, is itself fascistic both in its organisation and in its demands for loyalty and obedience. In a recent article Joseph Waldmeir points out that many American novelists pursue this irony further, to the appearance among the American forces of such actual fascist traits as racialism and sadism. He also suggests that the main division among novelists of the Second World War is between those who accept this "expedient fascism" in the superior interests of winning the war at all costs and those who utterly reject it.[10]

Wouk's acceptance is implicit in the resolution of *The Caine Mutiny*. In *Guard of Honor*, as we shall see, Cozzens makes his acceptance quite explicit; Marquand, too, though the issue is never really faced in *Melville Goodwin, U.S.A.*, would seem finally to incline in this direction. On the other hand, James Jones does not make a clear-cut distinction in *From Here to Eternity*, which for all its sincerity and vigour, exhibits an invincible emotional and intellectual confusion. The army is corrupt and brutal, founded

[7] Herman Wouk, *The Caine Mutiny*, London 1951, p. 477.

[8] *Op. cit.*, p. 459.

[9] Norman Mailer, *The Naked and the Dead*, New York [1948], p. 415.

[10] Joseph Waldmeir, "Novelists of Two Wars," *Nation*, CLXXXVII (1958), 304-07.

on the crude fear-psychology expounded by General Slater, who seems somewhat reminiscent of Mailer's General Cummings, and its values are rejected in favour of those of the oppressed and cast-out, like Prewitt himself and Malloy, his hero of the stockade. Yet Prewitt, the thirty-year man, loves the army: it is home, "inside" as opposed to "outside." In the end, we are forced to recognise in *From Here to Eternity* the fundamental ambivalence of a love-hate relationship, a restive acceptance of the army embodied not only in Prewitt, the perpetual odd man out,[11] but even in Sergeant Warden, the perfect soldier, who suddenly realises that he *has* to sleep with Karen Holmes, the wife of his company commander:

> not as vengeance, or even retribution, but as an expression of himself, to regain the individuality that Holmes and all the rest of them, unknowing, had taken from him. And he understood suddenly why a man who had lived his whole life working for a corporation might commit suicide simply to express himself, would foolishly destroy himself because it was the only way to prove his own existence.[12]

Chief among the novelists who reject "expedient fascism" are Norman Mailer and Irwin Shaw; they accept America's role in the war, but this does not automatically reconcile them to the American army. In Shaw's competent but over-extended novel *The Young Lions*, the worst of the villains is a German, but in Mailer's much more impressive *The Naked and the Dead* the villains, Sergeant Croft and General Cummings, are both Americans, and the rejection of the army and of its ethic, or lack of ethic, is emphatic. The nearest approach to a hero is a politically naïve intellectual, Lieutenant Hearn, who finds his ideas defining themselves in opposition to General Cummings's conception of a domestic American fascism:

> Cummings's tension altered. There had been a deep satisfaction in expounding this, a pleasure apart from all the other concerns of this discussion with Hearn. "I've been trying to impress you,

[11] Cf. Leslie Fiedler, "Dead-end Werther: the Bum as American Culture Hero," in *An End to Innocence: Essays on Culture and Politics*, Boston [1955], pp. 183-90.
[12] James Jones, *From Here to Eternity*, New York 1951, p. 107.

Robert, that the only morality of the future is a power morality, and a man who cannot find his adjustment to it is doomed. There's one thing about power. It can flow only from the top down. When there are little surges of resistance at the middle levels, it merely calls for more power to be directed downward, to burn it out."

Hearn was looking at his hands. "We're not in the future yet."

"You can consider the Army, Robert, as a preview of the future."[13]

What General Cummings preaches Sergeant Croft practises. The patrol sent behind the Japanese lines is clearly intended to be a microcosm of America: it is also, as Croft conducts it, a kind of laboratory experiment in Cummings's fear-psychology. Hearn, who is killed on the patrol, realises before he dies how disturbingly accurate is the analysis on which Cummings's ideas are based and how strong the American potential for fascism actually is.

Yet Croft's determination to climb the mountain is eventually defeated, and this, as Walter B. Rideout suggests, is perhaps intended "to demonstrate the inability of power moralists to manipulate history in opposition to mass will."[14] Mailer himself has said that he thought of Croft in terms of Captain Ahab,[15] but the interpretation Rideout offers is certainly in line with Mailer's personal commitment to a left-of-centre but non-Communist radicalism. This attitude, which colours Mailer's whole presentation of Cummings and of the army, was common enough in the thirties but is rare among contemporary writers. Mailer's affinities with Dos Passos, we realise, go beyond matters of technique—the similarities, for example, between the "Time Machine" passages in The Naked and the Dead and Dos Passos's Biographies—and he speaks in the postwar period with a voice remarkably similar to the voice which is audible in U.S.A. In The Naked and the Dead, as in U.S.A., all the characters seem to lead, in their different ways, confused, frustrated,

---

[13] Mailer, The Naked and the Dead, pp. 323-4.

[14] Walter B. Rideout, The Radical Novel in the United States, 1900–1954, Cambridge, Mass. 1956, p. 272.

[15] Breit, The Writer Observed, p. 200.

and unhappy lives, and the emerging impression of America is far from encouraging. At the same time, the fascists and power-fanatics do not have it all their own way. Hearn dies, but Croft is defeated and Cumming's victory is a hollow sham. The organisation is not inevitably triumphant and the individual, alone or in voluntary combination with his fellows, still has some kind of chance.

That *The Naked and the Dead* remains superior to Mailer's subsequent work, such as *Barbary Shore* (1951), which in effect is a fantasy-parable, and even *The Deer Park* (1955), which has a contrived air, seems in part the result of his greater familiarity with his material and, more importantly, to his more clearly defined moral intention. It is, perhaps, a rather simple-minded intention—James Gould Cozzens would certainly find it so—but to a novelist embarked upon a work as ambitious as *The Naked and the Dead* the intellectual sophistication of the moral intention is likely to be less important than the conviction, the assurance, the passion with which the intention is pursued. *The Naked and the Dead*, like *U.S.A.*, has such passion: Mailer's later novels, like the later novels of Dos Passos, do not have it. Yet with Mailer as with Dos Passos the conviction that seems to have been lost relates to means rather than to ultimate ends. It is clear, at least, that in all Mailer's novels it is the individual, and individual integrity, that must be fought for and preserved; the organisation—army, state, or industry—is the enemy.

3

This conflict between the individual and the institution is the central theme explored in the best of the Hollywood novels, most of them dating from the nineteen-thirties and early nineteen-forties but a few, including Mailer's *The Deer Park*, from the post-war period. The glamorisation of Hollywood may hinder our thinking of it in terms of industrial organisation, but Max Lerner has recently reminded us that "The qualities of the industrial process in Hollywood are the qualities of any big American industry: machine-tool technology, division of labor, mass production, bureaucracy, hierarchy." This "line-and-staff hierarchy," Lerner argues, "with its pyramiding of power and its constriction of creativeness for most of the people involved, represents the greatest weakness of the Hollywood system."[16]   These arguments may be open to question, but the evidence of all the serious novels about Hollywood certainly goes to suggest the accuracy of Lerner's diagnosis.

There are, of course, vast numbers of novels about Hollywood, though few of them are of any literary interest.   A large proportion of them, good and bad, use Hollywood mainly as a lurid backdrop for stories whose central interest lies in the romantic or sensational activity of the foreground: Ben Hecht's *I Hate Actors* (1944), for example, Niven Busch's *The Actors* (1955), William Saroyan's *Rock Wagram* (1951), and, on a somewhat higher level, Gore Vidal's *The City and the Pillar* (1948) and John O'Hara's *Hope of Heaven* (1938).   In other novels, such as *The Big Money* (1936) and *Most Likely to Succeed* (1954) by John Dos Passos and *So Little Time* (1943) by J. P. Marquand, Hollywood provides only one among a variety of settings.   There are also the many satires, both straightforward ones such as Anita Loos's lighthearted *A Mouse Is Born* (1951), and fantasy-satires such as Upton Sinclair's earnest but inept *They Call Me Carpenter* (1922), Henry Blake Fuller's *Not on the Screen* (1930) and the more successful *A Voyage to Purilia* (1930) by Elmer Rice.

Other novels about Hollywood exemplify rather too persistently the novel-as-guidebook or the novel-as-textbook approach.   For instance, practically every Hollywood novelist has attempted to capture in words the variety and peculiarity of Hollywood architecture, although none of them has done better than Edmund Wilson in his essay on "The City of our Lady the Queen of the Angels," recently reprinted in *The American Earthquake* (1958). Many of the novels have a tourist flavour, as if written for the actual or would-be visitor, and it would be possible, and amusing, to collect and collate the miscellaneous information on Hollywood which they offer.   It is John Dos Passos, however, in *The Big Money* who has the last word on Hollywood as a geographical expression: "They saw signs pointing to Hollywood, but somehow they got through the town without noticing it . . ."[17]

[16] Max Lerner, *America as a Civilization*, London 1958, pp. 823-4.
[17] John Dos Passos, *The Big Money*, in *U.S.A.*, p. 394.

The novel-as-textbook approach is particularly obvious in Robert Carson's *The Magic Lantern* (1952), which is little more than a lightly fictionalised account, ponderously written, of the history of the movies from their earliest beginnings to the advent of sound. It is only just saved as a novel by a few scenes, notably the one in which the hero, a film producer, leaves the hospital in which his wife has just died: "And then the clouds parted and the damned, rosy sun shone upon us, precisely as in the moving pictures."[18] With novelists who attempt to recount the history of the cinema or to describe in detail the actual processes of film-making— the "novel-as-trade-manual" approach—we may feel ourselves in a dilemma similar to that experienced by Henry James when called upon to review three "military novels": "These are delicate matters, I again remind myself, for, whatever else such books may be, they may be very good soldiering."[19]

Books like Richard Brooks's *The Producer* (1951), for example, may well be very good film-making, for Mr Brooks is himself a director, but this does not necessarily make them good fiction— though *The Producer*, it must be said, is a thoroughly competent sociological novel. "The 'military' work of art, of any sort," says James, "is in no degree a critical term, and we never really get near a book save on the question of its being good or bad, of its really treating, that is, or not treating, its subject."[20] James perhaps places more weight on the word "really" than it can properly support, but his emphasis is clear: a novelist can be immensely knowledge-able about a subject and even, in the superficial sense, informative, without ever exploring it in any depth. Only imagination can bring information to life, and imagination is what most Hollywood novels conspicuously lack.

4

A few Hollywood novels, however, are both serious and successful. Budd Schulberg's *What Makes Sammy Run?* (1941), for example, is full of realistic background detail of the Hollywood scene and probably describes more accurately and sensitively than any other

[18] Robert Carson, *The Magic Lantern*, London 1954, p. 440.
[19] *The American Essays of Henry James*, p. 228.   [20] *Ibid.*

novel the actual life in Hollywood—a "tough town," as Kit Sargent says, because "it still has the gold-rush feeling. . . . It's become a major industry without losing the crazy fever of a gold-boom town."[21]   In the novel as a whole, however, Schulberg makes imaginative use of this information in creating a twentieth-century parable of much wider relevance.   The ruthless rise of Sammy Glick from office-boy to impresario involves the fall of others, notably Sidney Fineman, the genuinely creative producer who had been "one of the few real old-timers still on top,"[22] and the force of the parable is made explicit in the final paragraphs of the novel as Al Manheim, the narrator, reviews what has gone before:

> Now Sammy's career meteored through my mind in all its destructive brilliance, his blitzkrieg against his fellow men.   My mind skipped from conquest to conquest, like the scrapbook on his exploits I had been keeping . . .   It was a terrifying and wonderful document . . .   And some day I would like to see it published, as a blueprint of a way of life that was paying dividends in America in the first half of the twentieth century.[23]

Schulberg's theme is economic individualism, pushed to such extremes of self-interest that it becomes "the most frightening ism of all."[24]   He not only presents Hollywood vividly and concretely as an actual place but also symbolically as the city where Sammy's way of life can most readily flourish and attain its full luxuriance, a kind of hot-house for the world's Sammy Glicks.

Budd Schulberg has written a second Hollywood novel, *The Disenchanted* (1950), which seems to have been largely based on the career and character of Scott Fitzgerald.   The novel has structural weaknesses and lacks the tautness and economy which distinguished *What Makes Sammy Run?*, but it is valuable for the sympathetic portrayal of Manley Halliday, the hero, and in the treatment of the relationship between Halliday and his producer, Victor Milgrim, Schulberg displays an intelligent approach to the problem which so much occupied Fitzgerald himself, that of the creative artist working within an industrial organisation.

[21] Budd Schulberg, *What Makes Sammy Run?*, New York 1941, p. 261.
[22] *Op. cit.*, p. 97.   [23] *Op. cit.*, p. 303.   [24] *Ibid.*

More considerable than either of Schulberg's books is Nathanael West's *The Day of the Locust* (1939). West, like Schulberg, worked in Hollywood, but he is less concerned with understanding the film world or presenting it realistically than with defining the meaning of Hollywood in its relation to American society as a whole. Thus he concentrates not on the more spectacular aspects of Hollywood but on the little people, the extras and miscellaneous hangers-on of the film-world, and those who have no direct connexion with the cinema and have simply "come to California to die." West, with his nightmare vision, sees Hollywood as a kind of limbo, populated by "the people who come to California to die; the cultists of all sorts, economic as well as religious, the wave, airplane, funeral and preview watchers—all those poor devils who can only be stirred by the promise of miracles and then only to violence."[25] Their chief representative in the novel is Homer Simpson, a huge but helpless schizophrenic, sunk deep in a despair which eventually finds vent in uncontrollable sobbing. Homer's sobs make "a heavy, hollow, chunking noise. . . . Each chunk was exactly like the one that preceded. It would never reach a climax."[26] As Homer sobs, so he lives. The cranks, cultists and sun-seekers, the people who come to California to die, are incapable of any kind of climax: they achieve ecstasy only by submerging their identities in a crowd and finding release in mob-violence. Tod Hackett, the book's central character thinks of them as the "cream" of America's madmen, but feels "almost certain that the milk from which it had been skimmed was just as rich in violence."[27]

It is Hollywood and the motion-picture industry, it appears, to which this cream naturally and irresistibly clings. All these marginal film-people are grotesques; from the Gringos, a family of Eskimos who had been brought from Alaska for retakes of a film about polar exploration but then refused to go home again, to Claude Estee, a writer, whose house was an exact reproduction of a Southern mansion and who himself "teetered back and forth on his heels like a Civil War colonel and made believe he had a

[25] Nathanael West, *The Day of the Locust*, in *The Complete Works of Nathanael West*, ed. Alan Ross, New York 1957, p. 420.
[26] *Op. cit.*, p. 398.   [27] *Op. cit.*, p. 335.

large belly." Yet, "He had no belly at all. He was a dried-up little man with the rubbed features and stooped shoulders of a postal clerk."[28]   West catches the grotesquerie in a tiny incident:

> While Tod mounted the steps to reach his outstretched hand, [Claude] shouted to the butler.
> "Here, you black rascal! A mint julep."
> A Chinese servant came running with a Scotch and soda.[29]

In similar vein West describes the riot of a preview crowd at the end of the book, the sad chaos of a studio lot—a crazy "Sargasso Sea,"[30] in West's phrase, of dreams made into plywood, filmed, and dumped—and the disastrous attempt to film an ambitiously reconstructed Battle of Waterloo. West sees Hollywood, in fact, as at once the symbol and the inner citadel of an insanity rampant throughout America.

The savage fantasy of *The Day of the Locust* brings Evelyn Waugh's *The Loved One* (1948) to mind. Several English novelists have touched upon the Hollywood scene—Aldous Huxley for example, in *After Many a Summer* (1940) and *Ape and Essence* (1949), and Christopher Isherwood in *The World in the Evening* (1954)—but only incidentally and with satirical intention. Isherwood's *Prater Violet* (1946) is a lively account of British film-making, while Gavin Lambert's *The Slide Area* (1959), though skilfully written, must be considered a series of sketches of Hollywood life rather than a fully-developed novel. *The Loved One*, in fact, is the one notable Hollywood novel written by an Englishman. Despite its obvious resemblance to *The Day of the Locust*, it is narrower both in scope and in intention, as the title itself, ironic where West's is prophetic, suggests. For Waugh the nightmare, though recognised as such, has no personal relevance, and the book seems to be a deliberate exercise in the macabre and the grotesque. West, the American, writes out of an intense inner compulsion: the nightmare is his own and demands to be written down. The book seems always on the edge of hysteria and ends in a scream. Tod thinks of making love to the screen-struck and intensely self-centred Faye Greener: "it would be like throwing yourself from the

[28] *Op. cit.*, pp. 271-2.   [29] *Op. cit.*, p. 272.   [30] *Op. cit.*, p. 353.

parapet of a skyscraper. You would do it with a scream. You couldn't expect to rise again. . . ." Tod "managed to laugh at his language, but it wasn't a real laugh and nothing was destroyed by it."[31] There is laughter in *The Day of the Locust*, but it is unreal laughter which destroys nothing and which fails to shake off the nightmare.

For Scott Fitzgerald Hollywood was not a nightmare world. His unfinished novel *The Last Tycoon* (1941) firmly confronts the problems of working creatively within an organisation which, while it lays claim to aesthetic value, lives by its ruthlessly economic purposes, which is in fact an industrial organisation, fundamentally hostile to the artist. At the same time, Fitzgerald persistently points out the contrast between Hollywood and the outside world, between the unreal and the real. There is a memorable scene in the opening chapter when a group of Hollywood people make an uncomprehending and almost accidental pilgrimage to The Hermitage, Andrew Jackson's home. It is shut; they cannot get in; they do not know what they are there for; one of them, Manny Schwartz, commits suicide nearby. "Manny Schwartz and Andrew Jackson—it was hard to say them in the same sentence."[32] Here Fitzgerald apparently intends to symbolise the debilitating lack of contact between the world of the movies and the traditional sources of American vitality, and throughout the novel he stresses the essential unreality of the cinema environment. Manny Schwartz speaks of having had a daughter once upon a time when he was " 'in the big money' "—as if, Cecilia comments, " 'she had been sold to creditors as a tangible asset' "[33]—and Wylie White assures him that, Job-like, he will get it all back one day. The situations multiply: Stahr and Kathleen make love in the unfinished villa among the ping-pong tables and the imported grass, the voice over the telephone which Stahr expects to be that of the President of the United States belongs in fact to an orang-outang, and on the night of the California earthquake a scene of fantasy occurs:

[31] *Op. cit.*, p. 271.
[32] F. Scott Fitzgerald, *The Last Tycoon*, in *Three Novels of F. Scott Fitzgerald*, p. 13.
[33] *Op. cit.*, p. 9.

"Under the moon the back lot was thirty acres of fairyland"[34] and the two women come floating by on the head of the Goddess Siva. There are even the near-grotesques: Birdie, stuffed naked into a closet in her boss's office in the middle of the day, and the famous but faded star whose eczema has to be covered over before each take.

Fitzgerald's principal aim, however, is to understand Hollywood; he wants to portray how the film industry actually works, to explore the making of motion pictures and the ways in which human factors are involved in the process. Among the notes for *The Last Tycoon* we find:

> People in the East pretend to be interested in how pictures are made, but if you actually tell them anything, you find they are only interested in Colbert's clothes or Gable's private life. They never see the ventriloquist for the doll. Even the intellectuals, who ought to know better, like to hear about the pretensions, extravagancies and vulgarities—tell them pictures have a private grammar, like politics or automobile production, and watch the blank look come into their faces.[35]

Fitzgerald, of course, is fascinated by the ventriloquist, above all by the super-ventriloquist, Monroe Stahr, and he prides himself on knowing the "private grammar" of motion pictures. The account of the actual processes of making motion pictures which takes up Chapters Three and Four ("A Producer's Day") contains an extraordinarily vivid description of Stahr at work. The interviews with Boxley, the touchy English novelist, and with Rodriguez, the successful star obsessed with his sexual impotence; the story conference; the luncheon discussion among the financiers; the removal of a director from the picture he is working on; the "rushes"—here is the core of what Fitzgerald had discovered about Hollywood and the making of motion pictures. The exhilarating description of the "rushes" becomes, in some ways, the climax of the whole book as we have it.

What principally fascinates Fitzgerald is Stahr's personal power and clear-sightedness, his ability to make decisions and to span the dichotomy of the film-as-art and the film-as-business. Stahr, both

---

[34] *Op. cit.*, p. 25.   [35] *Op. cit.*, pp. 158–9.

as artist and as man of action, is raised almost to the level of the cultural giants of the Renaissance: "he had a long time ago run ahead through trackless wastes of perception into fields where very few men were able to follow him."[36] Again, "he had flown up very high to see, on strong wings, when he was young. And while he was up there he had looked on all the kingdoms, with the kind of eyes that can stare straight into the sun."[37] He is invested with a quality which is felt as more than human, and it becomes an almost divine condescension that he should have come at last to earth, that, after his flight, "he came here from choice to be with us to the end."[38]

Stahr is the "last tycoon" himself, the "last of the princes,"[39] the last representative of a doomed line. When he speaks of deliberately making a film that will lose money none of his colleagues understand what he is talking about. In *The Last Tycoon* Fitzgerald laments the passing of a great era in the history of Hollywood and foresees that the new dispensation will be far less admirable than the old. Apart from Stahr's chief enemy, Brady, whose character is inadequately developed in the novel as we have it, there are no evil characters in *The Last Tycoon*. Among the notes for the unfinished novel we find this comment: "Remember my summing-up in *Crazy Sunday*—don't give the impression that these are bad people."[40] The allusion to the short story is not wholly clear, but presumably refers to the following paragraph:

> The singing reached Joel vaguely; he felt happy and friendly toward all the people gathered there, people of bravery and industry, superior to a bourgeoisie that outdid them in ignorance and loose living, risen to a position of the highest prominence in a nation that for a decade had wanted only to be entertained. He liked them—he loved them. Great waves of good feeling flowed through him.[41]

Joel is drunk, but it is at least clear that Fitzgerald did not see Hollywood as either mad or evil. On the other hand, the fact that Fitzgerald planned to destroy Stahr before the end of the novel

---

[36] *Op. cit.*, pp. 17-18.   [37] *Op. cit.*, p. 20.   [38] *Ibid.*
[39] *Op. cit.*, p. 27.   [40] *Op. cit.*, p. 160.
[41] "Crazy Sunday," in *The Stories of F. Scott Fitzgerald*, ed. Malcolm Cowley, p. 406.

reflects his conviction that the bad in Hollywood was steadily gaining ground upon the good. Stahr is in himself the last stronghold of the old order: once he has gone, everything is likely to go. According to Fitzgerald's outline for *The Last Tycoon*, Stahr's death was to be followed immediately by "Foretaste of the future in Fleishacker."[42] Apparently Fleishacker, the company lawyer, unscrupulous, uncreative, but powerful, was to indicate, by his words or actions, how Hollywood would develop after Stahr, the last of the heroic creators, had gone. Plainly it would not have been a happy prospect.

In *The Deer Park* (1955), Norman Mailer seems to have tried to take over where Fitzgerald left off and bring us up-to-date on Hollywood. Comparison between *The Deer Park* and *The Last Tycoon* is inescapable: in *Advertisements for Myself* (1959) Mailer speaks of being influenced by Fitzgerald and he has clearly learned a good deal both from Fitzgerald's successes and from his mistakes. For example, he has taken over from *The Last Tycoon* the first-person narrator who is involved with movie people but not actually in the movies: Sergius is more successful as a narrator than Cecilia Brady, however, because he is more detached than she could be, and because he has had an experience of life outside the movies (he comes to think of it as the "real world" in contrast to the unreality of the cinema's world) which provides him with a basis for comparison and judgment. There is a similarity, too, between Monroe Stahr and Mailer's principal character, Charles Eitel. Stahr is a producer, Eitel a director, but each has the same dilemma: he wants to make good pictures but everyone, in the name of commercialism, is against him and he is further distracted from his proper business of making pictures by the intrusion of politics into his life. This latter theme is of great importance in Mailer's novel: Charles Eitel's surname (Mailer is at pains to explain that it is pronounced "eye-TELL") foreshadows his final co-operation with the Congressional committee investigating subversive activities.

The most interesting character in *The Deer Park*, however, has no counterpart in *The Last Tycoon*. This is Marion Faye, the pimp, whom Mailer seems to be trying to make into a kind of nihilistic

[42] *The Last Tycoon*, p. 143.

saint. The life Faye leads is depraved, yet in his absolute and unflinching honesty with himself and with others he seems to serve as the vehicle for Mailer's own views, so that again and again we are brought to see that his judgments are the correct ones. Sergius tells him he is "just a religious man turned inside out." He replies: "Nobility and vice—they're the same thing. It just depends on the direction you're going. . . Just so you carry it to the end."[43] Faye plays a vital role in the development of the theme of personal and artistic integrity: Sergius is trying to discover what integrity is, Eitel is trying to forget that he once had it, but Faye actually *has* integrity, in however perverted a form. Thus it is that Faye is at first Eitel's "conscience," dissuading him from co-operating with the Congressional committee, but later turns against him when he does co-operate in order to get his job back: "you might have been an artist, and you spit on it," Faye snarls.[44] It is Faye too who keeps Sergius from marrying Lulu Meyers and so becoming entangled in the movie world, a world in which it is impossible to keep one's integrity—above all, because of the irresistible, insidious attractions of "professionalism," the satisfaction to be gained from doing really clever commercial work.

The trap of professionalism is the one into which Eitel, the potential artist, has fallen: "in brooding over his past, he came to remember the unadmitted pleasure of making commercial pictures. With them he had done well . . . despite all pretenses that he had been disgusted."[45] As Sergius comes to realise, this is why the movies cannot deal with the "real world"—the world he learned about before coming to Desert D'Or—but only with distortions of reality. Munshin's spontaneous reworking of Eitel's precious script is an excellent example of what such "professionalism" may mean in practice:

> Collie was talking rapidly now, the story being teased by his producer's mind, nimble as the fingers of a puppeteer. In the beginning Eitel's hero ought to study to become a priest. Personality-wise, he would have everything, Munshin stated, charm, intelligence, poise—everything but the most important thing.

[43] Norman Mailer, *The Deer Park*, New York [1955], p. 147.
[44] *Op. cit.*, p. 184.   [45] *Op. cit.*, p. 170.

"The guy's too cocky," Munshin said. "I see a terrific scene where the principal or the head monk or whatever they call him at a priest school, a kind of wise old priest-type Irishman, calls in Freddie"—one of Munshin's habits when telling a story was to call the hero "Freddie"—"and tells the kid that it's no go, he doesn't think Freddie ought to become a priest, not yet. Scholastically, he says, the kid's got everything. He's tops in Church History, in Holy Water, in Bingo Management, he's A plus in Confessional Psychology, but he doesn't have the heart of a priest. 'Get out in the world, son, and learn humility,' the old priest says. Do you see it now?"[46]

This is extremely funny, but it also rings terrifyingly true.

Throughout the novel Mailer lays great stress on the inversion of accepted values and of logical expectations. Most of the action takes place not in "the capital of cinema," Mailer's invariable term for Hollywood, but at a desert resort for movie people some two hundred miles inland. At Desert D'Or nothing is what it seems to be: "It was a town built out of no other obvious motive than commercial profit and so no sign of commerce was allowed to appear."[47] The stores look like anything but stores, the hotels cannot be seen from the outside, the bars are places of fantasy, "as different from the warm front of Desert D'Or as the inside of one's body is separate from the surface of one's skin,"[48] and in them it is impossible to tell whether it is night or day. The houses, built with walls of glass to give a view of the desert and the mountains, are so close together that they have to be shut in by high fences: "the result was like living in a room whose walls are mirrors."[49] Finally, Desert D'Or is "a place where no trees bear leaves."[50] The morbid introspection of Mailer's characters and the unnaturalness of their lives is reflected in the sterile fantasy of Desert D'Or and in the unreality of the motion-pictures they make.

The Deer Park concludes with an apparently hopeful but extremely enigmatic assertion of the positive value of sex—like other passages in the novel this has since received some illumination from the publication of *Advertisements for Myself*—but in the body of the

[46] *Op. cit.*, p. 179. [47] *Op. cit.*, p. 2. [48] *Op. cit.*, pp. 3–4.
[49] *Op. cit.*, p. 3. [50] *Ibid.*

novel the world of Desert D'Or and the cinema is one of hypocrisy
and corruption where integrity crumbles and only Faye's "beat"
nihilism has dignity: "Self-swindles roiled Faye; in this sense he
was absolutely opposed to the human race."[51]   So, looking into
the dawn towards the atomic testing grounds, he imagines the final
apocalyptic orgasm:

> So let it come, Faye thought, let this explosion come, and then
> another, and all the others, until the Sun God burned the earth.
> Let it come, he thought, looking into the east at Mecca where
> the bombs ticked while he stood on a tiny rise of ground trying to
> see one hundred, two hundred, three hundred miles across the
> desert. Let it come, Faye begged, like a man praying for rain, let
> it come and clear the rot and the stench and the stink, let it come
> for all of everywhere, just so it comes and the world stands clear in
> the white dead dawn.[52]

Powerfully suggestive of "the rot and the stench and the stink" is
the horrifying scene which opens with Herman Teppis, the great
and all-powerful producer, sitting at his desk, which once stood in
the Vatican but now contains liquor and a silent-running tape-
recorder. Seated there, and looked down upon by the portraits
of his mother and dead wife and by a famous painting of a mother
and child, Teppis first tries to force a marriage, for its publicity
value, between a homosexual and a nymphomaniac, and then,
without even moving from his chair, has a particularly sordid
passage with a call-girl procured for him by his son-in-law.[53]
Nothing as corrupt as this appears in the world of *The Last Tycoon*.
There, the very fact that Stahr himself is in charge constitutes a
guarantee that some creative work will be done, despite all opposition. But Stahr is doomed. In *The Deer Park*—would Fleishacker
have foretold this?—Herman Teppis is in power, and Teppis
stands for an utterly hypocritical and conscienceless commercialism.

5

Reality is distorted, human values are inverted or destroyed, and
commercialism is always and everywhere the enemy. This is the
essential theme of all the serious Hollywood novels. It is at the

[51] *Op. cit.*, p. 147.   [52] *Op. cit.*, p. 161.   [53] *Op. cit.*, pp. 263–85.

heart of the struggle between Stahr and Brady in *The Last Tycoon*, between Fineman and Sammy Glick in *What Makes Sammy Run?*, between Halliday and Milgrim in *The Disenchanted*, between Eitel and Teppis in *The Deer Park*. The struggles take different forms but are unhappily similar in outcome. Stahr, who somehow includes commercial acumen *within* his creative genius, is still powerful in *The Last Tycoon* as we have it, but the notes make it clear that when he dies the Brady-Fleishacker element will take over. Sammy Glick triumphs over Fineman, although he finds his victory hollow. Halliday is defeated, less by Milgrim than by his own weakness. Eitel, too, though in a quite different way from Halliday, loses to Teppis through self-betrayal: he "sells out." Nathanael West, without presenting a conflict of quite this kind, clearly suggests that the cinema has nothing to do with art: his whole emphasis, indeed, is on the grotesque artificiality of the film-world.

The fundamental ambiguity of the Hollywood situation is best expressed in *The Disenchanted*: "A strange business, Halliday was thinking. These men are in business but they're more emotional than business men. And they're involved with art but they're altogether too business-like for artists."[54]   The ambiguity itself is perhaps inevitable; the distortion and dishonesty arises from the failure to acknowledge the ambiguity, the refusal of Hollywood to face the facts of its own situation. In one of the earliest of Hollywood satires, Carl Van Vechten's *Spider Boy* (1928), Ben Griesheimer the movie magnate quickly gives himself away: "This firm . . . Griesheimer hesitated and then began again: This group of artists. . . ."[55] People in Hollywood apparently *want* to be deluded: "He's the greatest director in the world. He says so himself," says Capa Nolin, the screenwriter, of another character in *Spider Boy*. She goes on: "I don't take anything out here seriously, not even myself. You see . . . most of the houses out here are made of stucco. You can kick your foot right through them. You can kick your foot through everything else here too."[56]

[54] Budd Schulberg, *The Disenchanted*, New York 1950, p. 74.
[55] Carl Van Vechten, *Spider Boy*, London 1928, p. 108.
[56] *Op. cit.*, p. 84.

Every female star has a "mamma" who is anyone but her real mother; Ambrose Deacon becomes a great Hollywood success not despite, but because of the fact that all he wants to do is leave Hollywood and go to visit a friend in New Mexico; Wilhelmina Ford (it is not her real name, of course) gets into the movies by affecting to scorn the movies. So in an even earlier novel, *Merton of the Movies* (1922) by Harry Leon Wilson, the hero becomes a successful comic actor only because his director exploits performances which Merton had intended to be profoundly tragic.

This is perhaps the most important of the many themes from these early novels that later writers have taken up and developed. Fitzgerald underlines the divorce of the movie-world from reality in the scenes at the Hermitage and in the villa at Malibu. Mailer is even more specific in the description of Desert D'Or and in Sergius's insistence that the "real world" lies outside the boundaries of "the capital of cinema." Sammy Glick reaches the heights of Hollywood success by means of deception, the technique of "the big lie," a kind of extravert Machiavellism. The Hollywood world of *The Day of the Locust*, like the Hollywood houses of *Spider Boy*, is crazy and unsubstantial, and Claude Estee's impersonation is quintessential. From these novels the whole world of the movies emerges as a gigantic impersonation, and we are continually confronted with the utter contrast between Hollywood's private face and its public one. The values are all inverted: beauty equals eczema (the star in *The Last Tycoon*); screen he-man equals homosexual (Teddy Pope in *The Deer Park*) or impotent (Rodriguez in *The Last Tycoon*); "the nation's newest sweetheart"[57] equals ex-prostitute (Margo Dowling in *The Big Money*) or nymphomaniac (Lulu Meyers in *The Deer Park*); success comes most lavishly to those who do not deserve it (Sammy Glick in *What Makes Sammy Run?*) or to those who do not want it (Ambrose Deacon in *Spider Boy*).

All the serious novels about the motion-picture industry insist on this frightening contrast between the two faces of Hollywood. The general consensus seems to be that Hollywood is, if not monstrous, at least extravagant; if not grotesque, at least unreal; if not

[57] Dos Passos, *The Big Money*, p. 426.

evil, at least dishonest and hypocritical. From such a quasi-artistic but actually industrial setting, clever commercial pictures, the products of professionalism may come, but the odds against the honest and original picture, let alone the true work of art, are great and growing greater.

Yet, a few writers, notably Schulberg and Fitzgerald, are able to discern certain virtues in Hollywood, and it is surely a mark of maturity that they do so. We are told of Manley Halliday that "he himself had been critical of these Hollywood writers who sign long-term contracts and then save their best lines to excoriate the sources of their income,"[58] and we recall Cecilia's comment at the beginning of *The Last Tycoon*: "I knew what you were supposed to think about [Hollywood] but I was obstinately unhorrified."[59] Fitzgerald's observations and judgments of Hollywood are well-informed, deeply considered and always penetrating. Although he had *The Great Gatsby* very much in mind when he was writing *The Last Tycoon* he did not fall into the temptation of seizing upon what was most similar in his material: when we remember the party scenes of *The Great Gatsby* and think what Fitzgerald might have done with the even more spectacular material which Hollywood offered, the restraint, the sanity, the balanced appraisal of the studio world that we actually find in *The Last Tycoon* becomes doubly impressive. Fitzgerald is sometimes accused of having had a "Hollywood" mentality: yet he refutes this accusation nowhere more strongly than in *The Last Tycoon* where he deals so justly and so convincingly with Hollywood itself.

[58] *The Disenchanted*, p. 118.
[59] *The Last Tycoon*, p. 3.

10

Institutions in Fiction: the Academy

I

O f all the groups of modern institutional novels probably the largest is the one composed of novels about academic life. Indeed, the academic novel plays in the contemporary American literary scene a part very similar to that once played by the Hollywood novel. The universities and colleges have taken over from the film-studios as the leading employers of writers, and the typical academic novel is the work of a college professor of an arts subject. Although we shall use the term "academic" to describe novels *about* academic institutions, not simply novels emanating from them, the two categories coincide to such an extent that all the American novels we will be considering in detail have been written by past or present members of the teaching or administrative staffs of American universities or colleges.

Mary McCarthy, for example, taught for a time both at Sarah Lawrence and at Bard College and presumably drew upon these experiences when writing her novel *The Groves of Academe* (1952). Although this is usually considered the first academic novel in the current procession, in fact it only very slightly preceded a number of other novels about universities which appeared later that year: Robie Macauley's *The Disguises of Love*, for example, and Gerald Warner Brace's *The Spire* also came out in 1952. However, no subsequent academic novel has had quite the impact of *The Groves of Academe* if only because none of the others has been so skilfully written or so merciless in its satire.

The setting is Jocelyn, a co-educational college of the "progressive" type, and the central character is Henry Mulcahy, "called Hen by his friends, forty-one years old, the only Ph.D. in the Literature department, contributor to the *Nation* and the *Kenyon*

Review, Rhodes scholar, Guggenheim Fellow, father of four, fifteen years' teaching experience, salary and rank of instructor."[1] At the outset of the book Mulcahy is notified that his appointment is not to be renewed, but Mary McCarthy quickly freezes any incipient compassion which the reader might be experiencing by the description of Mulcahy which follows: "A tall, soft-bellied, lisping man with a tense, mushroom-white face, rimless bifocals, and greying thin red hair, he was intermittently aware of a quality of personal unattractiveness that emanated from him like a miasma."[2]

Mary McCarthy relies a little too heavily—as, to be sure, greater satirists have done—on physical ridicule, but in this instance she justifies the disgust she arouses by her portrayal of Mulcahy's behaviour. Finding himself cast in the role of victim, Mulcahy proceeds to exploit it to the utmost. He accuses President Hoar of dismissing him for political reasons and his liberal-minded colleagues, drawn variously by political indignation, pity, and guilt at the repugnance they feel for him, rally to his support. Sighing for "the old militant simplicities,"[3] the academics explore in discussion and in their consciences the contradictions inherent in the liberal position itself, and Mulcahy is able to play so successfully upon their earnest but muddled idealism, and upon the liberalism of President Hoar, that in the end it is Hoar who is forced to resign. The novel combines a study of political paranoia in the presentation of Mulcahy himself—a "damnable demagogue"[4] as Hoar comes finally and bitterly to realise—with a set of satirical variations on the liberal theme. In fact, it is in many ways less an academic than a political novel.

At the same time, the characters are very recognisably "academic": indeed, this is the essence of that mingled intelligence and naïvety which most of them display. There are also, in this somewhat episodic book, long sections describing Jocelyn itself, its ideals, organisation, and activities. In these sections the satire seems softened, the writing, always brilliant in its effects, more purely comic. The poetry conference, for example, is one of the funniest episodes in modern fiction, while the chapter entitled "Ancient

---

[1] Mary McCarthy, *The Groves of Academe*, London 1953, p. 3.
[2] *Ibid.*   [3] *Op. cit.*, p. 116.   [4] *Op. cit.*, p. 272.

History" contains an extremely effective critique of "progressive" college education: it demonstrates vividly the inevitable conflict between Jocelyn's announced aims for its students ("they were simply to be free, spontaneous, and co-educational")[5] and the inescapable fact of Jocelyn's institutional identity. Thus each student has to choose a topic for special study, and the "average entrant" is soon convinced "that he was not only going to be encouraged to express his individual bent, but that if he did not already have some personality-defining interest he had better work one up fast."[6] In fact most of them find themselves steered into similar and familiar paths:

> . . . the faculty, in practice, had arrived at a quiet gentlemen's agreement whereby each teacher offered two or three specialties, a limited choice, or else let the student roam, unsupervised, to some salt-lick of his own choosing. A student who did the latter was likely to get a high mark in Spontaneity but to rank low in Effort, Ability to Use the Tools of the Discipline, and Lack of Prejudice. The better students, in general, adjusted themselves without repining to what the faculty had to offer, pointing out to their juniors that it was better to allow Mr. Van Tour to teach you what he knew than what he didn't patently.[7]

The success of *The Groves of Academe* is such that we can discern a line of satirical academic novels stemming from it. Chief among these is Randall Jarrell's *Pictures from an Institution* (1954), an extremely clever book, marred by occasional over-writing, an indulgence in wit for its own and not the novel's sake. Where Mary McCarthy's book sometimes leaves an unpleasant taste Jarrell's tends to fray the nerves. This is perhaps a more humane book than *The Groves of Academe*, and it is often as funny, but it remains in the earlier book's shadow. Indeed, although Jarrell may have thought that he was challenging this fate, he in fact invites it when he chooses for the setting another progressive college, Benton, and for principal character a tough, malicious woman novelist, Gertrude Johnson, who is simultaneously teaching at the college and writing a novel about it. Jarrell presents a few "good"

[5] *Op. cit.*, p. 53.　　　　　[6] *Op. cit.*, p. 68.　　　　　[7] *Op. cit.*, p. 69.

characters in this novel, but he makes Benton itself an object of satire as well as most of its inhabitants, Gertrude above all. Indeed, Jarrell concentrates so much of his attention upon Gertrude and, to a lesser extent, upon President and Mrs Robbins, that the satire on Benton itself and upon progressive education seems of a comparatively perfunctory kind: the novel does, in fact, offer pictures from an institution rather than of one.

A clear impression of Benton does emerge, however. It is a little private world of its own, quite apart from "the world outside," a place where a great variety of people "lived together in amity and complacency. It was like, in many ways, some little community in the Middle Ages . . . almost all the people there were agreed about almost everything, and glad to be agreed, and *right* to be agreed."[8] At Benton the group-spirit prevails, what we would now call the "social ethic": "What mattered at Benton was the Approval of Your Colleagues, the respect of the community of Benton."[9] The influence of Benton as an institution is stifling, deadening, working against "life":

> The people of Benton . . . had not all been provincial to begin with, but they had made provincials of themselves, and called their province, now, the world. And it was a world in which almost nothing happened, a kind of steady state . . . Is an institution always a man's shadow shortened in the sun, the lowest common denominator of everybody in it? Benton was: the soldiers, as always, were better than the army in which they served, the superficial consenting nexus of their lives that was Benton. The people of Benton, like the rest of us, were born, fell in love, married and died, lay sleepless all night, saw the first star of evening and wished upon it, won lotteries and wept for joy. But not at Benton.[10]

A more recent novel in this particular line is Stringfellow Barr's *Purely Academic* (1958). Professor Schneider, head of the History Department of a small Middle Western university, is at the beginning of the book hen-pecked, underpaid, depressed—the embodiment of the popular academic stereotype. He subsequently achieves

---

[8] Randall Jarrell, *Pictures from an Institution*, London 1954, pp. 111-12.
[9] *Op. cit.*, p. 114.   [10] *Op. cit.*, pp. 234-5.

self-confidence and reputation, puts on his household's trousers again, and escapes from university pettiness and poverty to a much more lucrative position as head of the Division of General Education for the Winthrop Foundation. He gains his self-confidence by having an affair with the young and desirable wife of Thomas Nast, the powerful and despicable head of the Economics Department; his reputation by pretending to be employed on a top-secret job for the government; his new post by making friends with Denby, head of the Winthrop Foundation, who likes Schneider because almost alone among his colleagues he has retained his sense of the ludicrous. *Purely Academic* is a comic rather than a witty book and towards the end its tone wavers uncertainly between fantasy-farce and satire; but although it both attempts and achieves much less than either *The Groves of Academe* or *Pictures from an Institution* it is highly effective at its more modest level.

Professor Schneider's progression from university to foundation often reminds us of the career of Sinclair Lewis's hero in *Gideon Planish* (1943), and both authors choose similar methods and objects for their satire. Denby explains to Schneider why he had left teaching some years before:

"Campus life! My God! I couldn't take it. The place awash with perfectly decent boys and girls, sweating through the most ghastly textbooks, copying down in their notebooks the appalling stupidities and ineptitudes that tired, underpaid, repetitious, frustrated professors droned at them, trying to get a grade that would add up with other grades to get them a diploma, printed on imitation sheepskin for real sheep. Faculty wives, worn out with trying to make two ends meet, or gone hard and bitter and spiteful, carrying on social vendettas with each other. And, over all, an uneducated ex-general or ex-banker blandishing tax-evading donors into perpetuating their own egos. It's a truly hideous picture of perfectly nice people caught up in an absolute web of pretense."[11]

As in *Pictures from an Institution*, the people are far superior to the institution to which they belong. Denby declares that this educational mess is "a coast-to-coast operation,"[12] extending even into

[11] Stringfellow Barr, *Purely Academic*, New York 1958, p. 31.
[12] *Op. cit.*, p. 35.

the Ivy League colleges; Schneider thinks of it as a "squirrel cage,"[13] with himself inside it. Schneider also reflects that in order to achieve their social ambitions his colleagues "had done nothing more awful than to turn a noble profession, the profession of teaching and learning, into a retail business. And yet . . . what an appalling thing to do!!"[14] Eventually Schneider escapes from the "squirrel cage" into the Winthrop Foundation, but he has already been warned by Denby that a foundation is as much a racket as a university: "There's not much a foundation can do. Broadly speaking, it has even more means at its disposal than a university has. But it has an equally ill-defined end. In short, it's a microcosm of our society: abundant means but no ends."[15]

Vladimir Nabokov's *Pnin* (1957) belongs in this line of academic novels rather than any other, but it is a highly individual work of much humour and considerable, if rather coy, charm. The hero, Professor Timofey Pnin, a totally unassimilated *émigré*, teaches Russian at Waindell College, which is "a somewhat provincial institution"[16] and also something of an educational fraud:

> Two interesting characteristics distinguished Leonard Blorenge, Chairman of French Literature and Language; he disliked Literature, and he had no French . . . He gave a course entitled "Great Frenchmen", which he had had his secretary copy out from a set of *The Hastings Historical and Philosophical Magazine* for 1882-94, discovered by him in an attic and not represented in the College Library.[17]

When Pnin's career as a teacher of Russian is about to be terminated it is Blorenge who refuses him a job teaching French: he discovers that Pnin actually speaks and reads the language. And so Pnin leaves Waindell College, and at the end of the book we see him driving forlornly into the distance. But it is not altogether a sad ending, for Pnin, with his gentleness, his passion for recondite research, his "unforgettable digressions," does not belong in an institution, let alone an institution like Waindell College. Waindell may think that it has sacked Professor Pnin, but in fact it is Pnin who can do without Waindell.

[13] *Op. cit.*, p. 49.   [14] *Op. cit.*, p. 68.   [15] *Op. cit.*, p. 262.
[16] Vladimir Nabokov, *Pnin*, London 1957, p. 9.   [17] *Op.cit.*, pp. 140-1.

2

Not all the recent academic novelists have taken a highly critical view of their material. Indeed, we can pick out a group of novels of quite a different kind: these might be called the affirmative academic novels, and one of their chief representatives is Theodore Morrison's *The Stones of the House* (1953). Although the novel is too long and its style is deliberate to the point of mannerism, it deserves consideration as a humane book in which Morrison approaches seriously and intelligently the personal and professional problems of university administration. The hero, Acting-President Aiken of Rowley University, learns at the end of the book that he is to be President Aiken: he is diffident at the promotion, but happy. According to Dean Abner, Aiken's best friend, power is not the supreme goal; neither is it to be shirked: "A man who refused opportunities ran the risk of diminishing himself, of going stale and complacent."[18] At the same time: "There was a difference between trying to get to the top and trying to reach your own ceiling."[19] This sensible note of affirmation without naïvety is characteristic of the book. Aiken is troubled throughout by the conflicts which arise when one has an allegiance both to an institution and to individuals, and he is painfully aware of the contradictions of motive and effect that are inextricably involved in any attempt to do good through institutions. "What good does it do to do good?"[20] he asks himself, and at one point he discusses the question with Dr Holsberg:

> "It's an old problem, isn't it, how to do good, or try to do it, through an institution? Reconciling the needs of the individual and the needs of the institution. It's enough to make any man wonder what his motives really are. Mightn't the same be true of a hospital as well as a college?"
> "Often," the doctor assented.[21]

Throughout the novel Morrison attempts to treat the day-to-day and apparently trivial details of administration within this wider frame of reference, and he has consequently made *The Stones of the*

[18] Theodore Morrison, *The Stones of the House*, New York 1953, p. 86.
[19] *Ibid.*   [20] *Op. cit.*, p. 318.   [21] *Op. cit.*, p. 171.

House, despite its limitations, quite the most satisfactory of the affirmative novels. In Morrison's second novel, *To Make a World* (1957), Rowley University and President Aiken reappear, but the action mainly concerns the Stoughton Foundation, a wealthy body devoted to educational good works. The book's weakness, by comparison with its predecessor, is that neither the university nor the foundation are adequately presented as going concerns, as places where things happen and are done. Morrison's treatment of the foundation, however, may be largely deliberate; he seems to insist on its mysteriousness, its insubstantiality, on the difficulty of discovering what it is all about and where power really resides. At the end of the book it is seen as a kind of victory that the two main characters are able to escape from financial dependence on the foundation and from involvement in its complicated world of interweaving personal and hierarchical relationships.

Neither of Morrison's novels is as unhesitatingly affirmative as Carlos Baker's *A Friend in Power* (1958). The action revolves round the choice of a new president for Enfield University, but the political activities involved are of the mildest and most gentlemanly nature. The hero, head of the Modern Languages department, eventually accepts the presidency, but he is persuaded to do so not because he wants the position but because he sees it as a duty to which he has been called. The long discussions of power are entirely reassuring: if Lincoln had remained a country lawyer he could not have saved the Union or freed the slaves, while "the search for truth is the university president's whole business. . . . He runs the whole shebang in such a way that he helps others in their search for truth."[22] It is not surprising that reviewers of the book welcomed it as a timely demonstration that American education was fundamentally healthy.

The cosy academic world of *A Friend in Power* is very different from the world of Howard Nemerov's *The Homecoming Game* (1957), one of the ablest and, for all its humour, one of the most serious of recent academic novels. Although it clearly does not belong in the tradition of *The Groves of Academe*, its emphasis is by no means entirely affirmative: the central characters are not bad

[22] Carlos Baker, *A Friend in Power*, London 1958, p. 221.

men, but they are bewildered and defeated men. Nemerov often suggests a James Gould Cozzens with a sense of humour: both have an elegant style which tends to be involved and parenthetical; both constantly examine the complexity of the problems which arise in moral issues and the consequent near-impossibility of firm moral judgments. When the novel opens, the hero, Charles Osman, an associate professor of history, has just failed Raymond Blent, a star football player, in a departmental examination, thus making him ineligible to play in the Homecoming Game the following day. Pressure is brought to bear on Osman from all sides and eventually he agrees to let Blent play, only to discover that the situation is complicated far beyond anything he had imagined: deeper and deeper layers of confusion, mixed motives, dishonesty and corruption are progressively revealed. Osman, trying to do the "right" thing, finds himself committed to actions that are unquestionably "wrong": "Of course, Charles told himself, all this that happened today comes from trying to be good, trying to help others, trying to do the right thing; in a way, when one did that, one became unreliable; much as a driver would do who sought to anticipate the next move of another driver instead of simply assuming the worst."[23]

We are confronted again with the central question of *The Stones of the House*: "What good does it do to do good?" Nemerov, through one of his characters, suggests a moral for administrator and teacher alike in the example of " 'the ship's captain whom Socrates talks about in the *Gorgias*, who does his best for people in his own technical area, sailing the ship, but has the wit to realize he can't know whether he's done 'em good or harm.' "[24] The moral, of course, is that one can never decide what is good for other people; such attempts must always fail, and one can only go on doing one's job, as administrator or teacher, as well as one knows how.

3

Though Nemerov does not develop further the metaphor of a ship, many writers have noticed how appropriate it is for a college.

[23] Howard Nemerov, *The Homecoming Game*, New York 1957, p. 191.
[24] *Op. cit.*, p. 237.

Ideally considered, a college has that "freedom from all land entanglements" which Conrad found on shipboard: it is an obvious instance of an isolated, tightly-bound community where prolonged intimacy may provoke the appearance of human emotions at their most violent and most naked. Not surprisingly, the English novelist Ivy Compton-Burnett, whose later novels always deal with interrelationships within a single family, chose an academic setting for some of her earlier books: a women's college in *Dolores* (1911), a preparatory school in *Pastors and Masters* (1925), and a girls' school in *More Women than Men* (1933). As Robert Liddell has remarked, a school suited her purposes as "an example, like the family, of a group of people living too closely together."[25]

It is this aspect of college life which especially interests another English novelist, C. P. Snow, notably in *The Masters* (1951), which revolves round the election of a new master at a Cambridge college. While exceptionally exciting as pure narrative, *The Masters* also serves as the vehicle for Snow's ideas, and his intention in this novel, as in *The Affair* (1960) and, to a lesser extent, in *The Light and the Dark* (1947), is perhaps best expressed in a passage from yet another of his novels *The New Men* (1954). Lewis Eliot, Snow's narrator, is describing the deliberations of a committee charged with selecting a new head for a highly important scientific establishment:

> These men were fairer, and most of them a great deal abler, than the average: but you heard the same ripples below the words, as when any group of men chose anyone for any job. Put your ear to those meetings and you heard the intricate labyrinthine and unassuageable rapacity, even in the best of men, of the love of power. If you have heard it once—say, in electing the chairman of a tiny dramatic society, it does not matter where—you have heard it in colleges, in bishoprics, in ministries, in cabinets: men do not alter because the issues they decide are bigger scale.[26]

The college offers Snow a small group of above-average and sometimes brilliant men living in constant association and frequent rivalry with each other: in short, it offers him the perfect micro-cosmic situation in which to work out his chosen and constant

[25] Robert Liddell, *A Treatise on the Novel*, London 1947, p. 147.
[26] C. P. Snow, *The New Men*, London 1954, pp. 278-9.

themes of human ambition and "personal politics." No doubt Jocelyn College had something of the same interest for Mary McCarthy: having described a restricted community in *The Oasis* (1949) she seems to have moved on quite naturally to the more numerous but still confined world of a college in *The Groves of Academe*, her first full-length novel.

We cannot say how far the other American novelists have consciously adopted a similar attitude towards their material, but almost all of them reveal their constant preoccupation with what may be roughly called political issues. Many novels are concerned with the power-structure within the university, with the hierarchies within departments, and with the often feudal relationships of departments to each other and to the central administration. Morrison's two novels are largely concerned with internal university politics, and so is *The Homecoming Game*. *The Stones of the House*, *A Friend in Power*, and *Purely Academic* all deal, in their very different ways, with the process of choosing a new president. Wider issues also appear. *To Make a World* deals with the personal and institutional relationships that link a university with an educational foundation, and so, less seriously, does *Purely Academic*. More importantly, few American academic novels of recent years have not portrayed at least one character accused of Communism, and several books have taken as their subject the situation which arises when such external issues intrude into university life. This is a central theme of *The Groves of Academe* and the almost exclusive subject-matter of May Sarton's *Faithful Are the Wounds* (1955), which deals with the suicide of Edward Cavan, a distinguished Harvard professor of English, in October 1949. Because Cavan refuses to compromise his left-wing political beliefs in any way, he is threatened with investigation by a Congressional committee and finds himself alienated from his former friends, most of whom have in one way or another adapted themselves to the changed political situation. The novel, which is well written within the limits of its plain and unadventurous style, ends in a strong assertion of the liberal standpoint.

We should perhaps call *Faithful Are the Wounds*, even more than *The Groves of Academe*, a political thesis novel. The point of discussing it as an academic novel, however, is that it was obviously provoked by the post-war Congressional investigations into the political beliefs, activities and affiliations of teachers in schools and colleges all over the United States. Because these highly controversial investigations attempted to undermine the basic principles of academic freedom and integrity, they must have influenced powerfully, if less directly, many other novels of university life; indeed, it is feasible to argue that they have been one of the main causes of the recent spate of academic fiction. Certainly the experience of the investigations forced upon American teachers generally a greater political awareness, if only of a negative kind, than they might otherwise have had, and prompted many of them to attitudes of self-defence or self-examination. These attitudes appear in the novels, and it is perhaps discouraging to find that self-defence tends to appear as complacency and re-assertion of the *status quo*, as in *A Friend in Power*, while self-examination emerges as rather destructive criticism, as in almost all the other novels apart from *The Stones of the House*.

Especially in the later novels, however, there is clearly much more involved than a direct or indirect response to McCarthyite pressures. *Pnin* and *Pictures from an Institution*, for example, cannot be discussed only in such terms, nor can *Purely Academic*. In such novels the enemy is not anything external but the institution itself. In Jarrell's book the institution is stupefying, in Barr's stultifying: Benton is dead; Barr's university is a racket and those in power, seeking endowments and believing that beggars can't be choosers, pursue "the educational policy of a whore."[27] *Purely Academic*, indeed, is the nearest American equivalent to Kingsley Amis's *Lucky Jim* (1954), the funniest and most outspoken English attack on the pomposity and fakery of academic life: it has the same debunking tone as *Lucky Jim* and the same failure to provide any resolution except in wholly negative escape, Jim Dixon to his job in London, Professor Schneider to his post with the foundation.

Lucky Jim, however, stands almost alone among recent English academic novels: its only notable companions are Malcolm Bradbury's *Eating People is Wrong* (1959) and William Cooper's

[27] *Purely Academic*, p. 120.

The Struggles of Albert Woods (1952), an amusing exposure of an academic opportunist which has perhaps been a little unjustly overshadowed by *Lucky Jim*'s subsequent success. In general the attitudes of English academic novelists have differed considerably from those of their American counterparts. For example, almost all the American novels question how, or indeed whether, one can do good through institutions—to what extent, if at all, the good man can make institutions the instrument of his good intentions towards particular individuals or towards society in general. In most of these novels the authors are either intensely critical or, at best, as in *The Stones of the House*, self-questioning and self-doubting. They are concerned with the aims and purposes of the university and with the effectiveness of the methods employed to achieve those ends: some of them go so far as to question the whole *raison d'être* of the modern American university.

This is certainly not true of most English academic novels of recent years: even when these are most realistic in their discussion of academic power politics, as in *The Masters*, or of scholarly fraud, as in *The Affair* and Angus Wilson's *Anglo-Saxon Attitudes* (1956), there is no sense of the academic world itself being placed on trial. Even *The Struggles of Albert Woods* does not raise such issues, and Amis in *Lucky Jim* seems to be protesting against the abuse of the system rather than against the system itself. Characteristically, *The Masters* closes on an extremely positive note:

> When I arrived in the college, I had already moved about a good deal among the layers of society; and I had not come to the end of my journey yet. I had the luck to live intimately among half-a-dozen different vocations. Of all those I had the chance to see, the college was the place where men lived the least anxious, the most comforting, the freest lives.[28]

A little earlier, Lewis Eliot speaks of the college as "a society completely sure of itself, completely certain of its values, completely without misgivings about whether it was living a good life."[29] Snow's academics do not exercise their minds or consciences about whether or not they are doing good; indeed, in *The Light and the*

[28] C. P. Snow, *The Masters*, London 1951, p. 387.
[29] *Op. cit.*, p. 386.

Dark it is suggested that "Good people don't do good."[30] This is not complacency—no one has examined academic jealousy, hatred, and pettiness more rigorously than Snow—but it is assurance.

4

The many attacks on academic freedom in America in the years since World War II must be largely responsible for these differences between English and American academic novels, since recent academic novels in England and America are in other ways remarkably similar. For instance, both treat of adult and even elderly people rather than young ones. Rarely does either an English or an American novel mention, much less present, the actual business of teaching, and for the most part they depict students only incidentally and for purposes of humour or plot development. We certainly note a marked change from the more important academic novels of the past.[31] Universities have traditionally appeared in novels as a crucial stage in the hero's growth to manhood: thus we recall the Princeton of F. Scott Fitzgerald's *This Side of Paradise* (1920), the Harvard of Thomas Wolfe's *Of Time and the River* (1935), or, in England, the Oxford of Compton Mackenzie's *Sinister Street* (1913), to which Fitzgerald was much indebted, or the rather different Oxford of Evelyn Waugh's *Brideshead Revisited* (1945). In contrast to this, the typical academic novel of the last few years, in both England and America, has been faculty- rather than student-centred.

The obvious comment is that formerly novels about universities tended to be the work of past students; now they tend to be the work of present teachers. The novels themselves tend to be more "academic," in that many of them have the appearance of deliberate literary exercises, as if the success of *The Masters* and *The Groves of Academe* suggested to several would-be novelists that they might have material on their own doorsteps: a large proportion of academic novels are first novels. More importantly, the institution itself tends to be seen from above rather than from below and to

[30] C. P. Snow, *The Light and the Dark*, London 1951, p. 192.
[31] On this point see Mortimer R. Proctor, *The English University Novel*, Berkeley and Los Angeles 1957, pp. 1-2, and *passim*.

bulk much larger, arrogating the attention that in the earlier books belonged naturally to the hero. If what might be thought of as the central academic experiences, scholarship and teaching, have tended to be ignored in favour of questions of power and promotion, that may be due in part to authors first becoming seized with the idea of writing an academic novel and then discovering that they had little to write about except their own ambition and that of their colleagues. However, serious academic novelists have written of these same themes for quite different reasons: like so many modern American novelists, they have wanted to write novels attacking or defending institutionalism, and they have naturally turned for their material to the institutions they knew best.

In Snow's books and in the better American novels questions of power and promotion are placed in these wider contexts, but it remains true that almost all recent academic novels, English and American alike, are not novels about education but novels about careers—professional novels, in a quite narrow sense, as much concerned as novels about government or big business with the internal politics of the organisation, with the possibilities of personal manipulation, with questions of prestige and status within a quasi-bureaucratic hierarchy. What distinguishes the American novels from the English is their extreme self-consciousness about the nature of the academic society and their persistent questioning of its aims, values, and achievements.

II

James Gould Cozzens

I

N orman Mailer and Mary McCarthy have both written important novels about institutions; otherwise they have little in common as novelists. What they do have in common, however, and what they share with most of the earlier social novelists we have considered, is a readiness to use the novel as a vehicle of social criticism. With the obvious exception of the *exposé* novelists, much of whose work is of a sub-literary kind, the more widespread attitude among contemporary social novelists seems to be one of conservatism or of simple acceptance. Many of them take an entirely apolitical position: they accept society as it exists and are primarily concerned to present society as they see it. One such novelist, John Brooks, has spoken of his "passion to record," of the desire to ensure "That nothing should be lost, that the essences of one's time as well as its facts and figures should be set down, that the timeless struggles of the human heart should be seen exactly as they existed under a certain set of conditions."[1] While agreeing that "Such a novelist must admit at the outset that he shoots at smaller game than those whose target is to discover and enunciate new human truths,"[2] Brooks goes on to make impressive claims for the kind of novel he has in mind, a kind which

> might be called the social novel, had not that term been preempted to describe a group of books written chiefly during the thirties and having a distinct ethical and political bias. It could be called the novel of society, but only at the risk of suggesting, incorrectly, that

[1] John Brooks, "Some Notes on Writing One Kind of Novel," in *The Living Novel*, ed. Granville Hicks, New York 1957, pp. 44-5.
[2] *Op. cit.*, p. 45.

its setting is invariably the likes of upper Fifth Avenue or Monaco. It is so close to the old novel of manners, but manners have changed so much in the past fifty years that the term would be limiting and actually misleading. Therefore I'll speak of it as the recording novel; and in case that sounds too temporary and mortal, it may be well to recall Turgenev's *Fathers and Sons*, a recording novel about a specific and idiosyncratic society now nearly a century gone that shows as well as any the permanence of interest attainable within this form.[3]

Outstanding among modern authors of "recording novels" is John P. Marquand, who found his manner in *The Late George Apley* (1937) and scarcely deviated from it in his later books. All his work has the technical skill and assurance of the thorough professional, but the persistent recurrence of certain themes, situations, and techniques amounts almost to a formula. We encounter again and again the New England small-town upper-middle-class background of tradition, moderate wealth, Harvard, respectable business and the professions; the parents from whom the hero struggles rather unaggressively to be free; the girl he failed to marry but perhaps should have married; the no-more-than-satisfactory marriage he has in fact contracted; the children he cannot quite understand; the job with which he is on somewhat uneasy terms. We become thoroughly familiar, too, with the controlled, almost mannered, relaxation of the style, and with the memoir, the "Class life," the idea for a novel, the interview, and all the other devices for introducing a series of flashbacks which build neatly, like blocks in a children's game, into a total picture of the novel's "now."

The Late George Apley itself is a remarkable *tour de force* which has received inadequate attention and appreciation from American critics, but the unadventurousness of Marquand's later work must limit his claim to be regarded as a serious artist. Nevertheless, Marquand told an interviewer in 1949: " 'I would like, before I'm through . . . to have a series of novels which would give a picture of a segment of America during the past fifty years,' "[4] and he has given vivid, if sometimes brief, impressions of such varied fields

[3] *Op. cit.*, pp. 45-6.   [4] Breit, *The Writer Observed*, p. 47.

of activity as banking (*Point of No Return*), advertising (*H. M. Pulham, Esq.*), the literary life (*Wickford Point*), Hollywood (*So Little Time*), the theatre (*So Little Time*; *Women and Thomas Harrow*), radio (*Melville Goodwin, U.S.A.*), business (*B. F.'s Daughter*; *Sincerely, Willis Wayde*), the army (*B. F.'s Daughter*; *Melville Goodwin, U.S.A.*, and the stories "Good Morning Major" and "The End Game" included in *Thirty Years*). His portrayal of the more domestic aspects of New England society is accurate in its observation and rich in its variety and for this, rightly, his work is best known.

A novel like *Point of No Return* (1949) provides ample evidence of Marquand's percipience as a social observer. Marquand takes up much of the book with a nostalgic evocation of a New England small town, but its central theme develops around bureaucratic competition. Charles Gray, seen at work and in his suburban home, is what we have since learned to call an "organization man," and we watch in the novel his final submission to the organisation, in this case a big city bank. Marquand always kept up with the sociologists; in *Point of No Return* he was ahead, at least, of the popularisers among them. In *B. F.'s Daughter* (1946), it is true, he deals with business characters of a rather old-fashioned kind, but in a more successful novel, *Sincerely, Willis Wayde* (1955), he presents Willis as an individualist who cynically exploits the techniques of success in the age of the organisation man. The suggestion of parable which runs through the book emerges explicitly near the end:

He pushed back his chair and stood up, gently smoothing out the folds in his double-breasted coat, smiling, looking like someone who had been asked by the toastmaster to say a few words. He had that same professional assurance, and May had been right— his suit had undoubtedly been made in London by a tailor accustomed to American whims. For a second Willis dominated the scene, modestly and sincerely. His ease was the best thing about him. You could not tell, Steve was thinking, how much of his cordiality was real. There was no way of gauging the depth of his sincerity. It might very well have been that he did have a soft spot in his heart, and that he had honestly meant what he had said about loyalty, and about being deeply sorry. On the other hand he might have had no heart at all. Authority and success had made him strangely impervious, since success had smoothed down all his rough edges, turning him into a type interchangeable with any photograph on the financial page of the *New York Times*. It was hard to tell about those people, who had all been processed in the same way, but he was essentially an American type.[5]

As Steve thinks a little later, the whole story was "one that could only have happened in America."[6] Marquand never came nearer than this to an explicit social statement, and it is, perhaps, an emotional statement, expressive of distaste and dislike, rather than a precisely directed critical comment on society.

In his attitude towards society Marquand is much closer to Tarkington, say, than to Dreiser, tending to treat society without specific social or political intentions but simply as material, as grist for the novelist's mill. Although it is obvious that his tastes and attitudes are deeply conservative, Marquand remains, often to a point of extreme delicacy, an uncommitted writer. He habitually uses a plainly non-autobiographical first-person narrator of transparent obtuseness or hypocrisy—a device most brilliantly employed in *The Late George Apley*—and so leaves ample room for deliberate uncertainties of moral judgment, almost for the abandonment of moral judgment. Even a novel like *Melville Goodwin, U.S.A.* (1951), which begins with all the marks of an *exposé*, ends by being nothing of the kind: we learn that however stultifying the army may be, we must respect rather than judge it. Marquand does not so much satirise or expose as explain; we learn, above all, that this is the way things are.

Essentially, then, Marquand is a recording novelist, with a fundamentally conservative commitment to a society whose superficial follies and ironies he can nevertheless recognise and identify. He seems to have remained restricted by his upbringing in the upper-middle-class of New England, much as Sinclair Lewis was permanently trapped within the mental confines of the Middle Western middle-class; like Lewis again, he worked out his "natural," autobiographical material in his earlier books and subsequently turned, in a thoroughly professional way, to working-up

[5] J. P. Marquand, *Sincerely, Willis Wayde*, Boston and Toronto 1955, p. 501.
[6] *Op. cit.*, p. 503.

the careers of men in business and the professions. His characters lack the vitality of Lewis's most successful creations, but it can at least be said of them that they appear within a social context which has been clearly observed and firmly presented. John Brooks recognised that the recording novel was not the highest form of literary achievement, yet done with the constant skill and frequent grace which Marquand brought to his work, it is by no means one to be despised.

2

When John Brooks spoke of the "passion to record" he had his own work mainly in mind. Much of his writing has been in the area of direct reportage, but his novels equally exemplify the passion of which he speaks; indeed, they are firmly in the Marquand manner as to both style and content. He is best known for his first novel, *The Big Wheel* (1949), which deals with a mass-circulation magazine of the *Time* variety, but perhaps his most successful novel is *The Man Who Broke Things* (1958), in which a Western financier attempts to take over control of an old-established firm in New York. In this novel Brooks quite skilfully creates suspense out of the technicalities of a "take-over bid," and we may be reminded not only of Marquand but of earlier novelists such as Winston Churchill and Booth Tarkington: it is much the same formula of smooth, almost bland writing, an "interesting" setting informatively presented, and a cautiously affirmative compromise at the end.

A considerably more important novelist than Brooks is John O'Hara, one of the few contemporary American writers who comes near to being a true novelist of manners. His work often challenges comparison with Marquand's—there are remarkable similarities, for example, between O'Hara's *A Family Party* (1956) and Marquand's *Life at Happy Knoll* (1958)—and there is no doubt that, if not always a more interesting novelist than Marquand, he is consistently a better writer. His first novel, *Appointment in Samarra* (1934), and, to a lesser degree, *Butterfield 8* (1935), are genuinely distinguished works quite outside Marquand's range; in both books, but more especially in *Appointment in Samarra*, he employs his social material economically and evocatively, rather as Fitzgerald does in *The Great Gatsby*, and he structures the novel in such a way as to keep this material always in focus and always under control.

O'Hara grows repetitious in his later work, for while he is immensely knowing about the society he depicts, he only knows a relatively restricted area, both vertically and horizontally, and he seems unable to make it yield sufficient fresh insights and meanings. Lionel Trilling has spoken admiringly of O'Hara's "passionate commitment to verisimilitude,"[7] and in his best work this is undoubtedly a major source of O'Hara's strength. However, the later novels, and especially the longer ones such as *A Rage to Live* (1949) and more especially *Ten North Frederick* (1955), add little to the original insights of *Appointment in Samarra* but simply pile up an immense weight of sociological documentation at each point of the narrative.

3

One of the most distinguished of contemporary American social novelists is James Gould Cozzens, more impressive and more politically engaged than Marquand, but, like him, seized with the passion to record. Cozzens did his best work of that kind in his days of comparative obscurity before the publication of *By Love Possessed* (1957). Clearly that novel was greeted with inordinate enthusiasm, but the attacks of Dwight Macdonald[8] and others, followed somewhat cannily by the book's English reviewers,[9] have done a useful job in cutting Cozzens down to size. There now seems some danger of the reaction going too far, of Cozzens being expelled beyond the intellectual pale as a hopelessly middle-brow writer, his very real if limited virtues unjustly ignored.

By any reasonable standards, Cozzens is an important novelist, even if he is unlikely ever to write a great book. For example, although *The Son of Perdition* (1929) does not now seem a particularly

[7] Lionel Trilling, Introduction to *Selected Short Stories of John O'Hara*, New York [1956], p. viii.

[8] Dwight Macdonald, "By Cozzens Possessed," *Commentary*, xxv (1958), 36-47.

[9] See Michael Millgate, "By Cozzens Unpossessed," *New Republic*, cxxxviii (9 Jun. 1958), 21.

distinguished work, *S. S. San Pedro* (1931), an excellent, tightly-written story of the sea, greatly surpasses such a book as *The Caine Mutiny* which it somewhat resembles in theme, while *Castaway* (1934) is a terrifying fantasy, a cross between Poe and Kafka, of a man locked in a huge department store: in the midst of over-whelming material abundance it is his mind, obsessed with the irrational fears of solitude, that cannot hold up. Apart from *Ask Me Tomorrow* (1940), perhaps the least successful of Cozzen's mature works, all of the later novels are centrally concerned with the cohesion of the social structure. In *The Last Adam* (1933: the English title is *A Cure of Flesh*), *Men and Brethren* (1936), and *The Just and the Unjust* (1942) the heroes are, respectively, a doctor, a parson, and a lawyer, and the three novels form something of a group in which Cozzens points out the sad inadequacies of conventional moral values and professional ethics when confronted by the often shocking demands of actual living.

In *Men and Brethren* an Episcopalian minister, Ernest Cudlipp, encounters just such a difficult situation when he tries to help Carl Willever, a well-known Christian apologist who has been expelled from his order for homosexuality. Cudlipp asserts that he has a right and duty to be charitable, but Dr Lamb, his immediate superior, replies that this must not be "at the expense of your good name and reputation. The parish you serve has first claim on both. You have no right to risk your reputation. Your position makes it an integral part of the parish's, the whole Church's reputation."[10] Later Dr Lamb declares: "It would appear to be high time for you to realize that you aren't free to consult only your likes and dislikes. . . . You will have to make up your mind whether your ministry is to act as my Vicar; or whether you feel that you have an independent mission to help such people as Father Willever."[11] The clash is not so much between duty and desire, as between two conflicting conceptions of duty itself, and it arises directly from the bureaucratic situation: how unreservedly should a man commit himself to the organisation, especially when he disagrees with fundamental aspects of its policy. For a priest such as Cudlipp the

[10] James Gould Cozzens, *Men and Brethren*, New York 1936, p. 221.
[11] *Op. cit.*, p. 223.

dilemma has unusual difficulties and refinements, and these Cozzens explores with some acuteness, but it is essentially the same dilemma of the moral man in the bureaucratic situation which Cozzens presents again and again in this group of novels.

Cozzens gives this theme its fullest expression in *Guard of Honor* (1948), his last novel before *By Love Possessed*. The action of *Guard of Honor* takes place during the early part of World War II at Ocanara, an air base in Florida largely concerned with experimental projects. Cozzens limits his time-span to three days, although it seems doubtful whether the novel greatly gains from this or from the notoriously pretentious style. Much more successful is the choice of setting, which gives scope for a great variety of often violent incident, but at the same time strictly defines the human limits of the action. This is a single self-contained military installation with a clear-cut hierarchy of command. Although it is war-time, we hear of the fighting only as a distant though constant rumour, and Cozzens directs our attention not to man fighting, but to man commanding, obeying, intriguing, and to man refusing to command, obey, intrigue. The world of Ocanara air base itself is richly and vividly created, with a convincing profuseness of detail in the descriptions of flying, administration, and day-to-day military life. Cozzens displays considerable technical skill in the intricate interweaving of characters, incidents, and sub-plots, and in the management of the dual presentation whereby we see the action primarily from the angle of Colonel Ross, who acts as deputy to General Beal, the base commander, but also at times through the eyes of Captain Nathaniel Hicks, who occupies a humbler position in the hierarchy. Both Hicks, a magazine editor in civilian life, and Ross, a judge, are typical of Cozzen's upper-middle-class moral men and they serve admirably as vehicles for the author's moral comment and judgments.

Guard of Honor is an extensive and penetrating investigation into the operations of military bureaucracy—into the effects of the hierarchical system; into the responsibilities, and the permissible irresponsibilities, of command; and into the often curious and devious processes by which decisions are reached. As in his other "professional" novels, Cozzens forces his characters to face up to the unattractive, sometimes brutal, nakedness of irremovable fact, and the process leads him at times to somewhat reactionary conclusions; for example, we learn that ideally one can claim justice and equality for Negroes, but as long as more Southern whites than Negroes serve in the Air Force the need to win the war demands that ideals of justice must give way to the prejudices of the Southerners. The theoretical must give way to the practical, even at the very highest levels of decision making. General Nichols, telling Colonel Ross of his experiences at the Quebec Conference, picks up the Colonel's remark about politics being called the art of the possible:

> General Nichols gave him a quick, complimentary look. "Yes," he said, "the possible! That engaged them a lot. The problem is always, as I see it, to find out what that is; because that's all. You have to work inside that. The top echelon rides in the whirlwind, all right; but sometimes the storm seems to do the directing. That limits your choice, your freedom. Certain things that it might be wise to do can't be done. Of course, it doesn't mean you haven't, at the top, a good deal of choice, a good deal of freedom. You can't order a man to flap his arms and fly; but you can always order as many qualified pilots as you have to take as many planes as you have and fly the wrong way to the wrong place at the wrong time."[12]

Ross is greatly impressed with this. Later, explaining to his wife Nichols's views both on the large issue of the Quebec Conference and on the small, local issue of the Negro officers, he says:

> "His thought in both cases was that you will not do what you cannot do. Do you find the thought impressive?"
> "No," said Mrs. Ross.
> "It is quite important, however, if you have to make the decisions. A great many people, maybe most people, confronted by a difficult situation, one in which they don't know what to do, get nowhere because they are so busy pointing out that the situation should be remade so they *will* know what to do. Whether you like it or not, there are things you can't buck—no matter how

[12] James Gould Cozzens, *Guard of Honor*, New York 1948, p. 393.

much you want to, how vital it is to you. A parachutist who jumps from an airplane cannot climb back, no matter what. Even if he sees he'll be killed when he lands, he can't. Gravity is a condition, not a theory."[13]

This may seem a little obvious—like Stahr's advice to the airline pilot in the first chapter of *The Last Tycoon*—but it is Colonel Ross himself who comes to realise "that wisdom, though better than rubies, came to so little; that a few of the most-heard platitudes contained all there was of it."[14] We accept the "wisdom" of *Guard of Honor* more readily than that of *By Love Possessed* largely because Cozzens states it clearly as simple truth, and because he does not so insistently thrust it upon our attention. In *By Love Possessed* Cozzens probes into the many forms which "love" may assume, but he rarely attains that profundity to which he seems to pretend; there is nothing so heavy-handed in *Guard of Honor* as the long, verbose, ponderous discussions between the priggish Winner and the improbable Penrose.

There has recently been considerable comment on Cozzens's philosophy,[15] but he is not really a very reliable guide in the realm of general principles. Cozzens would make an indifferent legislator, but an excellent, if stern, judge: despite his insufficiently generous conception of man, one must respect his knowledge of men. His scrutiny of individual men is penetrating and implacable, and his final judgments, though severe, are not unfair. Colonel Ross, or Judge Ross, provides him with his most successful and appropriate mouthpiece:

There never could be a man so brave that he would not sometime, or in the end, turn part or all coward; or so wise that he was not, from beginning to end, part ass if you knew where to look; or so good that nothing at all about him was despicable. This would have to be accepted. This was one of the limits of human endeavor, one of those boundaries of the possible whose precise determining was, as General Nichols with his ascetic air of being rid of those

[13] *Op. cit.*, p. 439.
[14] *Op. cit.*, p. 533.
[15] See, for example, John W. Ward, "James Gould Cozzens and the Condition of Modern Man," *American Scholar*, XXVII (1957-8), 92-9.

youthful illusions, viewing with no nonsense the Here and the Now, always saw it, the problem. If you did not know where the limits were, how did you know that you weren't working outside them? If you were working outside them you must be working in vain. It was no good acting on a supposition that men would, for your purpose, be what they did not have it in them to be; just as it was unwise to beguile yourself, up there on top of the whirlwind, with the notion that the storm was going to have to do what you said.[16]

In this passage Cozzens gives us the core of the book and of his own position. It is, however accurate, extremely discouraging. Yet neither Colonel Ross himself nor the book as a whole entirely succumb to this conclusion. An opposition seems to develop between the action of the novel and Colonel Ross's reflexions upon it. You will not do what you cannot, says Nichols, and Ross must agree; but the action tends to show that, despite everything, you will do what you can. If the book as a whole gives a rather negative overall impression that is not so much because of its "message" as of Cozzens's limitations as a novelist. He has less assurance in presenting intimate personal relationships than in analysing the fine shadings of hierarchical relationships. His women are not very convincing, nor, for the most part, are the more passionate of his male characters. Indeed, passion seems to carry a negative connotation in Cozzens's moral world, and in such cases he tends to constrict the character's behaviour within the limits of a rather simple basic formula.

Thus Lieutenant Edsell seems akin to the typical "angry boy" of Jacobean drama, and hardly more subtle—indeed, almost a "humour" character. Cozzens seems to give him a representative importance in the novel as a disgruntled liberal: acting impetuously, insolently, self-righteously, and always on incomplete information, he is constantly creating confusion and disorder which Colonel Ross and others must set right. Try as he does, Colonel Ross cannot feel sympathetic towards Edsell, and the book is so dominated by Colonel Ross's conservative and bleakly realistic viewpoint that Cozzens often strikes us as too dispassionate, too limited in his

[16] *Guard of Honor*, pp. 532-3.

sympathies, too unresponsive to "the promises of life." In *By Love Possessed*, for all the book's preoccupation with passion, Cozzens displays a fundamental lack of human warmth, raising doubts as to his qualifications to write on such a theme at all.

By Love Possessed is altogether a more self-conscious book than *Guard of Honor*, and the idiosyncracies of Cozzens's style become even more exaggerated. Perhaps the style is an appropriate vehicle for the tortured self-doubtings of Cozzens's characters as they oscillate between the horns of their moral dilemmas; [17] even so, Cozzens seems imprisoned within his manner, and only by breaking out of it is he likely to write a novel of the first rank. Yet nobody has delineated more sensitively than Cozzens the moral predicaments of professional men—professional by vocation, or, as in the military world of *Guard of Honor*, by necessity—at the times when the demands of living and of human sympathy come into conflict with the rules within which they must work or the ideals to which they are dedicated.

4

This concern with the moral problems of professional men suggests certain similarities between Cozzens's work and that of the English novelist C. P. Snow. The "wisdom" which emerges from Snow's novels has a good deal in common with the "wisdom" we have discerned in Cozzens, and Snow, who greatly admires Cozzens,[18] would certainly accept, in its magnificent and revealing simplicity, the accuracy of "You will not do what you cannot do." On the other hand, Snow has insisted throughout his work on the importance, and the reward, of doing what you can do. His heroes— George Passant, for example, in *Strangers and Brothers* (1940), Roy Calvert in *The Light and the Dark* (1947), Charles March in *The Conscience of the Rich* (1958)—are often defeated, often deprived of success, wealth, love, happiness, hope itself. But whatever else they may lose they always retain some last spark of passion, an

[17] This is the view argued by D. W. Harding in his review, "The Limits of Conscience," *Spectator*, 6773 (18 Apr. 1958), 491.

[18] See C. P. Snow, "Mr. Cozzens Hits the Jackpot," *Sunday Times*, 8 Dec. 1957, p. 8.

ultimate resilience. Cozzens seems not to share this eagerness of Snow's; he never gives any very satisfactory idea of *why* you go on doing what you can. His characters seem curiously without ambition, either for themselves or for the world.

Although we cannot take the comparison with Snow very far, it may help to define other of Cozzen's achievements and limitations. The great distinction of *Guard of Honor*—as to a lesser extent of *The Just and the Unjust* and *By Love Possessed*—is that the world of the novel, a confined but by no means small or narrow world, is presented with extraordinary vividness, precision, and richness of concrete detail. The world of the typical Snow novel—the lawyer's world of *Time of Hope* (1949), for example—is sufficiently convincing, but Snow does not attempt such profusion, such comprehensiveness of notation. Indeed, Snow's strength lies in quite another direction: in a kind of austerity, a plainness of manner and of treatment which, while it has obvious limitations, has the great virtues of keeping the narrative line clear and concentrating our attention on the essential human situation. Lionel Trilling speaks of *The Masters* as "a paradigm of the political life."[19] What prevents *Guard of Honor* from being a paradigm of the military or the bureaucratic life is its very richness, the marvellously presented circumstantial hullabaloo of Air Force life. The authenticity of Ocanara itself does not so much confuse the issues as stamp them as unique.

This last difference between Snow and Cozzens may represent, in large measure, the difference between a novelist who feels he can take his society for granted and one who feels he cannot.[20]

---

[19] Lionel Trilling, *A Gathering of Fugitives*, Boston [1956], p. 130.

[20] For an interesting sidelight on this point see C. P. Snow, "Which Side of the Atlantic: The Writer's Choice," *New Statesman*, LVI (1958), 287-8. Snow says that if he were making the choice between being an American writer or an English writer there is one argument which would be decisive in keeping him in England: "It is simply that here we know our audience. In America the writers don't really know whom they are writing for—apart from their fellow writer-scholars . . . Any reading public is a tiny minority of the whole population; with us, in a much more homogeneous society than the American, that minority shares enough assumptions to be a good audience, and is also pleasingly wide-spaced" (p. 288). In England, he concludes, "we know, almost in a personal sense, whom we are writing for. An American writer can't; he feels much more lost." (*Ibid.*)

Certainly *Guard of Honor* is characterised by an attempt, akin to that made in many other American novels, to create a social world through profusion and precision of detailed notation. The attempt succeeds to a remarkable degree, and *Guard of Honor* remains not only Cozzens's outstanding achievement but one of the finest novels to appear in America since the end of the Second World War.

12

American Novelists and American Society

I

In English social novels, almost without exception, society is presented in terms of human relationships, not patterned by an abstract concept. In the nineteenth and twentieth centuries, at least, there have been few examples of the "moral fable" in English fiction, and English novelists, broadly speaking, have approached society in three principal ways. Some of them have undertaken a close and comprehensive examination of society, acting on the unspoken assumption that society is interesting for its own sake, as the way men live: Dickens and Thackeray do this in *Our Mutual Friend* and *Vanity Fair*; George Eliot declares it to be her aim in *Middlemarch*; and it provides the central concern of C. P. Snow's "Strangers and Brothers" sequence. Other English novelists have presented society mainly as a background or setting for the action of their novels. Often a careful and lengthy description of the social scene in the opening pages serves to establish it for the whole book; in subsequent chapters "society" is something that can be assumed, taken as read. George Eliot uses this method in *The Mill on the Floss* and *Felix Holt*, so does D. H. Lawrence in *The Rainbow*. Finally, there are those novelists whose sense of society and its sanctions is so integral a part of their whole conception that it is almost impossible in their work to separate out any presentation of society as such. In novels of this kind, notably those of Jane Austen and Ivy Compton-Burnett, we become aware of society, almost exclusively, through the interplay of characters.

With good reason, then, Richard Chase spoke of "great practical sanity"[1] as a characteristic feature of the English novel. Not only

[1] Chase, *The American Novel and Its Tradition*, p. 2.

does England lack a significant novel called *The Englishman*;[2] it also lacks novels called *The Titan*, *The Octopus*, and *The Turmoil*. The titles of English social novels are likely to be more factual, less metaphorical and romantic; *Hard Times*, *North and South*, *The History of Mr. Polly*, *The Man of Property*. The gradualness of change in England, the relative permanence of the basic social structure, the background of a long and comparatively settled history, have all made it possible for the English novelist to take society more or less for granted: that is to say, he has been able to assume that he and his readers share a large area of common knowledge about the structure of society, the nature of social relationships, and so on. For the American novelist this has not been possible to anything like the same extent, and to this fact can be traced a great many of the differences between the English social novel and the American.

It is not difficult to see some of the reasons why American novelists have lacked assurance in their treatment of society: the instability of the society itself; the extreme self-consciousness of the whole American experience; the part played by the novel in developing America's awareness of herself as a nation. American writers have repeatedly been worried, confused, or angered—rarely amused—by the irreconcilability of American ideals and American experience, and one result of this sense of the gulf between the way things should be and the way things are, has been a readiness to regard the novel as a political instrument. English reform movements have tended to be dominated by intellectuals, whose preferred media have been the essay and, occasionally, the problem play. In seeking to achieve radical alterations in society, they have not directly sought mass support; in fact, much of their attention has been directed to the problem of restraining popular unrest and of guiding it into the most profitable channels. Most American reform movements, on the other hand, have been "grass-roots" uprisings led by demagogic personalities of sincere but simple pieties and

---

[2] Constance Rourke observes of Henry James's *The American*: "Even the title was a fulfillment. Who ever heard of a significant English novel called *The Englishman* or of an excellent French novel called *Le Français*?" (*American Humor*, New York [n.d.] p. 194.)

programmes: Mary Lease's "raise less corn and more hell"[3] is typical of the slogans which have gained circulation and allegiance. And just as the stories of Horatio Alger were among the most influential propagators of the American "success" myth, so in their day the novels of Ignatius Donnelly, Edward Bellamy, William Dean Howells and many others were the often unsubtle but nonetheless powerful advocates of a wide variety of political doctrines and Utopian dreams. At the end of the nineteenth century, writers such as Gustavus Myers, Jacob Riis, and Lincoln Steffens showed that straight reporting might in certain circumstances be more effective than fiction, but Jack London and Upton Sinclair, more doctrinaire in their approach to social problems, continued to preach socialism through the medium of the novel—presumably because it was wider in its circulation, simpler in its appeal, and less hampered by the discipline of observable fact.

In addition to these narrowly political writers there have been the many novelists of social protest. Early in the century there were the "muckrakers," such as Winston Churchill, William Allen White, Robert Herrick, and Ernest Poole; later came Anderson, Dos Passos, Steinbeck, the "proletarians," and Norman Mailer. For all the differences between them, such novelists of social protest have at least one thing in common: they approach society not in a responsive or sensitive way but with their minds already made up; they come armed not only with their talents but with a theory. It is of the essence of the novelist's job that he should impose a pattern upon his material, but these novelists impose a pattern not of art but, in the broadest sense, of politics.

It is often a very simple pattern. In Churchill and Poole, in Howells, Anderson, and Dos Passos, more recently in such novels as Norman Mailer's *Barbary Shore* (1951) and David Karp's *All Honorable Men* (1956), we recognise again and again the clear outlines of pastoral, morality, parable, or polemic, for the American social novel has frequently taken the form of the "moral fable." As Arnold Kettle has pointed out, one great limitation of the moral fable is that "If you start with an abstract 'truth,' even a profound

---

[3] Quoted in Frank Thistlethwaite, *The Great Experiment*, Cambridge 1955, p. 262. Mary Lease was one of the leaders of the Populist movement.

one, it is difficult to avoid the temptation to mould life to your vision": for example, in *Candide*, "it is the vitality of Voltaire rather than of the world that comes across."[4]   Of course, Voltaire frankly presents *Candide* as fantasy-parable, but many American novelists who are highly "realistic" in their treatment of surface detail found their themes, quite as plainly as Voltaire, upon some entirely abstract political or economic "idea."

These generalisations apply most obviously to such "angry" and directly "intentional" novels as Upton Sinclair's *The Jungle* and *The Metropolis*, Jack London's *The Iron Heel*—though that novel is set in the future—and John Steinbeck's *The Grapes of Wrath*.   In these novels a steady accretion of shocking events, a rhetoric of action, often takes the place of thought or, except at a journalistic level, even of observation.   The limitations of the moral fable are equally apparent, however, in such important novels as *U.S.A.* and *The Naked and the Dead*.   Dos Passos and Mailer are not so much responding to the social fact as trying to fit the social fact to their particular social "idea."   Dos Passos especially shows a marvellous knowledge of American life in breadth and in detail, but we have seen that his overall portrait of America suffers severely from political stylisation and that, as in *The Naked and the Dead*, the stylisation is actually underlined by the introduction of obtrusive structural devices.

Such novels are particularly obvious examples of an extreme self-consciousness about society which has led American writers, again and again, to undertake some sort of large cultural statement about American society as a whole.   Indeed, American social novelists have commonly failed not because of their timidity in the face of society but because of their temerity.   Refusing to work within the social area they know, they attempt to encompass American society as a whole.   Their very titles—*An American Tragedy*, for example, and *U.S.A.*—testify both to the magnitude of their undertaking and to the underlying pre-occupation with cultural definition.   We may now find at once comic and tragic the

---

[4] Arnold Kettle, *An Introduction to the English Novel*, London 1951, I. 18-19. Kettle (II. 172) mentions Graham Greene's *The Heart of the Matter* as a recent example of the moral fable; to this we might add William Golding's *The Lord of the Flies*.

spectacle of Thomas Wolfe facing up to continental America and, like a photographer at the Grand Canyon, being frustrated into fury at being unable to get it all in, but Wolfe is only an extreme example of a tendency to grandiosity that is both widespread and continuing.

2

Most American social novelists have lacked a sense of proportion in their treatment of society, and we may relate this to the extraordinary importance in the history of the American novel of "realism" and, in the non-philosophical, literary sense of the term, of "naturalism." In America the novelists' use of "realistic" techniques has often represented a self-conscious attitude towards society rather than a genuine understanding; their preoccupation with a realistic presentation of the social surface, in which everything tends to become of equal importance, may often disguise an essential ignorance of deeper social realities. Such is undoubtedly the case with many "muckraking" novels, with most of the "proletarian" novels of the nineteen-thirties, and with a large proportion of contemporary "tough" or *exposé* novels about such subjects as politics, business, the entertainment industries, and advertising.

The most persistent tendency in American realism is for the realist to become obsessed with his material. He not only fails to shape it, he allows the novel to be shaped by it: the material takes charge. This is what happens in Abraham Cahan's *The Rise of David Levinsky*, for example, and, again, in the work of Theodore Dreiser. We noticed earlier Dreiser's preference for basing his novels on an actual incident or case-history, because of the greater sense of reality this gave him. Dreiser's immersion in the social fact is perhaps his greatest source of strength, but his failure to organise his material is his greatest weakness. His passion for social documentation becomes an obsession which, in such novels as *The Financier*, *The Titan*, and *The "Genius,"* operates in complete disregard of literary form.

Lionel Trilling, himself the author of an impressive socio-economic novel, *The Middle of the Journey* (1947), has spoken recently of the job the contemporary novel should do "of giving us reasonably accurate news of the world, of telling us the way things are."[5]   This is, perhaps, peculiarly the job of the contemporary American novelist, and in the same essay, a review of David Riesman's *Individualism Reconsidered*, Trilling seems to suggest that it is proving too much for him: "No American novel of recent years," says Trilling, "has been able to give me the sense of the actuality of our society that I get from Mr. Riesman's book."[6] Riesman, of course, is a sociologist, and his book is a collection of essays: he does not have to face the problems of artistic verisimilitude —specifically, the problems involved in the presentation of feasible human relationships—which make it difficult for any novelist with primarily sociological ambitions to produce anything of lasting interest.   In the first place, he cannot hope to compete with the sociologist proper: for example, *The Hucksters*, which enjoyed a certain vogue as an exposure of advertising, in fact reveals less than a single chapter of such a journalistic survey as Martin Mayer's *Madison Avenue, U.S.A.*   More importantly, it can be argued that the delineation of society as such is a dubious undertaking for any artist.   Again and again the material takes charge, as it does in Dreiser; or the political intention takes charge, as in so many of the novelists of social protest; or there is a tendency for the social material, the "information," to become separated out from the ostensible action of the novel, as happens in *The Pit* and in Tarkington's *The Magnificent Ambersons*.[7]   So many institutional novels are weak because their authors, having first decided to write, say, an academic novel, have only then looked round for a suitable story and characters.

The proper function of social description in a novel must be to define and illuminate the human predicament.   This is something which English novelists seem almost automatically to have accepted. Many American novelists have not accepted it, and they have often squandered their powers as a result.   The examples of James Gould Cozzens and C. P. Snow are relevant here.   Whatever reservations we may make about their work we do not doubt that they are

---

[5] Lionel Trilling, *A Gathering of Fugitives*, p. 92.

[6] *Ibid.*

[7] Booth Tarkington, *The Magnificent Ambersons*, Garden City, New York 1918. Chapter 28, for example, is almost entirely given over to potted social history.

both engaged in a serious attempt to see society as it is and to understand the forces which condition and motivate men as social beings. However, Cozzens favours a technique of rich and detailed social notation while Snow keeps such notation to a minimum, and these differences in approach are highly suggestive of the problems which still face the American social novelist. Even today an English novelist, such as Snow, Angus Wilson, or Anthony Powell, seems to take his society more or less for granted. Some of the best among recent American novelists, notably Saul Bellow and William Styron, attempt to do this in some of their books, but for the most part the American novelist remains highly self-conscious about his relation to society and often makes an ambitious attempt to create and sustain the whole social area in which his characters move. Hence we find the profusion of technical detail in Cozzens's books, the minute documentation of O'Hara, the emphasis on information in the contemporary "institutional" novel, in the *exposé* novels of Budd Schulberg and others, and in the "recording" novels of Marquand and Brooks.

3

In the Preface we referred to Lionel Trilling's observations, from "Manners, Morals and the Novel," on the poverty of American social fiction. We might now suggest that the social novel may be more common in America, and commonly more distinguished, than Trilling allows, and that whatever the limitations of the American social novelists, they have been astonishingly successful in evoking, recreating, and investigating many different areas of American society. What American social novelists have failed to do—and this may be partly to blame for their being so consistently underestimated by American critics—is produce impressive examples of either of the two major traditional forms of the European social novel, the picaresque novel and the novel of manners.

America, as Cooper, Hawthorne, and James long ago complained, has never favoured the novelist of manners. Except here and there for brief periods—for example, in late nineteenth-century Boston and in parts of the South before the Civil War—American society has never stood still long enough for manners to become

settled and readily identifiable.   Scott Fitzgerald's extraordinary
achievement was that he created a novel of manners out of the
material offered by a society in a state of extreme flux.   Even in
such American novels of manners as do exist, there is an inversion
of our normal expectations of the form.   These expectations, of
course, were created by familiarity with European examples,
although it is interesting to notice that many recent novelists of
manners in England—for instance, Kingsley Amis, John Wain, and
Iris Murdoch—seem to have more in common with American
novelists than with most of their English predecessors.   In the
traditional European novel of manners, supremely exemplified by
Jane Austen, defaulters such as Frank Churchill are judged according
to standards which are fundamentally social.   In the American novel
of manners, the values of society are almost invariably rejected and
the defaulter becomes the hero.   We are on Gatsby's side, on Lily
Bart's side.   We are even, with qualifications, on the side of George
F. Babbitt and Silas Lapham.   We sympathise with Marquand's
George Apley and H. M. Pulham when they deviate from the
standards of their society rather than when they adhere to them.   In
his essay "On Social Plays," Arthur Miller writes:

> The fact remains, however, that nowhere in the world where
> industrialized economy rules—where specialization in work,
> politics, and social life is the norm—nowhere has man discovered
> a means of connecting himself to society except in the form of a
> truce with it.   The best we have been able to do is to speak of a
> "duty" to society, and this implies sacrifice or self-deprivation.
> To think of an individual fulfilling his subjective needs through
> social action, to think of him as living most completely when he
> lives most socially, to think of him as doing this, not as a social
> worker acting out of conscientious motives, but naturally, without
> guilt or sense of oddness—this is difficult for us to imagine, and
> when we can, we know at the same time that only a few, perhaps
> a blessed few, are so constructed as to manage it.[8]

Although Miller is speaking of all industrialised societies, not only
of America, this sense of radical maladjustment to modern society

[8] Arthur Miller, "On Social Plays," Introduction to *A View from the Bridge*,
New York 1955, p. 6.

seems peculiarly strong in American writers. Almost all American novelists have presented the relationship between the individual and society as a struggle between irreconcilables, and it has often been noted[9] that American literature is rich in images of isolation and escape: its typical figures are Natty Bumppo alone on the prairie, Huck Finn lighting out for the territory, Babbitt wanting to escape back into a safe man-world, Holden Caulfield planning to act deaf-mute and live in a hut on the edge of the woods. There seems little doubt that this situation, in part, reflects the American writer's perennial sense of insecurity in a society to which he has himself been unable to adjust—a society, moreover, which has scarcely ever been able to offer him an audience which he could confidently identify and directly address. This sense of alienation, experienced by almost all the important nineteenth-century writers apart from Mark Twain, has in the twentieth century become virtually institutionalised under such heads as Progressivism, "The Lost Generation," the Communist Party, Southern Agrarianism, and "The Beat Generation." An attitude of "protest" has become almost *de rigeur* for the American writer.

We are not surprised, then, to find the novel of manners poorly represented and the sanctions of society rejected. What is surprising, and much harder to explain, is the absence of distinguished picaresque novels. Richard Chase's observation that "the American social scene has not been so interesting, various, and colorful as the European"[10] may be true of the vertical cross-section through society, which principally interests the novelist of manners, but it hardly applies to the horizontal sweep across the land as a whole, which might be expected to appeal to the picaresque novelist. Although Whitman was the first writer to point out the richness of these horizontal contrasts of American life, Mark Twain was the first novelist really to exploit them. *Huckleberry Finn* (1884), like other books by Twain, is essentially a picaresque novel, but this aspect of Twain's work seems not to have been influential. Thomas Wolfe, of course, wrote picaresque novels and Dos Passos,

[9] See, for example, Henry Bamford Parkes, "Metamorphoses of Leatherstocking," in *Literature in America*, ed. Philip Rahv, New York 1957, pp. 431-45.
[10] Chase, *The American Novel and its Tradition*, p. 160.

though he has not one but several main characters, often achieves a picaresque effect through sheer variety of action and scene. Few other serious writers have written novels of this kind, but recently we have had Saul Bellow's *The Adventures of Augie March* (1953), Ralph Ellison's *Invisible Man* (1952) and Jack Kerouac's *On the Road* (1957), all of which, though differing greatly in quality and in their approximation to the picaresque, at least share the appealing virtue of responding positively and often vividly to the richness and variety of American life. This virtue also distinguishes such novels as Thornton Wilder's *Heaven's My Destination* (1934) and J. D. Salinger's *The Catcher in the Rye* (1951), which both contain elements, of the picaresque, and even Vladimir Nabokov's *Lolita* (1955), though Nabokov's intentions are largely satirical.

English picaresque novelists have often had to go abroad to find material for picaresque novels; American novelists have long had such material available within their own borders, but they have made little use of it until comparatively recent years. We might have expected that the very conditions which worked against the novel of manners in America—the shapelessness and instability of society, the stress on individualism—would have made the picaresque novel a popular form. This, however, is to look at the American novel with preconceptions formed by familiarity with the European novel, and it is essential that the American novel be discussed on its own terms. It is more valuable to see it, not in relation to the European novel and European society, but in relation to the peculiar characteristics of American society and, above all, to the position of the novelist within that society.

The comparatively few American writers who have seen man and society in proper proportion, and who have had the power to realise their vision in terms of the novel, seem to have chosen two principal methods of coping with the peculiar difficulties presented by the vastness, newness, shapelessness, and instability of American society and by their own inescapable self-consciousness about it. They have chosen, as in *The Great Gatsby*, *The Catcher in the Rye*, and *Appointment in Samarra*, a primarily poetic method, dependent upon imagery and allusion. Or they have chosen, like Fitzgerald in *The Last Tycoon*, O'Hara in his later novels, Sinclair Lewis and

Howells in their best work, Edith Wharton and Cozzens in almost all their books, a technique of social saturation, of working deeper and deeper into a single, carefully delineated social area. Dos Passos in *U.S.A.* might be said to have attempted a development of this second method by putting down a series of sample borings all over the surface of America.

Sociologists, historians,[11] and even literary critics such as Bernard DeVoto[12] have complained that "highbrow" American fiction gives an inaccurate image of American life as a whole. They may very well be right: the popular magazines always provide a more accurate indication of what the great mass of people are thinking and doing. In the last analysis, what we ask of the social novelist is not so much that he should reflect our view of society, but that he should make us see society his way. In admiring the novels of George Eliot, we need to remember that what seems to us the accuracy of her social observation is in some degree an indication of her greatness as a novelist, of her power to make us accept the image of society she presents. It matters little whether or not William Faulkner's novels give an "accurate" picture of the South; what matters supremely is that Faulkner presents his South, the world of Yoknapatawpha County, solidly and vividly, both as a setting and as a conditioning environment. Of the American novelists we have considered in detail, perhaps only two, Edith Wharton and Scott Fitzgerald, have unmistakably achieved this kind of power in the social novel, though others have approached it in their best work, and it is in their handling of the business theme that the distinction of Edith Wharton and Fitzgerald is most clearly seen.

4

In the last quarter of a century or so, more especially in the years since World War II, American social novelists have been especially concerned with the development of bureaucracy and institution-alism and with the implications of this development for the

[11] See, for example, John Chamberlain, "The Businessman in Fiction," *Fortune*, Nov. 1948, 134-48; Robert A. Kavesh, *Businessmen in Fiction*, Hanover, N. H., 1955; and especially Allan Nevins, "Should American History be Rewritten?" *Saturday Review of Literature*, XXXVII (6 Feb. 1954), 7-9 etc.

[12] Bernard DeVoto, *The Literary Fallacy*, Boston 1944.

individual and for society as a whole. It is a development which has profoundly affected the world of business, as it has every area of the national life, and Walter Prescott Webb has observed:

> The rugged individualists of the late nineteenth century ... were in perfect harmony with the society in which they operated because every individual in that society was acting as they were, and hoping to follow their examples. The rugged individualist has now disappeared within the business corporation; the little fellows have before them no such living examples, and have given up all expectation of being giants. Personality has been submerged by organization on all sides. But what remains in the business corporation is the old motive of profit, the old method of competition, the old philosophy of a free and unfettered world. In a sense the business corporation has institutionalized the old individualism and is seeking to preserve it especially for itself as a survival from an extinct period.[13]

The problems facing characters in modern business novels are likely to be almost identical with those facing characters in novels about the army, about government, even about universities, although enough of the old ideology of business remains for someone like John Brooks, in *The Man Who Broke Things*, still to squeeze from descriptions of modern business activities something of the excitement that gripped Dreiser and his contemporaries.

For earlier social novelists, the business theme was not simply "available" but almost inescapable. American writers, with their extreme self-consciousness about their society, have been haunted by the archetypal figure of the "American-as-businessman," and have often fallen into the mistake of regarding the American businessman as an entirely unprecedented and extraordinary phenomenon. H. L. Mencken praised the portrait of Cowperwood in *The Financier* as "wholly accurate and wholly American,"[14] but in fact the main difference between American nineteenth-century businessmen and their European predecessors and contemporaries lay simply in the scale on which they worked and in the lack of organised opposition they encountered. The American businessman

[13] Walter Prescott Webb, *The Great Frontier*, London 1953, p. 133.

[14] H. L. Mencken to Theodore Dreiser, 6 Oct. 1912, quoted in Robert H. Elias, *Theodore Dreiser: Apostle of Nature*, New York 1949, p. 164.

had not merely a country but a continent to exploit; he had ideology on his side, in the doctrines of individualism and self-help; and he was opposed by no strong settled power of church, court, law or society at large. In Europe capitalism supervened upon an already long-established social system, with all that such a system implied in terms of manners, culture, and vested interests. In America capitalism grew up with the country, and in the process of expansion there were vast virgin areas to be taken over, rich natural resources to be developed, countless economic power vacuums which the forces of uncontrolled speculation inevitably filled. But if the opportunity offered by continental America made it possible for American businessmen to be bigger than their European counterparts, they did not necessarily differ in other ways. Describing the extravagance of the Parisian financiers in the reign of Louis XVI, Miriam Beard writes:

> Not entirely incongruous, therefore, was the craze of the new-rich American millionaires of the "Gilded Age," after the Civil War, for châteaux and salons decorated in the French styles. In fact, they were but following fashions set originally to a large extent by Florentine and French financiers . . . there is no real reason why any beef-baron or tinplate czar should not indulge to the limit in the period of Louis XVI, with rococo gilt chairs, pink damask and mirrors in profusion, since such dainty objects were created especially to suit the tastes of men like the Crozat brothers, patrons of Watteau, the financier Paris de Montmartel, close friend of La Pompadour, and the rich banker Sam Bernard.[15]

This is to put the matter too simply, perhaps, but the juxtaposition does help to put Cowperwood and his "palace of art" into proper perspective.

In thinking of the American businessman as unique, American novelists made two other fundamental mistakes. The first of these, and one made by nearly all novelists before the nineteen-twenties, was to regard the businessman as necessarily a great man, a type of the "epic hero." In the days of the captains of finance and industry the epic hero undoubtedly offered a far more obvious subject for fictional treatment than the obscure hero and, superficially at least,

[15] Miriam Beard, *A History of the Businessman*, New York 1938, p. 202.

a more attractive one.   But in the early years of this century the "romance of fact" which surrounded the big businessman represented a direct challenge which few novelists were capable of meeting.   The question was, first, whether any fictional character could convincingly match the careers and personalities of such men as Rockefeller, Carnegie, and Ford, and, secondly, whether any novelist could hope to impose any image upon the popular imagination as powerful as the images of real-life businessmen which were being built up year after year by mass-circulation newspapers and magazines and by cheap "inspirational" literature of the Horatio Alger type.[16]   It is a measure of Dreiser's achievement as a novelist that in Frank Cowperwood he did come near to creating such an image.   The fact that Sinclair Lewis, an inferior novelist, created in George F. Babbitt an image of far greater currency and permanency only serves to underline the obvious truth that whereas the epic folk-heroes of modern society tend to come from real life, the obscure folk-heroes, almost by definition, can hardly do so: they must be created by the cinema, as in the films of Charlie Chaplin, by the theatre, as in Arthur Miller's *Death of a Salesman*, or by the novel, as in *Babbitt*.   Whereas the name of Cowperwood had to fight for attention in competition with such names as Rockefeller and Morgan, the name of Babbitt was immediately accepted as giving an identity to the obscure hero, who had previously been both nameless and faceless.

The other mistake these novelists made was in assuming that business itself was necessarily an interesting activity.   To read business novels and books about business is to become gradually aware that, as often as not, there are few grounds for such an assumption.   The outsider is dazzled, as was Dreiser, by the sheer scale of business operations and by the magnitude of their effects, but there is little to suggest that the operations themselves are intrinsically exciting.   "I'm still convinced that successful business is devastatingly uninteresting"[17] says George Passant in C. P. Snow's *Strangers and Brothers*, and most American business novels, contrary

[16] See Sigmund Diamond, *The Reputation of the American Businessman*, Cambridge, Mass. 1955.

[17] C. P. Snow, *Strangers and Brothers*, London 1951, p. 93.

to their authors' intentions, suggest that he may very well be right. Their central theme is usually one of growth, but growth, as William Allen White observes in his own over-long novel *A Certain Rich Man* (1909), "is so still and so dull and so undramatic that it escapes interest and climax."[18] These words could be aptly applied to Robert Carson's *The Magic Lantern*, to Abraham Cahan's *The Rise of David Levinsky*, which Dreiser much admired, and to the long chronicle of Frank Cowperwood's business and amatory affairs. All the painstaking documentation of *The Financier* and *The Titan* adds little insight into those essential elements of any fictional work, character and conduct.

Apart from Zola, whose example was too eagerly seized upon by American novelists, European writers have not been especially excited by business or by businessmen. The "success" theme appears in crude form in England as early as Thomas Deloney's *Jack of Newbury* (1597) and reappears during the Victorian period,[19] but in English and European literature the businessman most often appears in the guise of the *nouveau riche* and as an object of satire. Miriam Beard writes of the nineteenth-century European business-man: "Despite his technical triumphs and his brand-new name, the capitalist entrepreneur could not for a moment startle the literati of the century into taking him for a fresh species of mankind. They persisted in regarding him as the eternal blundering parvenu, who had reappeared in all ages for at least two thousand years, now in classic Rome as *Trimalchio*, in Renaissance Italy as *Pantalone*, and in Baroque France as the *Bourgeois Gentilhomme*."[20] To this list we might add such English figures as Sir Giles Overreach in Massinger's *A New Way to Pay Old Debts* and the whole gallery of get-rich-quick enthusiasts in Ben Jonson's *The Alchemist*. Trimalchio, Pantalone, M. Jourdain, Overreach, and Sir Epicure Mammon are all comic figures, the objects of satire; Dickens used satire as a weapon in attacking the Bounderbys and Gradgrinds of the Victorian business world; and business characters in modern

[18] William Allen White, *A Certain Rich Man*, New York 1909, p. 225.
[19] See J. F. C. Harrison, "The Victorian Gospel of Success," *Victorian Studies*, I (1957), 155–64, and Asa Briggs, Introduction to Samuel Smiles, *Self-Help*, London 1958, pp. 7–31.   [20] Miriam Beard, *op. cit.*, p. 700.

English fiction, such as Denry Machin in Arnold Bennett's *The Card* and Uncle Ponderevo in H. G. Wells's *Tono-Bungay*, are often satirically or humorously treated, though sometimes with admiration as well.

In the American novel, business characters are scarcely ever comic or humorous. We must of course except Colonel Sellers and Silas Lapham and acknowledge a certain whimsicality about some of James's businessmen and about David Marshall in Henry Blake Fuller's *With the Procession*, but the vast majority of businessmen in American fiction are treated with grim dislike or with an equally grim admiration. English novelists, taking society and its values more or less for granted, have tended to see the big businessman, with his egregiousness, his offences against moderation and the social order, as an object of satire. American novelists, lacking a developed sense of the social order, have lacked assurance and a sense of proportion in dealing with the businessman. Contemplating him they have often felt distaste and even revulsion, yet they know that the United States is founded upon and continues to proclaim a system of principles which lays great stress on individualism and enterprise, and they recognise that, when measured against this national scale of values, the apparent offences of the businessman may begin to look like virtues and even take on heroic proportions. Again and again we find American novelists attempting to grapple with the dichotomy between American ideals and American reality, and we discern all too often in their work the kind of confusions and ambiguities likely to occur in any novel in which the author insists on laying down ideals and principles and relating them to reality. In the work of Howells, Sherwood Anderson, and Dos Passos, for instance, we can discern a firm underlying commitment to traditional American values best described as Jeffersonian-agrarian, but, for all their moral indignation, their social criticism is blunted by the limitations inherent in the agrarian position and by its lack of relevance to the problems of an urban-industrial civilisation. It is perhaps indicative of this weakness that this criticism is often enforced, especially in Howells and Anderson, not by argued exposition or the revealing interaction of character but by the methods of the moral fable, and, in particular, by the use of heavily charged images of virtue and corruption.

American writers have often failed to realise that a novelist is probably wiser to explore not the making of money but rather the way individuals are affected by the possession of money and of the power which money gives. At the same time the morality of money-making undoubtedly is important—the question of whether it has been honestly or dishonestly acquired—and characters must be presented as credible social beings, the conceivable products of their particular environment. Henry James's businessmen are unsatisfactory in this respect—it is incredible, says one historian, that Newman and Verver "could have made fortunes in the Gilded Age and at the same time remained so innocent and so benevolent."[21] Novels like *Washington Square*, *The Europeans*, and *The Bostonians* show clearly that James had a rich awareness of American social reality, but when his concern for cultural definition led him to approach what he recognised as the quintessentially American world of business, he seems to have been handicapped by his very familiarity with and respect for the English and European social novel. With Edith Wharton, less self-conscious both as artist and as American, these difficulties do not arise to anything like the same extent: she presents her businessmen just concretely enough to secure full credibility. While not especially well informed about the world of affairs, she dealt with it in her novels confidently and effectively, and her whole example suggests that James too hastily assumed that business was outside his range.

In the novels of Scott Fitzgerald we find perhaps the most skilful management by an American writer of the whole problem of the businessman in fiction. Both the persistence of the Lincoln motif in *The Last Tycoon* and the reference to Gatsby as "Trimalchio"[22]—Mizener tells us that projected titles for the book included *Trimalchio* and *Trimalchio in West Egg*[23]—suggest that Fitzgerald held his material in clear historical perspective; this must have helped him, especially in *The Great Gatsby*, to perform

[21] Henry Bamford Parkes, *The American People*, London 1949, p. 263.
[22] F. Scott Fitzgerald, *The Great Gatsby*, p. 86.
[23] Arthur Mizener, *The Far Side of Paradise*, p. 171.

what we have already called his "confidence trick." Fitzgerald realised from an early age that business was in itself relatively uninteresting, and he gave Gatsby and Stahr business acumen as only a single facet of their whole character. This at once gives them added stature and puts business in its proper place. However, it is essential to our understanding of Gatsby that we should know his business is crooked, and we are repeatedly reminded of this not by tedious passages of business detail—if Fitzgerald learned nothing else from Dreiser he learned to avoid these—but by brief, telling allusions: for example, the encounters with Wolfsheim and the overheard remark about the man whose "idea of a small town" was Detroit. The distinction of Fitzgerald and Edith Wharton as social novelists lies largely in their ability to create within their novels, in terms of the novel's world, a new scale of values capable of including the businessman in an organic way. They refuse to become obsessed by the vastness and occultness of business activities, and instead of treating the businessman as a demi-god or a villain they succeed in placing him in a social perspective which enables him to be viewed critically but with a sense of proportion.

American social novelists, obsessed with the special nature of the American experience and with the necessity for bringing that experience closer into line with American ideals, have rarely looked beyond it to the universal human experience of which it is inevitably a part. Almost alone among these novelists, Edith Wharton and Scott Fitzgerald can be said to have a sense of history as distinct from a merely nostalgic sense of the past. While they are fully alive to the "Americanness" of the American experience they do not forget the universality of all human experience. While they are fascinated by the social surface they are always aware of the forces at work below the surface. While they criticise society they do so in society's own terms, not in terms of an irrecoverable agrarian past or an unobtainable Utopian future.

INDEX